The
Anxious Lawyer

The
Anxious Lawyer

*An 8-Week Guide to a Joyful and Satisfying Law Practice
Through Mindfulness and Meditation*

Jeena Cho
Karen Gifford

Cover design by Elmarie Jara/ABA Publishing.
Interior design by Betsy Kulak/ABA Publishing.

Printed in the United States of America.

20 19 18 17 16   5 4 3 2 1

ISBN: 978-1-62722-624-0

Discounts are available for books ordered in bulk. Special consideration is given to state bars, CLE programs, and other bar-related organizations. Inquire at Book Publishing, ABA Publishing, American Bar Association, 321 N. Clark Street, Chicago, Illinois 60654-7598.

www.ShopABA.org

This book is dedicated to Justin Broglie, our colleague, collaborator, fellow student of meditation, and dear friend. The insight, creativity, immense kindness, and unique spark you brought to all you did continues to inspire us. You passed through this world much too quickly.

Contents

Introduction

DID THE TITLE OF our book bring a crooked smile to your face? That smile of reluctant recognition? As much as we like the title, *The Anxious Lawyer* is far too apt, and far more resonant with practicing attorneys than we would like it to be. Many lawyers have been conditioned to constantly strive to be perfect, and feel as though they live in a world where they're constantly failing. Anxiety and stress have a tendency to become absorbed into the fabric of our lives, and it may be hard to remember what life felt like before.

Ironically, anxiety is such a common condition for lawyers, yet rarely is there room to talk about the difficulties and challenges of being a lawyer. What's worse, there's an insidious, unstated attitude in our profession that if you experience anxiety, depression, or other stress-related challenges, it's a character flaw. We've talked to many lawyers suffering from burnout, anxiety, overwhelming stress and depression and everyone has shared that the worst part of it is the feeling of isolation—that she is the *only* one with this problem.

It's Tough to Be a Lawyer

Most lawyers have been through a Continuing Legal Education (CLE) class for Substance Abuse Prevention (or something similar) where the speaker rattles off statistics documenting how unhappy or downright miserable lawyers are. Lawyers rank fourth among professionals with the highest suicide rates. Lawyers suffer from depression at twice the rate of the general population. Of 1.2 million lawyers in this country, 240,000 are depressed. The rate of substance abuse among lawyers is twice that of the general population. What's puzzling is that despite these rather gloomy statistics, there is little, if any, effort to either find the root cause or help for the lawyers who are suffering.

In many ways, the structure of our legal system promotes conditions ripe for high degrees of substance abuse, depression, anxiety, and, perhaps most tragic of all, suicide. The economic pressures on legal practitioners are greater than ever. We constantly push ourselves to work harder, to do more, to bill that extra 0.1 hour. Lawyers are expected to take the client's position, no matter how disagreeable it may be, put personal feelings aside, and win at all costs. We refer to litigation as going to war, and we're expected to be warriors in that war. In fact, we're often trained to see our opposing side as the "enemy."

Comments like "don't ever let the opponents see your weakness" or "leave your emotions at the door" are all too common in our profession. This disconnect between how we feel and the facade we're required to put on can make us feel isolated. It can appear as though everyone but you has it all figured out and they're coping just fine. This can lead, in turn, to feelings of inadequacy and even shame. We feel there must be something wrong with us if we can't check our emotions at the door and perform with robotic precision. The denial and suppression of how we feel can run so deep we lose touch with our own emotions. In fact, attorneys may fear their own emotional lives.

While lawyers are beleaguered in many ways, they have few tools to deal with the strains. While interest in meditation has skyrocketed in recent years, successfully engaging the business community, the benefits of meditation have not been recognized as widely by the legal profession. This is unfortunate, because a lawyer's mind is arguably his most used and valued instrument.

A Meditation Book for Lawyers, by Lawyers

Chances are you decided to pick up this book because you too may be struggling with anxiety or stress. You may have also decided to get the book because you're curious about mindfulness and meditation. Both of us decided to try meditation after many years of living in constant states of anxiety and stress. Jeena decided to try meditation after being diagnosed with social anxiety disorder and having struggled for many years with constant, persistent anxiety. Karen decided to try meditation during a particularly challenging time at a very demanding job while also balancing the responsibilities of motherhood.

With this book we are aiming to support our fellow professionals by presenting a simple and straightforward introduction to meditation for those engaged in the practice of law. Since we both came to meditation as practicing attorneys, we know firsthand the difficulties and rewards of legal practice, what the daily life of a lawyer is like, and the common challenges lawyers face in dealing with clients, colleagues, opposing counsel, and the court system. We've experienced how meditation can support a more effective and enjoyable legal practice, and make the stresses of a demanding professional life more manageable. At the same time, we've seen how, as a group, our fellow lawyers are often reluctant to attempt meditation. In our experience, meditation is often presented in a way that feels artificial and inaccessible to most lawyers, and, as a result, can end up feeling antithetical to a professional culture that places great value on logic and reason.

Our deepest hope in writing this book is that meditation can serve as a tool to help you, our readers—our fellow colleagues—thrive. This has certainly been our experience. When we practice being still, and making room for reflection, we experience a ripple effect in the other parts of our lives. We are certainly not suggesting meditation is a substitute for getting medical or psychological help, but we do believe it's extremely helpful. Meditation and its related practices can be part of an approach to a life and a career that includes achievement, constructive engagement, expanding self-knowledge, and personal fulfillment.

Why Do We Meditate? Why Should You?

There are many reasons for beginning a meditation practice, and there is certainly no wrong or right one among them. What follows are our stories of how we came to meditation, as well as some more general reasons that often provide the motivation to start meditating.

Jeena's Story

"There is nothing wrong with you. Not physically," said the doctor. Waves of relief washed over me. "I'm not dying of some horrible disease." This relief was quickly followed by feelings of frustration. I was losing hair—clumps of hair for reasons my doctor could not find. When I look back on this period in my life, I can see the hair loss was just the tip of what I wasn't acknowledging to myself. Despite having an outwardly great life, I was suffering. I had almost daily insomnia and I was increasingly becoming more anxious. I managed the insomnia with Ambien. As the anxiety persistently took control over more and more of my life, I became more isolated. I reduced my social interactions (which triggered the anxiety) such that the only people I was interacting with were my clients and my fiancé. I could have tried to relieve the stress and anxiety with anti-anxiety and antidepressant medicines. But I didn't want to continue to medicate my way through life. *Something* had to change. That change came through meditation and mindfulness.

My first interaction with meditation was during law school. I stumbled upon the Himalayan Institute of Buffalo, NY, and a wonderful teacher, Rolf Sovik. My experience at the Himalayan Institute planted a seed that wouldn't sprout until much later in my life and apparently at the precise moment when I really needed it. After the doctor failed to find any physical cause for the hair loss, I had to acknowledge that perhaps stress was causing it. Much of the stress was caused by intense anxiety I felt in certain situations such as public speaking, speaking in groups, talking on the phone, and general free-floating anxiety. In 2011, I was diagnosed with social anxiety disorder. Through rather random luck, I learned about a study at Stanford University for treating social anxiety. At the initial meeting, the researcher explained there were two treatment programs. The first was cognitive behavioral therapy (CBT), which focuses on being in anxiety-provoking situations while in a safe environment and noticing "thinking errors." The second program was a mindfulness based treatment program.

As she explained the two treatment options, I instinctively knew I would benefit more from the mindfulness program. It intuitively felt more familiar and more suited for my mind. Since it was a research study, the participants were randomly assigned and I completed the CBT program. The program was highly effective and I noticed huge improvements in the intense anxiety I felt during social situations. However, I still wanted

4

to explore the mindfulness program. Fortunately, Stanford University also offers a course on Mindfulness Based Stress Reduction (MBSR). The course was life-changing.

I devoted myself to the practice of daily meditation and mindfulness with the same zeal that got me through law school. It awakened a sense of hunger for inner exploration and becoming more fully present to my life. I began to explore difficult questions around life's meaning and purpose. I became much more intentional about how I spent my time.

It is often said people come to meditation practice because they are suffering. I was certainly no exception. However, what I got from the practice of meditation and mindfulness is so much richer and unexpectedly more remarkable than simple stress and anxiety reduction. There is a fuller and richer sense of opening up to my life and the world around me. I experience more feelings but am no longer enslaved to emotional reactions. I feel more centered and grounded. I don't worry as much, especially the pointless, incessant worries that used to keep me up at night.

Mindfulness and meditation practice have helped me be a better lawyer. I can be with my clients' suffering without losing myself in it. I am able to stay calm during stressful events, such as a hearing. My relationship to opposing counsel has changed. My mood is no longer swayed by what the opposing counsel says or does. I have an unshakable sense of resilience—that no matter what happens, everything will be okay because I can rely on myself.

Before I started my journey into mindfulness, I just wanted the stress and anxiety to end. This has happened, but in a different way than expected. Stressful and anxiety-provoking situations are still plentiful in my life. Opposing counsel with whom I had difficulties in the past still act in ways I find challenging. Clients still come in with overwhelming sadness and despair. Judges still rule against my clients.

Ultimately, what has changed is my relationship to these triggering events. I can observe myself getting emotionally triggered without getting lost in the feelings. I am better able to acknowledge and comfort myself when things don't go as planned. I can observe my heart and pulse quickening, the heat rising to my face, or the shaky legs as I take the stage for a public speaking event, without going into full panic mode. This isn't to suggest I am always able to do this skillfully but I also learned to be gentler with myself. The expectation of perfection has lessened, which allows me to take risks and try new things instead of living in constant fear of failure.

Karen's Story

I began meditating when I was a litigator in the enforcement section of the New York Fed's legal department. I led investigations into misconduct in the banking industry and brought civil enforcement actions based on what I found. My cases involved activity such as embezzlement, loan fraud, and misconduct on trading desks, which were a recent addition to banks at that time.

I loved my work. It was fascinating and I was lucky to have brilliant colleagues. I also believed—and still do—that what I was doing made the financial system run better and more fairly.

At the same time, my job came with obvious stresses. Cases that can result in significant fines, injunctions, and bans from the industry are extremely contentious, to say the least. The bankers I brought cases against thought I was ruining their lives and took my enforcement actions personally. Shouting and swearing were very much part of my day; my opponents were often the best lawyers in the country who could outspend me by many multiples.

While I was managing this challenging but rewarding legal practice, I was raising young children with a spouse who traveled four days a week. We were lucky to have a wonderful nanny; still, the demands were intense. Many nights I fell asleep on the floor of my children's room, so exhausted I didn't realize what happened until I woke up hours later with creases from the rug on my face.

And of course my internal life didn't slow down just because I was very busy in my external life. Just like anyone, I had my own maturing to attend to, as well as some fairly challenging events in my personal history that needed processing.

Over time, all these pressures wore on me. I became terribly crabby and hard to deal with at home. I didn't realize at the time how lucky I was to have such a patient spouse! Still, for quite a while I managed to put on a good face at the office.

Inevitably though, my stress levels caught up with me. When I chewed out a junior attorney for a minor mistake, the voice coming out of me sounded like the worst kind of senior lawyer—exactly what I'd sworn I'd never be. I apologized later, but the incident left me shaken. It was a wake-up call I couldn't ignore. I knew *something* had to give, and I really didn't want it to be my job. I'd heard meditation helped with stress, so I began trying to meditate every day.

The hardest part for me was getting started. I had many reasons to be motivated, but sitting still and watching my thoughts didn't come naturally to a "do-er" like me. At first I sat for just two minutes a day—and that was hard! Eventually I found my way, and meditation became one of the pillars of my day. No matter how crazy things were at work or at home, I could go inside and find a place of deep calm, sweetness, silence, and even joy.

So meditation helped me stay at my job and I was happy. I didn't realize the calm I felt was just the beginning. Far from tamping down my nervous system so I could endure the difficult parts of my life, meditating made me more aware, present, and open to change—and many changes happened!

Why Should You Meditate?

You are the only one who knows whether meditation is right for you or why you are interested in trying it. Still, it's interesting to hear why someone might begin a meditation practice. Some common reasons include:

- **Stress or anxiety management**—Many people begin meditation as a means of managing stress or anxiety, and perhaps this is an even greater motivator for lawyers than for others, since stress is such a defining aspect of our professional lives. It's telling that both of us, the authors of this book, began meditating to manage stress-related issues. If stress is the reason for your beginning your meditation practice, welcome! You're in good company.
- **Increasing focus and productivity**—Our computers, laptops, phones, iPads, e-readers, and myriad other devices can make us more productive, but they also enable continual interruptions. These never-ending sources of distraction can leave us frayed and even undermine our fundamental ability to pay attention. Many professionals take up meditation as an antidote, to help navigate the disruption that is part of the modern working world without sacrificing their effectiveness.
- **Letting go of unwanted habits**—Meditation is often a crucial support for people who are giving up habits like smoking, overeating, or other behaviors that don't serve them well.

- **Dealing with difficult events**—Tragedy strikes all of us at one point or another, and its timing is not something we choose. Dealing with a sad event or a challenging time in one's life is often the catalyst for beginning a meditation practice. Meditation can feel right at this time, both because it can be calming and soothing and because it can help us connect with the deeper questions that can arise in these situations.
- **Seeking meaning and self-knowledge**—We all want to know why we're here and what our lives are about. This inquiry may come up as a need to understand our deeper purpose, or better define our values. Or we may feel we want to see reality more clearly, without the fog of neurosis and self-deception we suspect separates us from the world as it really is.

This list is certainly not meant to be exhaustive. Beginning a meditation practice is personal to you; and whatever your own reasons for meditating, they should be honored. We'll return to the reasons we've set out here again at various points throughout the book, taking each in more detail. All are very valid reasons for meditating—and meditation has a good track record with all of them.

It's also possible the reason you meditate may change over time. You may begin a meditation practice to reduce stress or anxiety and increase concentration or focus; but with practice, you could find additional and perhaps deeper reasons to motivate your practice.

Meditation Changes Us

Reading through all of the many scientifically documented benefits of meditation, you may feel that improved physical health, mental focus, and the heightened compassion that can help us act in the world in a better way are more than enough reason for developing a meditation practice. However, all of these benefits—as impressive and welcome as they are—are essentially side effects. It's important to bear in mind that meditation practice originally began as a means of transformation. Ultimately that is the most important thing meditation does, and the changes it brings are far more extensive than the health and self-improvement goals that up to now have been the main focus of scientific study. Over time, meditation can fundamentally change the way we understand our own minds, how we see ourselves, and how we experience our connection to others and the world.

How does this change take place? While no one knows for certain—and science has only recently begun to investigate this question—one very simple way of understanding the process is this: by sitting quietly on a regular basis, we give ourselves a chance to see our own minds more clearly, and that begins a process that gently but inevitably changes us.

Jeena's Story:
How to Know Anxiety

I was at the Golden Gate Club to give a talk. What was expected to be a small group of thirty to fifty people had grown to more than 100. Luckily, I had over an hour before taking the stage. Most people fear public speaking. Supposedly, most fear it more than death. At the peak of the time I suffered from social anxiety disorder, what I was about to do—stand up in front of a group of people to deliver a speech—would have been unthinkable.

Anxiety is painful to live with. It's the constant fortune-telling, trying to foresee all the things that can go wrong in every situation. It's the fear of screwing up. Trying to predict the future. It's the feeling of never being at ease because your mind is constantly catastrophizing—on high alert.

When I started MBSR, I did it searching for a cure for the unbearable pain I was living with. I expected the treatment program would stop my feelings of anxiety. Just like taking an Advil for a headache, I expected the symptoms to disappear. After all, practicing sitting in silence everyday—there has to be some compelling reason for putting yourself through that.

After four years, here is what I've learned about anxiety:

I'll never be anxiety-free. What *can* change is my relationship to the anxiety. Instead of having my brain go into complete freak-out mode, I can catch the anxiety much earlier on. I have a much better awareness of how anxiety works. When there's an anxiety-triggering event, I notice my stomach tightening/turning, heart racing, and other somatic experiences. At this point, I can start to panic and interpret the somatic experience as "anxiety," or I can simply recognize it as a set of physical experiences and work on calming the body.

Practice. Practice. Practice. In addition to three MBSR courses, an MBSR Teacher Training Practicum, and CBT, I also took two public speaking classes. I joined Toast Masters. Yes, every step was excruciatingly painful. But as with everything, what you practice gets easier.

As my time to speak neared, I noticed my old friend—anxiety. In that moment, I recognized anxiety is neither bad nor good. It's just a physiological experience plus unhelpful, unproductive thought patterns. And I can survive with the slight tightening of the stomach, a feeling of swelling in the chest, and tingling in the arms, without the narrative ("I'm going to fail," "This is going to suck," etc.). I was simply able to accept this is my body's natural reaction to a significant moment, and a signal I should pay attention. Anxiety no longer keeps me from participating in activities I value and instead has turned into a friend I can rely on.

10

When we sit quietly day after day, we see our thoughts and how they play out. We start to notice our mental patterns: *when x happens, I always think y.* For example, maybe when something goes wrong, you always worry it's your fault; or maybe when someone praises you, you always feel like a fraud. Whatever our particular mental patterns, eventually we begin to see they *are patterns*, not the result of a reasoning process or a choice. As we are able to see more and more of our thoughts as just reflexive thinking, we realize we don't necessarily have to believe them. By taking our thoughts less seriously, we give ourselves more power to choose what to believe, rather than simply being at the mercy of whatever might pop into our minds at any given time. This shift in how we interact with our own thought process can have surprisingly broad-reaching consequences, giving us much more freedom of action in personal and professional settings.

As our meditation practice continues, more and more of our beliefs— perhaps even those that are very deeply held—reveal themselves to be based on reflexive thinking. We begin to hold all of our beliefs more lightly, approach the world from a more open stance, and even begin to take ourselves less seriously. For most people, this feels pretty wonderful! There is a reason why classical meditation texts describe the goal of meditation as "liberation"—it is liberating to let go of the heaviness most of us carry around our sense of self. Eventually, we begin to see that our understanding of ourselves as alienated, fragile beings who are at the receiving end of life is mistaken. We see that, in fact, we are whole, we are fundamentally free, and we are deeply connected to each other and the world, and we see this understanding is the true source of happiness.

Bringing about this shift in understanding is, in our view, the true purpose of meditation and its highest goal.

What Do We Mean by Meditation?

Even though you've heard a lot about the benefits of meditation, you may not be entirely sure about exactly what meditation is. Different people may mean different things by meditation. While many meditation traditions come with philosophies, religious beliefs, rituals, and specialized equipment, meditation itself is simply a form of mental training. All of the many different meditation practices that exist, at their essence, boil down to the same thing: they are all means of settling and focusing the mind. By sitting quietly with your own mind day after day, you get to know it better.

11

One reason meditation can have such a powerful effect on people's lives is because our mind is one of the very few things we have the ability to control. We may not be able to control what happens to us, but by getting to know ourselves and our own thought patterns better, we can learn to control how we react to and process the events in our lives—and developing this ability changes how we experience life. We can retain inner strength and a sense of well-being even in very difficult situations. We can savor life more fully when we aren't distracted by unnecessary worries about what might or might not happen in the future.

Building this kind of mental skill is particularly useful for lawyers, since we are always working to attain outcomes on behalf of our clients, and yet have limited control over those outcomes. We can't be certain of how the judge will react to our arguments, how our opposing counsel will receive our negotiating proposal, or even how the witness we've prepared will actually testify when faced with the spotlight of the courtroom. And, of course, we have no control at all over the facts that brought our client into our office in the first place.

The difficult reality is that regardless of how well we do our jobs, our ability to effect any particular outcome is highly constrained. Under these circumstances, getting to know our own minds and building our ability to deal with our mental reactions can be sanity-preserving!

In this book, we will be focusing on three basic meditative practices:

- *Mindfulness*, which is bringing our attention to what is happening in the moment, often by focusing on some type of physical sensation, like the movement of the breath, or the sounds around us
- *Metta*, which involves offering good wishes, or what has been called "loving-kindness" to ourselves and others
- *Mantra*, in which we focus our attention by repeating a word or phrase

We'll explore each of these meditation practices in greater depth later in this book, and we'll also try some related variations of each. All of these practices have the same general effect of calming the mind and focusing our attention, but each has its own feeling tone and will highlight different facets of the meditative experience.

As you follow the program set out in this book, you'll have a chance to experience each of these three meditation methods in enough depth to get a sense of how you respond to each one. It's very likely one will stand out as the practice you connect with most easily or that just feels right in some way. Once you've found a practice that resonates with you, we encourage you to keep practicing with it for some time—at least several months—before moving on to investigate others. Sticking with a single practice for a relatively extended period will help solidify your practice, and also will give you a chance to experience more of the subtleties and depths of meditation without the distraction of needing to focus on the basics.

Science and Meditation

Lawyers are naturally very interested in evidence, and you may reasonably want to know what objective means have been used to measure the effects of meditation. Fortuitously, considerable research on the topic of meditation is now available to help answer that question. As meditation became more integrated into Western society, Western scientists were increasingly interested in investigating its effects on the mind and body, on subjective experience and behavior, and on the brain itself. Scientists' curiosity and the perspective they bring to their investigations have opened a fascinating window into how meditation may work to transform us over time.

Thousands of studies of meditation have been conducted over the past fifty years, employing modern scientific techniques such as randomization and control groups, and tools such as functional magnetic resonance imaging (fMRI) and electroencephalogram (EEG) to observe changes in the brain and body of the meditator.[1] These studies point to a wide range of benefits that can flow from a regular meditation practice. Meditation appears to affect us organically, acting on many of our physiological and mental systems over time. It seems almost every week a new study appears revealing another area in which meditation shows promising possibilities of improving human experience: heart health, immune system function, diet, addiction, concentration—the list continues to expand. Perhaps the most exciting aspect of these continuing revelations is that scientific study is only beginning to uncover the contours of how meditation affects the entire human system.

Most recently, scientists are beginning to turn their attention to the neurobiological effects of meditation, and how they may underlie the behavioral changes we often see in people who establish a meditation practice. These studies seek to shed light on the mechanics of how meditation changes the ways in which the brain perceives and processes every experience. What they have found is neural networks and even physical structures of the brain are measurably affected soon after a person begins a meditation practice. We actually change our brain when we meditate.

We will be highlighting the outcomes of scientific studies on various aspects of meditation throughout the book. While we will be touching on a number of different areas where scientists are exploring the effects of meditation on physical and mental health, our summaries are by no means exhaustive. If you are interested in digging deeper into the science of meditation, there is a wealth of information available; and we've included some sources in our Resources section to get you started.

13

How to Use This Book

This book provides a general overview of the concepts behind meditation and related practices, the science behind them, and the nuts and bolts of cultivating a meditation practice through an eight-week, self-guided program. The book itself is meant to be a workbook. Think of this program like you would a gym membership. Buying the membership (or the book) won't do any good unless you actually show up to do the work.

There are many different ways of approaching the exercises in the book. You can read through the book once and then begin the exercises sequentially. You can also read a chapter, practice the exercise for a week, and then proceed to the next. Some people may find it useful to skip around and do the exercises out of order. While the exercises are listed by week, you may wish to spend more than a week on a particular exercise, particularly the ones around cultivating compassion for yourself and others, as this is a practice we have found is difficult for many attorneys.

As you work through the exercises, you may find you have a strong preference for one exercise while finding others less to your liking. We encourage you to at least try each week's exercise. The practice of mindfulness is to *notice* our mind's natural tendency to judge experience as something we like or dislike, and instead accept those experiences as-is. Therefore, if you find you have a strong dislike for one exercise, it doesn't mean you shouldn't do the exercise. See if you can simply notice and say, "How interesting. I wonder why I have such a dislike for this exercise." Be curious about each experience.

Sitting Practice Versus Off-the-Cushion Practices

All meditation traditions center around some type of formal, usually seated, meditation practice. In formal sitting practice, we set aside time on a regular basis to step away from our daily activities. During that dedicated time, we quiet and focus the mind by working with a specific meditation practice. Seated practice time is the basic building block of any meditation path. Devoting time exclusively to meditation gives us a chance to watch the mind without interruption and get to know it better. Spending a period of continuous time working with the meditation practice we have chosen also helps build our concentration and allows us to go deeper with that practice.

In addition to sitting practice, many meditation traditions also make use of a variety of practices that are done in our day-to-day life, off the meditation cushion. In this book, we'll be working with several different sitting practices; and as we introduce each one, we'll also ask you to work with some related practices. For clarity, we'll use the word "meditation" to refer to sitting practice. When we discuss practices that make use of meditation techniques or insights outside of our sitting practice, we'll use the term "off the cushion" to distinguish them from seated meditation.

Off-the-cushion practices harness the basic elements of specific meditation techniques. For example, you may consciously choose to bring a more mindful awareness to everyday activities that engage your senses like eating, washing, talking, or listening. Or if you meditate using a mantra, you may choose to repeat the mantra at various points during the day when you are engaged in an activity that leaves your mind relatively free, like driving, standing in line, or walking.

While they can't substitute for sitting practice, off-the-cushion practices are essential for integrating the insights of meditation into our lives. They reinforce the mental habits we build during our sitting practice time. They encourage us to recognize that the inner quiet and spaciousness we experience in sitting practice is available to us at any time, and in whatever setting or circumstances we may find ourselves. In fact, the main benefit of doing the off-the-cushion practices may be that they help break down any unconscious sense we have that our meditation practice is in some way separate from our so-called real life. The goal of meditation practice is, after all, not to master techniques for their own sake but to change the way we experience and live our lives.

Getting Ready
to Meditate

Dare to quit the platform, plunge into the sublime seas,
dive deep and swim far, so you shall come back with self-respect,
with new power, with an advanced experience,
that shall explain and overlook the old.

—Ralph Waldo Emerson

SO HERE YOU ARE—YOU'VE read through the introduction and have at least a general idea of what meditation is. You've also read about how a meditation practice can affect your life in both expected and unexpected ways. This chapter will help you prepare to start your eight-week meditation program, which begins in Week 1.

You'll be happy to know there's not much preparation necessary for an activity that, at its essence, is nothing more than spending quality time with your own mind. To get you going, we'll begin with a simple breathing technique and discuss a few useful tools that can help you set up your practice. We'll also discuss a number of common misconceptions about meditation, as those can be needlessly distracting or even discouraging when you're starting to meditate. Finally, and perhaps most importantly, we'll encourage you to take some time to set an intention for your meditation practice.

What We Do When We Meditate

The actual mechanics of meditation are quite simple. At a fundamental level, all meditation traditions and practices involve the same basic practice, and this is true for the meditation practices we'll be learning in this book. When we meditate, we use an object of attention such as the breath, sensory experience, or a word or phrase (often called a mantra) to focus and quiet the mind. Every time we notice we are getting caught up in our thoughts or our mind is wandering, we gently bring our focus back to the object of meditation we've chosen to work with.

Meditation does *not* mean we stop thinking, maintain a blank mind, or attain a perfectly peaceful state of nirvana. What does happen over time as we meditate is that we begin to change our relationship with our thoughts and feelings. We learn to observe our own mind. We increase our ability to focus. As we come back to the object of meditation over and over again during our sitting practice, we begin to experience more spaciousness in our own minds and come to see we are not our thoughts and feelings, regardless of how compelling those thoughts and feelings may seem in the moment we experience them. This very simple insight can be quite transformative.

18

Starting with the Basics—the Breath

A very good and practical place to begin a meditation practice is to spend some time connecting with and focusing on the breath, the most fundamental cornerstone of meditation. Because the breath is always with us and is easily accessible, we often use the breath as our object of attention during meditation. We intentionally bring our attention to the breath; instead of breathing on autopilot, we observe and become familiar with the breath.

Here are some of the reasons the breath is a good focal point for meditation, and why it is such a beautiful and practical tool:

- **The breath is always in the present.** One of the things that takes us out of our direct experience of life, with all its vibrancy, is our tendency to get caught up in reliving events of the past or projecting our thoughts into the future, worrying about what may happen next, or making plans for what we want to do someday. The sensations of the breath are tangible connections to what is happening right now; and by focusing on those sensations, we bring our minds back into alignment with the present moment.
- **The breath is a physical reminder and practical example of how we're all connected.** It literally connects us with the web of life around us. We exhale carbon dioxide, which is poisonous to us and could kill if we had too much exposure to it. This same carbon dioxide is nourishment for the plant life around us. Plants expel the oxygen that is a waste product for them but is vitally necessary for us. We could think of each breath we take as participating in a physical conversation we are having with the world, one that starts on the day we are born and continues through our entire life.
- **The breath reminds us we don't have to do everything.** The breath is always there, allowing all the millions of cells in your body to operate, without you ever having to consciously direct it. When you stop to consider what happens when you take a breath, it is a fairly miraculous process, transforming the air around us into nourishment for the body. Yet we don't have to do anything to make it happen. We don't have to get to the office, file a motion, execute a contract, or put dinner on the table in order for the breath to take care of us. During the time we're sitting, we can sit back and enjoy the effortlessness of that process.

Diaphragmatic Breathing

As you'll see as we go through our eight-week meditation program, one of our principal mindfulness practices uses the breath as a focal point. But before even beginning any formal sitting practice or gathering any

19

equipment, we can do a simple exercise that allows us to connect with this key meditative tool we always carry with us. And we'll see that by simply paying attention to the breath and perhaps making some small adjustments to it, we can begin to regulate our physical and mental states. So just by bringing some attention to the breath, we can already get a taste of the well-being meditation can bring into our lives.

You may be wondering, "What's the big deal with the breath? I've been doing it all of my life. Why does this matter?" Your breath, specifically the *quality* of your breath, hugely matters. How we're breathing can give us a lot of information about our physical and mental state. Consider the last time you had to engage in a physically strenuous activity such as running. What happened to your breath? It probably increased in speed and your lungs started working overtime to help supply much-needed oxygen to your body. Similarly, when under stress, your heart rate increases. As your heart rate increases, more oxygen is sent to the muscles. In order to keep up with this demand, you begin to inhale and exhale with greater frequency. The opposite physiological response is also true. When you're relaxed, the heart rate slows and breathing becomes more relaxed.

As you're reading this, notice how you're breathing. What part of your torso is moving? Is the movement mainly in the chest area or is your stomach rising and falling as you breathe? Take a moment to sit in a comfortable position, place one hand over the chest and one hand over the stomach, over the belly button. Notice which hand is moving. If you notice movement only in the hand over the chest or if both hands are moving, intentionally bring your attention to the hand over the belly and intentionally relax your breathing so the hand over your belly moves the most. It's important not to over-breathe or take big gulps of air. Continue to breathe this way for a few minutes, allowing your belly to move your hand, and take a moment to notice how you feel. Did changing your breath affect your sense of well-being?

The breathing style you just experimented with is often referred to as abdominal breathing, or *diaphragmatic breathing*, because it is done by contracting the diaphragm, a dome-shaped sheet of muscle and tendon between the chest and stomach. This style of breathing, in which the abdomen moves more than the chest, allows us to breathe more deeply and take in more air. Regulating the breath in this way can also help calm and settle the nervous system.

It may take some focus to do diaphragmatic breathing, since many people unconsciously engage in shallow breathing or chest breathing, drawing in minimal air into the lungs. This habit may have developed from years of compounded stress. Initially it may feel uncomfortable to breathe deeply, engaging the diaphragm and allowing your stomach area to rise and fall as you breathe. Some people, particularly women, may habitually suck in their stomach to maintain their body shape. It's common to have hesitancy in letting the stomach hang out, but go ahead and let it be loose.

To practice diaphragmatic breathing, sit in a comfortable position, with the back upright, roll the shoulders back, aligning the head, neck, the spine, and the hips. Place a hand over the stomach, over your belly button. As you breathe in through your nose, you should feel your hand rise. As you breathe out, your hand should fall. Your entire stomach should expand, including the sides. Another way to practice is to lie down on a firm surface with a mat or a blanket, either face up or face down. As you breathe in and out, you should feel your lower torso rise and fall. There should be little or no movement in the chest area.

With practice, you may find diaphragmatic breathing soothing, especially when you're feeling stressed. Diaphragmatic breathing can have an extremely calming effect and stop the fight-or-flight reaction. If you're used to breathing only from your chest, this can take some practice. It's also possible you may feel dizzy when you begin to practice diaphragmatic breathing. This is very common. If you do notice dizziness, stop the exercise, rest, and try again later. Once you intentionally begin to notice and pay attention to your breath, you may find yourself becoming preoccupied with thoughts about whether you're breathing correctly. Again, this is very normal. If you notice this, simply acknowledge it for what it is—a passing thought.

An easy practice you can incorporate into your day is to take a couple of seconds periodically to observe your breath. If you notice your breath is shallow, you can intentionally deepen your breath and practice diaphragmatic breathing. The beauty of this practice is you can do it anywhere. You can practice while commuting to and from work; you can practice while checking your e-mail, doing legal research, writing a motion, or even when you're speaking with someone. With practice, you'll get better at it and the good news is you have the remainder of your life to practice!

Common Misconceptions about Meditation

We hope the diaphragmatic breathing exercise gave you a sense of how enjoyable it can be to calm the mind for even a few minutes. If you're still feeling nervous or hesitant about beginning actual meditation, it could be because you're operating under a misconception about what meditation practice requires. The biggest misconception many professionals hold about meditation is that it's just something they can't do. Nothing could be further from the truth! In fact, you already have many of the basic skills necessary to build a strong meditation practice. In order to establish your meditation practice, you will need the ability to concentrate, some discipline, the ability to set a goal and work toward it, and the tenacity to keep working toward your goal even if you encounter a few setbacks. These skills are the basic currency of any professional life, and chances are they are very familiar to you.

If you still are concerned you may not be able to meditate, it's worth spending a little time considering what might be behind that concern. Many people who have never meditated simply have wrong ideas about what meditation requires.

22

It's Okay to Have Thoughts

Perhaps you believe you think too much to meditate. One very common misunderstanding about meditation is that it requires a completely silent mind, with no thoughts. Many lawyers have said things to us like, *I'd love to meditate, but I can't make my mind stop thinking.* Behind that statement seems to lurk another view—these lawyers don't *want* to stop thinking. Lawyers are good at thinking; we think for a living and, much of the time, thinking is something we enjoy. If that's how you feel, we're delighted to be able to tell you that meditating doesn't require you to stop thinking. In fact, it would be impossible to stop your mind from producing thoughts for any sustained amount of time.

As your meditation practice deepens, you may find when you meditate you experience periods of time when the mind is very quiet—and that often feels very good. At some point, however, your thoughts will begin again. This is completely normal. After all, the function of the mind is to produce thoughts. Just as our hearts beat and our lungs breathe, our minds are constantly creating thoughts. To continue the analogy a little, you can force yourself to stop breathing, but eventually you always start breathing again. Even if you were so good at holding your breath you passed out, once you lost consciousness, the breathing process would very naturally start on its own. The same is true of thinking—it is a natural process that restarts on its own.

So what do we *do* in meditation, if we aren't stopping our thoughts? As we noted above, the goal of meditation is not to rid ourselves of thoughts, but to change our relationship to our thoughts. We will be discussing this in more detail in the next few chapters, but for now consider the fact that many of us live entirely in a world created by our thoughts and mental constructs. We may think our opposing counsel is deranged, our clients are angels (or devils), or we are trapped by circumstances in a particular job. Whatever our particular beliefs about our situation, we often have no sense we have agency over those beliefs or that anything other than what we think about our circumstances might be true. As we meditate more regularly, we begin to see thoughts and the mental frameworks we create with them are just something produced by the mind. They can be useful tools, but they are not reality, and we have much more choice than we may have realized about whether to believe them or not. This simple insight can bring enormous freedom.

Meditation Doesn't Have to Take a Lot of Time

Many busy professionals shy away from meditation because they dread the idea of taking on another obligation. Their schedules are full to overflowing, and they can't see adding yet another task to their already over-full days. They picture a meditation practice as something similar to taking on a new sport or a major project. Meditation is a step into such new territory and the changes it can bring are so dramatic, surely it must require a big chunk of time, they imagine. In fact, meditation needn't be an elaborate and time-consuming task. A regular practice does require commitment, but the time you set aside to meditate can be as little as a few minutes per day, particularly in the beginning.

Once you begin to sit quietly on a regular basis, you may find as we did—that time spent on meditation is quite different from time spent on other activities. It is your time, in a way that time spent on almost anything else can never be. It is a respite from all the other demands of life and has a simplicity other activities don't offer. And its rewards come

23

with relatively little investment: building up your sitting time to half an hour per day is really all you need to have a very productive and engaged meditation practice.

If half an hour per day seems impossible, don't worry. You can start with as little as two minutes to get yourself going. However, we do ask you to consider whether it's really true you can't take half an hour for yourself and your mind. How much time do you spend watching television you really aren't enjoying or addictively clicking on social media links? If you give your mind a chance to experience the refreshment that can come with taking a true break from everyday stimuli and stresses, you may find it becomes much easier to find the time to sit.

You Don't Need to Leave Your Own Culture Behind

Another misunderstanding we hear a lot from people who are new to meditation is a concern that it may require them to enter an unfamiliar culture. Perhaps you associate meditation with Asian spiritual traditions. Many people in the West have learned meditation through one of these traditions. You may have seen their meditation areas with images of the Buddha or deities from Indian, Tibetan, Japanese, or other Asian traditions. If you haven't had exposure to any of those traditions, this may feel alien, particularly if you have no family or other personal connection with Asian culture and this imagery is unfamiliar to you.

While many great meditation traditions and practices do have roots in Asia, the good news is anyone from any culture can meditate. No particular culture has a special lock on meditating, which, after all, amounts to taking some time to sit quietly every day. If you are drawn to the teachings or imagery of a particular tradition, by all means, explore it. But if you aren't, that's fine. You can just meditate.

Highly Productive Meditators

There has been much attention in the popular press on meditation's benefits for career success. Nonetheless, you may still have some concern that by helping you to "tune in" and relax, meditation might blunt the edge you've carefully cultivated in your working life. Lest you worry that meditation will give you so much perspective you won't want to participate in the challenges and achievements of the professional world, the list below of highly accomplished business people and professionals who are also avowed meditators should put your mind at ease. Meditation is no barrier to professional success!

Steve Jobs, the late founder and CEO of Apple

Marc Benioff, CEO of Salesforce.com

Mark Bertolini, CEO of Aetna

Jeff Weiner, CEO of LinkedIn

Rick Rubin, former president of Columbia Records

John Mackey, CEO of Whole Foods

Evan Williams, Cofounder of Twitter

Bill Ford, Chairman of Ford Motor Company

Padmasree Warrior, former CTO of Cisco Systems

Oprah Winfrey, Chairwoman and CEO of Harpo Productions, Inc.

Ray Dalio, founder and Co-CIO of Bridgewater Associates USA

Robert Stiller, CEO of Green Mountain Coffee Roasters, Inc.

Arianna Huffington, President and Editor-in-Chief of Huffington Post Media Group

Andrew Cherng, Founder of Panda Express

Bob Shapiro, former CEO of Monsanto

Bill George, former CEO of Medtronic

Mary Cranston, former CEO and retired Senior Partner of Pillsbury Winthrop Shaw

Russell Simmons, Founder of Def Jam

Roger Berkowitz, CEO of Legal Sea Foods

Ramani Ayer, former Chairman and CEO of Hartford Financial
　Services Group

Rick Goings, CEO of Tupperware

You Don't Need to Change Your Beliefs about Religion or Spirituality

If you feel connected to a particular spiritual tradition or hold certain religious beliefs, you can continue to do so and have a meditation practice. There's no need to change any of your beliefs in order to benefit from a sitting practice. In fact, it's interesting to note virtually every religion includes a practice that involves sitting quietly with the eyes closed or softly focused. Those practices may be called prayer, meditation, or some other type of contemplation, but all are designed to quiet the mind. Sitting quietly and observing your own mind is compatible with religious faith, and, in fact, many people who consider themselves believers find their faith deepens as their meditation practice progresses.

On the other hand, there is no need to adopt any new religious or spiritual beliefs in order to meditate. There are a number of well-known atheists, including Sam Harris and Stephen Batchelor, who are also meditators. Their meditation practice does not appear to have interfered with their atheism or vice versa.

Useful Tools

One of the great things about meditation is that it is something you can do anywhere, any time. You don't need any equipment, and there are no membership fees. That said, there are a few simple tools that can support you in your practice and make it much easier to get regular about sitting.

A Timer

A timer is the one tool we highly recommend. At least initially, you are going to sit for a predetermined amount of time, and having a timer elimi-

26

nates the distraction of wondering how much time has passed. Most people find even after they're in the habit of meditating for a certain amount of time every day, a timer is still a nice tool to have.

While some people enjoy having a special timer for their meditation practice, there's no need for you to have a dedicated meditation timer. Most phones now have timers on them, and a kitchen timer will also work well for this purpose. If you'd like to have a timer specifically for meditation, there are many options including clock-like timers, online timers, and apps you can download to your phone.

If you decide to buy a timer, make sure you listen to its bell or chime before you purchase it, since this feature will directly affect how you experience the end of your meditation time. Besides the sound of the chime, some apps have other helpful features you may want to make use of, like keeping track of your sitting time or providing a journal. A couple of downloadable apps we like are Insight Timer and Mindfulness.

Something to Sit On

Many people like to use a meditation cushion or bench to sit on during their meditation time. Whether you choose to do so is up to you—having a special item to sit on is entirely optional. While we both have used meditation cushions or benches at various times, each of us has spent years at a time meditating without any special equipment. And, of course, when we teach meditation to lawyers, it is mostly in conference rooms of law offices, sitting on the very un-meditative office chairs.

It's important that any meditation cushion you use properly support your posture. We'll discuss sitting posture in Week One and we'll have more to say about how to go about choosing a meditation cushion then.

A Meditation Log or Journal

Keeping a meditation log or journal is a simple way to keep track of your meditation practice. First and most practically, it creates a record of just how much you're sitting. With the busyness of work and the many other commitments most of us juggle, it can be all too easy to fall into skipping sitting time without being fully aware of it. A written record keeps us honest.

A written record also allows us to see our journey. It may feel as though nothing is happening when you sit and you're not making any progress. But when you review your journal, you may realize you have, in fact, learned things about yourself, see trends, or notice moments before a big breakthrough. Because the state of meditation can be so different from the ordinary waking state, it's easy to forget even dramatic experiences unless you write them down. We both are continually surprised to find meditation students arrive in class discouraged and frustrated, only to find on reviewing their notes that they had deep insights and remarkable experiences over the course of the week they'd forgotten all about.

This book includes pages for a meditation log at the end of each of the chapters devoted to the eight practice weeks. The log asks you to record, for each time you meditate, the date, the time of day you sat and for how long, and leaves space to record a few reflections on your sitting time. Your entries need not be long. Just a sentence or two is sufficient. This is a good general outline for how you can keep a meditation journal going forward, once you've completed the program in this book.

28

Setting an Intention for Your Practice

Although not required, it's useful at this point when you are beginning to engage with meditation to set an intention for yourself and your practice. You may wonder what exactly we mean by an intention for a meditation practice. By asking you to set an intention, we're suggesting you identify something you're aiming for in your practice; something that's more than just a goal or a milestone. As nice as it is to achieve a goal, a goal doesn't necessarily reflect our values or deeper desires. By contrast, what we mean by an intention is something much more true or real that you want for yourself. So, while a goal might be to sit for five minutes longer each week, an intention would be to find more contentment in your life. An intention can be concrete—an example of a concrete intention might be to stop bickering with your spouse at the end of the day—but it should reflect a more deeply held value or wish for your life rather than something you would check off a to-do list.

Setting an intention is a little like setting your compass: it is always there in the background guiding you in a certain direction, even though you may not consciously be thinking about it at any given moment.

There's something a tiny bit magical about setting an intention—you may be surprised to find the world may seem to reflect your intention back at you, once you've taken the time to define it. Many people, ourselves included, have had the experience of setting a clear intention only to stumble on a helpful book or have a very useful conversation about the object of that intention almost immediately afterward. Or we may have a very satisfying experience, only to realize it almost exactly fulfills an intention we set for ourselves some time ago. An experience like that feels uncanny in the best possible way—like the universe is taking care of us and wants to support our best hopes for ourselves.

There have been plenty of new age books and workshops that try to capitalize on the feeling of magic we're describing. We want to be clear that we're not invoking that kind of sloppy or wishful thinking when we say an intention can set magic going. While you may genuinely experience a subjective feeling of magic when things fall into place around an intention, objectively speaking, the magic you set into motion may have a much more straightforward explanation. Think about it this way: simply by taking the time to think clearly about exactly what you are looking to get from your practice, you focus your efforts, even if you do so unconsciously. And by defining in a clear way what you're hoping for, you are much more able to take advantage of opportunities to fulfill those hopes than if you begin your practice without really knowing what you are trying to get out of it.

With that in mind, take a moment to consider what lies behind your decision to begin meditating and what a meditation practice can bring to your life. Maybe you're in a difficult juncture in your life and need a way to get some ground under your feet. Maybe you want to explore your own inner world and get a better sense of what's in there. Maybe you want to see reality more clearly. Or maybe you want to tap into the many benefits you've heard meditation can bring.

29

Exploring Your Intention

Identifying an intention for meditation practice can be surprisingly challenging for some people. It's often difficult to know what motivates us in the most prosaic aspects of our lives, so uncovering what we are hoping to gain from a practice like meditation can be very hard to do. If you're having trouble defining what your intention is, it may be helpful to spend a few minutes sitting quietly, so distractions can fall away and you have a chance to hear the voice of your own wisdom.

Try this short exercise. You'll need a quiet place to sit for a few minutes and something to write on:

Sit comfortably on a chair or cushion. Let your spine be as straight as possible without feeling stiff or rigid. Allow your eyes to close. Notice the feeling of the floor under your feet, or the cushion you are sitting on. For a minute or two, let your attention settle on the sounds around you. Notice the closer sounds and the sounds that are further away. Enjoy the sensation of hearing. After a few minutes, let go of the sounds, and just allow yourself to relax and enjoy a minute or so of doing nothing at all.

When you're ready, bring your attention back to the room and to your own body. Gently open your eyes. Now, from this more settled place ask yourself, what is my intention for my meditation practice? Write down what comes up for you. You may want to spend a few minutes refining this idea. Keep working on the idea until you can express it clearly in a phrase or sentence. The more clarity you can bring to your intention, the more power it will have for you.

If you like, you can see if there is something else beyond this first expression of the intention that came to you—the intention behind the intention. For example, perhaps you initially identified "getting more and better sleep" as the intention for your practice. If you look further you might realize a deeper or truer intention is "more well-being and peace of mind." If exploring your intention further feels appealing, you can repeat the exercise, this time asking yourself, what is the deeper intention for my practice? See if something new suggests itself.

Be sure to end this exercise with a clear, written summary of what your intention is. If you can't find the words to describe your intention right now, return later and see if you can articulate it. It's worth taking the effort to write your intention down—doing this will force you to clarify exactly what your intention is, and you can return and reread it later to see whether it is still valid for you, or to get a sense of how far you've come.

One note on the practical benefits of meditation: if you're drawn to meditation because of what you've read in popular media about the many physical and psychological benefits of meditation, that's wonderful. As we acknowledged earlier, these positive effects are truly impressive, and the attention they're now receiving may prove to be of great value to society by identifying a powerful, accessible, and inexpensive tool for addressing many of the most common physical and mental health challenges we face in the modern age. All the popular attention focused on these very pragmatic benefits can, however, lead to misunderstanding about meditation and what is possible—and realistic—to expect from a meditation practice. So if you're enthralled by the possibility of meditating your way to senior partner in just three years, a few words of caution are called for.

First, it's possible to fall into thinking the benefits of meditation end at the physical or psychological. Viewed through the lens of practicality, meditating can be seen as the equivalent of going to the gym or brushing your teeth: something you do to help yourself get through the day in a healthy way. As we pointed out in the introduction to this book, while there's nothing wrong with meditating for purely practical reasons, meditation was invented as a means of personal transformation, and that remains the most powerful way we can engage with it. Remember the people who first began meditating were asking themselves the big questions every person grapples with: Who am I? What is this world? Why am I here? These questions are worth asking, so we hope you won't limit your goals for your practice by over-focusing on the pragmatic.

Second, the current enthusiasm for bringing meditation to bear on real-life issues, and particularly the drive to bring meditation into the workplace, can lead us to see mediation as a kind of panacea and guarantor of success in the working world. We both have personally experienced some of the very significant benefits a meditation practice can bring to our working lives. At the same time, our experience has been that these benefits didn't necessarily unfold in a linear way. Although it's true that welcome and occasionally unexpected successes have come our way since we began meditating, meditation has not been a career cure-all for either of us. Setbacks are still very much part of our lives. When we identify the benefits meditation has brought to our working lives, we both tend to point to internal rather than external measures, for example, qualities like greater confidence, spontaneity, and pleasure in our work than to specific professional milestones like winning a case or making partner.

Returning to your own intention for your practice, our last bit of advice is, be bold. Whatever you choose as the focus for your practice is up to you, and whatever you choose is fine. In setting your intention, we do hope you take into account that meditation is deceptively powerful. It doesn't seem like just sitting quietly every day could have a big effect on one's life, but both of us, and many, many others, have experienced huge shifts in our inner and outer lives after taking up meditation. Remember this is a transformative practice. We suggest setting an intention that reflects your highest wish for yourself—maybe even something you think may not be possible. What happens may surprise you.

You're Heading into Safe Territory—Yourself

We often say meditation is a transformative practice, and it is. But what do we mean by transformation? If you're basically happy with the contours of your life, the idea of transformation can sound a little intimidating, or even unappealing. The important thing to remember here is that all this talk of transformation points back at you—you are the author of any transformation you may go through.

Some people worry if they start a meditation practice, before they know it, they'll end up on top of a mountain somewhere, fasting and wrapped in a sheet. A judge who arrived at one of our introductory meditation sessions remarked that meditation is all well and good, but she has things to do. She wasn't so concerned about the time needed to attend class and meditate over the course of each week, but rather that somehow meditating would interfere with her ability to attend to all the genuinely important and time-sensitive matters she has to deal with. The idea that meditation can impede a person's ability to be a productive and contributing member of society is surprisingly widely held. Perhaps it comes from the many popular books and movies about people who have dropped out of civilization in pursuit of inner wisdom. Hopefully, though, you've noticed the books about running away from society to meditate are written by people who *wanted* to run away from society. If you're not looking to drop out, meditation is highly unlikely to change that.

Karen's Experience of How Meditation
Changed Her Working Life

When I began to meditate, I was grateful to realize that it helped me relax at a time when I was dealing with the multiple demands of a young family and a busy legal practice. What surprised me was the degree of change meditation brought to my life. The changes didn't happen suddenly, they were consonant with my temperament and personality, but, nonetheless, they were profound. I certainly never expected meditation to affect my working life in the way it has.

As I got further into meditation practice and started to know my mind a little better, I started to see my thoughts in better perspective. Over time, I felt much more comfortable questioning my preconceptions rather than always trying to defend them. This shift in perspective had a radical effect on my experience of work. I began to view difficulties at work not as something to push away, but as opportunities to engage with my own mental constructs. And, believe me, I had lots of opportunities! If you want to see your own patterns and assumptions, working in a demanding job will bring them to the fore over and over again. My office became a place for deepening self-knowledge, rather than just a place to get things done.

Ironically, all this inner work ended up making me much more effective at my job. Learning to watch stressful feelings come and go during meditation gave me tools I put to use in many situations: I was less reactive in negotiations, less intimidated by the big guns my opponents brought into my cases, worried less about outcomes, and therefore was more able to do my best work. I was more authentically myself in court, and I believe that made me more persuasive.

Did meditation turn me into the best, most invincible lawyer ever? Probably not. But I know it helped me become the best lawyer I was capable of being. My meditation practice certainly made it possible for me to continue at a challenging job for years longer than I would have otherwise. I'm very grateful for that time and the chance to do work that was meaningful to me.

Later on, meditation gave me the mental space to question the all-work-at-all-costs ethos that dominates the legal profession, and find a way to practice part-time. And eventually, when I decided it was time to move on, meditation helped make the move out of legal practice—

33

a notoriously fraught transition—pass relatively smoothly. Many lawyers report that giving up legal practice turns their sense of identity upside down, and I was no exception. Leaving the law was a great exercise in seeing how I had limited myself professionally by hanging on to a concept that no longer reflected who I was, and meditation helped me recognize that.

Since leaving legal practice, I've consulted in the financial industry, held leadership roles at a number of companies, and currently serve as an advisor and investor in the financial technology space. I couldn't have made transitions to any of those roles if I hadn't been able to muster some comfort with uncertainty and connect with my sense of adventure. I credit my meditation practice with teaching me to love adventure, and in many ways it's felt like the biggest adventure I've ever been on. I'm looking forward to seeing what happens next.

One big reason meditation brings real and satisfying change into our lives is the changes we make as a result of our meditation reflect who we are at a fundamental level. You could think of meditation as a way of getting to know yourself better, and any transformation that meditation brings comes from that self-knowledge. Meditation doesn't—and can't—make anything appear in your mind that isn't already part of you. So you're headed into profoundly safe territory—the land of yourself. The people we know who've had long-term meditation practices report they feel more like themselves than ever.

On the other hand, it's possible you've wanted to make some changes to your life for some time, and, for one reason or another, you haven't done so. In that case, your meditation practice may well be a catalyst for change, by helping you to clarify your own thinking and gain perspective on fears you may have had about taking action. But it's important to be clear that you're driving the bus here. All meditation can do is put you in better touch with what you want for your life. Anything you decide to do as a result of that knowledge will be the result of your judgment and will reflect your values, temperament, and preferences.

The external changes we've seen long-term meditators make are not so different from the changes anyone makes over the course of life. The biggest changes we've noticed in ourselves and our peers who meditate don't have to do with changing jobs, but with changing attitudes. Over time, many meditators experience that fear, anger, and impulsive reaction play less and less of a role in their decision making. Limiting thoughts like "I can't try something new" or "I'm just not that kind of person" similarly hold less sway, with the end result that decision-making can happen with more clarity and ease.

Again, this evolution happens very naturally. Sitting with your own mind and getting to know it has a way of helping you see through limiting thoughts, emotions, and impulses. As your practice progresses, you'll have a chance to experience the many layers and subtleties of your mind. For example, when you experience physical pain, the first layer is the actual pain itself. The layer on top of that is the idea of pain and your reaction to the perceived pain. When you experience pain, the natural inclination is to push it away. So, as you practice meditation, you can observe the aversion to pain, the idea of pain, the reaction to the pain, and the pain itself. There may also be additional layers. As you begin to see past the more superficial layers of the mind, you realize there are many deeper layers, and you may not be able to see all these layers at once. Noticing how your body reacts, feels, or processes these layers is a useful way to access the complexity of human experience. You'll also likely experience insights. To continue this example, noticing the various layers of how you react to pain may lead you to see your idea of pain and reaction to that idea are far more limiting than the pain itself. This insight can have very big repercussions for the kinds of challenges and opportunities you are willing to take on. Having this experience of insight in turn opens your mind up to the possibility of having other insights, and learning from them. So you may find yourself living with an expanded sense of opportunity and agency, but this sense is something that comes from you and your own understanding of yourself, not from any outside force.

35

Beginning to Meditate

Away, O soul! hoist instantly the anchor!
Cut the hawsers – haul out – shake out every sail!
Have we not stood here like trees in the ground long enough?
Have we not grovell'd here long enough, eating and drinking
like mere brutes?
Have we not darken'd and dazed ourselves with books long enough?
Sail forth! steer for the deep waters only!

—Walt Whitman, *Leaves of Grass*

THIS WEEK YOU'LL BEGIN your sitting practice. This first week, you'll be working out where and when to sit and starting to establish the habit of meditating. In this chapter, we'll describe the meditation practice you'll be using for the first week of this course: mindfully noting the sensations of the body. We'll touch on some of the initial insights and challenges you may encounter in this initial week of practice. As you go through the week, you may also want to return to the suggestions and tips outlined in the previous chapter as you deal with the practicalities of setting up your practice.

Meditation Practice: Body Scan

In the first weeks of this course, we'll be using mindfulness based meditation practices. In Week 2, we'll discuss the practice of mindfulness more generally, as well as some of its underlying philosophy. For now, we'll focus on having a practical experience of mindfulness. To do so, we'll use a common introductory mindfulness practice: a simple body scan. In this exercise, you'll direct your attention to the physical sensations of various parts of the body, moving your attention slowly over your whole body. Many people find this exercise to be very relaxing—we hope you enjoy it.

In asking you to focus on different parts of the body, we should be clear this doesn't mean thinking about the body. Your focus should rest on physical sensations. Thoughts will come and go during the time you're sitting, but try not to get too fixated on them. Instead, notice the feeling of each part of your body as you move your attention from one area to another. What do you notice about your ankle? Your hips? Where do you notice the breath moving your body? See if you can bring a sense of wonder to noticing your own body. Enjoy the simplicity of just focusing on sensation—there's nothing else you need to do in this moment, nothing to get right or wrong. Let yourself take a break from everything else and get completely absorbed in the sitting exercise.

We suggest you start by sitting for just ten minutes everyday. This is long enough to reach a meditative state, and it should be relatively easy to fit into your day. Do this for at least three days, and then evaluate. Could you sit for a longer period of time? Is ten minutes really too much right now? Depending on your answer to those questions, you can adjust the amount of time you devote to meditation. Far more important than how long you sit is that you spend at least some time meditating every day. Eventually you'll want to aim to sit for half an hour per day, but unless you find this easy to do, don't worry about it for now.

Engaging with Meditation Practice

So, we have our meditation practice. What exactly do we do with it? A meditation practice is a gentle focal point for our attention during our sitting time. When we sit to meditate, we take a few minutes to settle ourselves into a quieter state, and then we use the practice as a touchstone, to help keep our minds relaxed and focused. You don't want to grind into the practice or hold on to it so tightly your mind has no room to relax. A useful analogy might be the feeling you have when you allow your peripheral vision to widen. You can still focus on an object within your line of sight, but your eyes take in more information, and the feeling quality associated with that wider view is more relaxed than a tight and narrow focus.

We want to hold the focal point of our meditation lightly, in part to give ourselves room to see our mind when it is in a relatively relaxed and open state. What is your mind like when you aren't asking it to perform a task? This may be the first time you've had a chance to observe your mind in this state, or it may be years since you've done so, and it's one of the most significant things you'll do as you build your meditation practice.

39

Meditation and Stress Reduction

Meditation's ability to help people cope with and reduce their experience of stress is one of the most studied and best documented of its effects. Hundreds of studies have shown the benefits of meditation in reducing stress in a wide range of settings.[2] Meditation training has been shown to have a measurable and continuing ability to reduce the experience and effects of stress even in people who are coping with such challenging situations as cancer treatment, HIV, and chronic pain.[3]

In the 1960s, Herbert Benson, a physician at Harvard Medical School, undertook the first breakthrough studies demonstrating meditative practices could be used to elicit what he termed the "relaxation response," in which a constellation of physiologic and psychological responses to stress can be decreased.[4] Building on this foundation, Jon Kabat-Zinn, an MIT-trained doctor and molecular biologist, later conducted clinical studies that helped to bring meditation further into mainstream medicine.

Kabat-Zinn established the Stress Reduction Clinic at the University of Massachusetts Medical Center in the 1970s and coined the term "mindfulness" to describe the fundamental skill of meditation, paying attention to what is happening in the moment. He also developed the Mindfulness Based Stress Reduction (MBSR) program that has now introduced millions of people to the basics of meditation.[5]

Kabat-Zinn's work has shown that physiological changes begin to take place in the brain after only eight weeks of meditation practice. Recent studies have shown regions of the brain that are important for learning, memory, and executive decision making grow measurably larger after meditating regularly in this relatively short time frame, and that other areas of the brain, such as the amygdala, grow smaller.[6] The amygdala, sometimes referred to as our "reptile brain," is involved in the fight-or-flight response, so the fact that it shrinks after even a relatively small amount of regular meditation practice suggests meditation can powerfully alter the way we deal with external threats and the extent to which we find ourselves living in fear.

40

One of the principal skills we build in the practice of meditation is the ability to observe our mind and become familiar with it—as it is. This focus on the mind as it is may be unfamiliar to you and require a little adjustment, as it is somewhat different from the way you may be accustomed to approaching mental exploration. Our modern Western culture tends to analyze the mind from the point of view of psychology. While psychology and meditation do share the goal of freeing us from dysfunctional mental patterns, they employ different means of doing so. Psychology generally examines the contents of thoughts, and uses this analysis to aid us in letting go of unhelpful mental patterns. In meditation, unlike psychology, we generally don't work directly with the contents of thoughts, but rather see thoughts as phenomena. Meditation posits that by simply observing the mind and the thoughts flowing through it, we begin to see thoughts for what they are—thoughts, not reality. This insight helps us to see we are free to believe or reject any particular thought, and can step away from mental patterns that aren't working for us.

This mind you are getting to know better has already done so much for you. It's gotten you through law school and helped you pass the bar exam. It's been a great tool for advancing your professional career. This practice will give you a chance to see what your mind is like when you're not asking it to do work for you.

Noticing the Moment of Choice

One aspect of the mind you will certainly be encountering this week is the cycle of thoughts and the mind's repeated return to clarity. These moments, when the mind returns to itself, are key to building your practice. It is in these moments we have the opportunity to exercise choice about where to direct our practice.

What we mean by the cycle of thoughts is the mind's tendency to drift from whatever it is doing, become lost for a few minutes in a series of associations, and then return to awareness. The mind does this over and over again, all day long. When you sit to meditate, you get a chance to see this pattern more clearly because you're not distracted by other things. The cycle of thoughts might happen something like this:

41

> You sit, focusing on the sensations of the body. You notice how your leg meets your hip socket. You notice how your torso is moving with the rhythm of the breath. It feels good. You're relaxed. You need to go grocery shopping after the timer goes off. You wonder if the store will have fava beans in stock. It's the right time of year. Spring. The last time you made favas was last spring; the day the decision came out in that case you'd worked so hard on. In many ways the decision was great, but that judge never understood one of the arguments you made. He was just never going to get that. It was disappointing. What if you'd included the affidavit from that other witness? It was a little off point, but it might have pushed the judge to dig deeper into the issue. Oh,—you're meditating right now.

This last moment, when the mind returns to awareness, is what we call the moment of choice. That moment, when you're simply aware of yourself and your surroundings, is a moment of clarity. It is a brief glimpse of pure awareness, which is the ultimate goal of meditation. It's also the time when you can make a choice about where to place your focus. In the example above, once you remember you are sitting to meditate, you can choose to return to your practice, to think more about that old case you worked on, or to be upset with yourself that you forgot you were meditating. Oddly, many people choose this last option, and spend the balance of their meditation period berating themselves for having forgotten to meditate!

Making good use of the moment of choice is one of the most important things you can learn from practicing meditation. So often we come to clarity, only to be upset with ourselves for drifting into thought. This is essentially giving the mind negative reinforcement, punishing it for being self-aware, when that's actually the state we want to encourage. Rather than being harsh with ourselves for allowing our attention to wander, a better response is gratitude our attention has returned, and we're again aware of what is happening in the moment. The reality is that even the most experienced meditator's mind will wander at times. So when you return to clarity, if you can remember to take a brief moment to appreciate the mind, that will encourage it to come back to itself more and more often.

As you get more practice in identifying the moment of choice, you may find you notice it during the day, when you are off the cushion. Recognizing the moment of choice and exercising choice over where you will put your focus can be very powerful and very freeing. That moment is when you can decide whether you are going to continue to ruminate about that difficult client or instead enjoy the view out your window for a few minutes. It's when you can choose between worrying you might be late to meet a friend and appreciating the pleasure of the brisk walk to meet her. It's when you can choose to continue a quarrel with your spouse or to shift the tone. Over time, these choices add up and can change the quality of your daily experience.

Your Sitting Posture

Whether you sit on a chair, a cushion, or on the ground, your meditation posture should be comfortable enough for you to hold without becoming a major distraction during the time you are sitting. This should be relatively easy in this first week, as you are probably only sitting for ten minutes at a time. Nonetheless, it's a good idea to take the time to find a sitting posture that works well for you. You are embarking on a practice that could continue for many years, so the patterns you establish now could have long-term effects. Finding an easeful posture will prevent injuries in the long run.

Because you'll be sitting for a relatively short amount of time, this is a good week to try out a few different postures and places to sit. You could try sitting cross-legged one day and see if that's for you. If you decide you want to try sitting on a meditation cushion, we've included some tips here on picking a cushion that's right for your body.

However you choose to sit, a few things should remain constant: your spine should be as straight as possible without being unnaturally stiff or uncomfortable, while the rest of your body should be as relaxed as possible. You can rest your hands on your thighs or fold them in front of you, with the palms up, resting in your lap. It's a good idea to support your lower back either by sitting in a chair, or if you are sitting on a cushion, sitting against the wall. You may want to have a small cushion to provide extra support for your lower back. Your knees should be below your hips so that your hip flexors can relax.

43

Choosing a Meditation Cushion

As we noted in the previous chapter, you don't need to have any special seating equipment in order to meditate. If you decide you'd like to have a special sitting cushion or bench, the genuine advantage of doing so is that it will permit you to find and give you sitting support that helps you stay physically aligned in a posture you can maintain comfortably. You are now in the process of establishing a practice that will hopefully continue for many years, so it may be worth spending a little time and money to help ensure that the position your body is in during your sitting time doesn't strain your back or joints.

There are many different types of meditation cushions and benches available online or in meditation centers, yoga studios, and specialized stores. We strongly recommend that you actually try out the cushion or bench you choose before buying it, to make sure that it actually is as comfortable as it looks. Some of the softer meditation cushions look nice, but don't provide enough support.

Any sitting aid should allow you to sit with your spine straight, but not rigid or stiff. The rest of your body should be able to be relatively relaxed.

Your knees should be below your hips so that your hip flexors can remain loose. If you notice that you have to tense up in order to stay upright, you probably have the wrong cushion. Finding the right cushion allows you to have a sitting support that helps you stay physically aligned in a posture you can maintain comfortably.

When you sit to meditate this week, take a few minutes to pick a posture and settle in to it. Once you've chosen it, commit to it for the time you're sitting. Unless you become very uncomfortable, try not to wiggle or fidget during your meditation time. As you settle in, take a few deeper breaths, and with each breath, try to allow your body to relax a little more. Let your shoulders slide down your back. Swallow and allow your jaw to relax. Consciously relax the muscles in your face and the top of your head. When you feel relaxed and settled, you can turn your attention to your meditation practice.

As with noticing the moment of choice, paying attention to posture when you sit for meditation may spill over into other areas of your life. Once you get into the habit of taking time to find a comfortable and relaxing posture for your meditation time, it may seem natural to want to have that feeling of ease at other times of day. For example, you may notice for the first time your desk at work isn't set up ergonomically and make some changes to it. Or you may notice you're instinctively taking a more upright and easeful stance when you sit on the bus or in meetings.

Establishing a Sitting Practice

This week as you sit every day, you're beginning to establish your sitting practice. As you'll see, establishing a regular sitting practice is essentially no more complicated than creating any new habit. It requires a little discipline, a lot of patience, and is much easier if you make it as pleasant for yourself as possible. If you consciously make meditation into a special time for yourself, time you have to relax and leave aside your daily worries and preoccupations, you'll probably find it is much easier to make it a regular part of your life than if you think of it as one more task you have to accomplish.

One minor adjustment you may need to make is aligning your approach to mastering a new skill with the nature of meditation practice. While lawyers tend to be very goal oriented, the practice of meditation doesn't have any goals or destination. It's not about getting the mind to *do* anything. It's the practice of *non-doing*. Being gentle with yourself and letting go are far more important to your practice than focusing on accomplishment. As you work through the exercises outlined in this book, as tempting as it may be to think of them as something to tick off on your to-do list, do remember the primary reason for engaging with meditation is to create a time in your day for yourself where you can sit silently and simply practice being.

In this regard, the most important thing you can do to get your meditation practice up and running is simple: sit every day. Just like physical exercise, the most crucial part of cultivating a meditation practice is just that—practice. The more you practice, the more opportunities you create to deepen your understanding of your mind, and that is how you'll eventually gain mastery over its patterns and reactions. The daily act of sitting yourself down with the intention to meditate will do far more to anchor your practice than any kind of meditation cushions, bells, any special atmosphere you create, or even any amount of instruction. Again, don't worry if you don't have a lot of time for your practice. It's much better to sit for ten minutes every day than to sit half an hour once per week. Similarly, you don't need to feel discouraged if you are very distracted or think nothing is happening during your meditation time. If you build the habit of sitting quietly every day, your mind will follow.

45

Getting the Meditation Habit Started

- **Sit every day!** Even if you can only sit for a few minutes, sitting daily will get you in the meditation habit.
- **Use positive reinforcement.** Connect your sitting time with something you already like—sit in your favorite chair, wrap yourself in a soft shawl, wear a comfortable sweater.
- **Find a meditation buddy.** We know two people who have a weekly date to meditate together over Skype once a week. They say hello, sit silently together for half an hour, hang up, and go about their days. Just being accountable to each other for their weekly meditation date helps both of them stay steady with their practices.

- **Set a meditation alarm.** If you have a hard time remembering to sit, set an alarm on your phone to go off ten minutes before the time you've designated for meditation. Those ten minutes will give you a chance to bring your other tasks to a stopping point before you turn to your sitting practice.
- **Don't be a meditation perfectionist.** If anything is making it too complicated to meditate—you think you don't have the right cushion, or you don't have time to create a serene atmosphere, or missed sitting at the time you usually sit—just drop that thing off your list. All you really need to meditate is yourself and your mind. Keep it simple and sit.

Another important aspect of establishing your practice is getting through the initial bumps. Once you start meditating, there will likely come a day when you forget to sit. This is a point when many people let themselves become demoralized and stop meditating—and that would be a mistake. Letting yourself be thrown off your meditation practice by the normal difficulties of settling into a new habit would be like giving up on a long-awaited trip to Bali just because you forgot to pack your sunscreen. Don't let the little frustrations keep you from your big adventure. Remember every experienced meditator has had to get past the early challenges, and know this is an area where you have an advantage over most people. If you are reading a book on meditation for lawyers, you already know that a key part of meeting any goal is not letting yourself be thrown off if you have a setback or two. How would you have gotten through law school if you quit the first time you forgot to do the reading for a class? So if you do miss a day of meditation, there's no need to be discouraged. Just sit the next day.

Most people find it becomes easier to meditate if they sit in the same place and at the same time every day. Find a place that is pleasant for you, is relatively quiet, and where you aren't likely to be interrupted. This could be a quiet room in your home, a comfortable corner or a chair, or it could be somewhere outside your home, like a park, a church, or a quiet room in your office. It's much more important to pick a spot that works for you than to try to create the absolute perfect environment or sit in a place that fits your image of a meditation space. A woman who attended one of our classes told us she meditates in her car between client meetings or before starting depositions, and this was perfect for her.

When you're starting your practice, you may want to experiment with sitting at different times of the day. Many people prefer to meditate first thing in the morning, before their minds become crowded with the tasks of the day. Others find sitting in the evening is a relaxing way to wind down before going to bed. Still others like a mid-day meditation and find taking a break from the busyness of the working day allows them to re-center themselves. Notice what works for you.

Some Common Challenges

While, of course, we hope your first week of sitting is easy, deep, and bliss-ful—and that could well be the case for you—it's also relatively common to encounter some challenges when you first begin to sit. In engaging with these challenges, remember to be gentle with yourself. As we noted earlier, you may find you need to step back from strategies you're accustomed to using when facing down a challenge. While your persistence and discipline can come in handy in getting your meditation practice started, this is not the time to engage in self-criticism or competitiveness. You may have used those feelings very effectively to get yourself through law school—perhaps they are still strong motivators for you—but it's better to focus on other means of motivating yourself while building the meditation habit.

47

Finding Time

Anyone who works in a service-oriented profession like the law struggles with the issue of finding time for other activities. The pressures to bill hours in a modern legal practice are enormous. Not only can your output always be improved—there are always more cases to read, journal articles, professional newsletters, or CLE materials that could add depth to your analysis—but your standing in the firm, compensation, and the professional recognition you receive from your peers are directly and often explicitly tied to the number of hours you spend at work. Navigating this demanding professional life while also leaving time for a strong, loving relationship, let alone a busy family life, is more than many lawyers ever manage, and the high divorce rate in our profession is a testament to that challenge.

So how can a meditation practice be added to the mix? As we noted in the introductory chapter, meditation does not require a big time commitment. Meditation is not a "more is better" practice. You may hear about people who go on three-month meditation retreats, and the depth to which they have taken their practices. You may want to emulate their commitment and spend hours on your cushion every day. While it's wonderful to have the luxury of time to devote significant parts of the day to meditation, it is by no means necessary. If you can work up to making meditation a half-an-hour per day commitment, you will have invested all the time necessary to have a fulfilling and productive practice—and you can take that practice as deep as you like.

Separate from the question of whether you actually have the time to meditate may be the feeling you are too busy to sit. This feeling of "busyness" is both a seduction and a major source of dysfunction for many lawyers. Apart from the objective reasons we often find ourselves with too little time, we can also allow a self-created sense of busyness to creep into our lives. This self-created feeling that "I'm very busy all the time" serves unconscious needs, but doesn't do so very effectively. If we are very busy, we secretly believe we must be doing something important—in fact, we must be very important. We're also too busy to confront what is painful or not working in our lives. Far from making us important or giving us control over the things we don't like, unnecessary busyness actually creates a barrier between us and the insights and changes that could make our lives more important and meaningful. If you find you repeatedly get to the end of the day without having made time for your meditation period, you may want to ask yourself if you are unconsciously making yourself feel busier than you really are. After all, on most days, even the busiest people have ten minutes.

Sleepiness

Some people find themselves drifting off to sleep during meditation. They sit down and settle in, only to have the bell jolt them back into awareness at the end of the meditation period. Or they find themselves repeatedly nodding off, struggling to stay conscious while maintaining a state of meditation. If this is your experience, there are a few questions you may want to ask yourself.

First, you should determine whether you really are falling asleep or not. Surprisingly, it is possible to experience something that feels like sleep during your meditation time when you are not asleep at all. There is a deep meditative state that can be confused with sleep, but is not actually sleep. It feels very dark, silent, and peaceful. Few, if any, thoughts occur. If you experience this state, you may even notice yourself nodding off, with your head falling forward periodically. Yogic traditions refer to this state as being in the "causal body." We like to think of this as a time when you may be working out old issues without having to consciously focus on doing so. It is a beautiful and gentle idea. Western science has validated the existence of this state in the laboratory, known as theta waves.[7] The best way to know whether you have really been asleep during a meditation period is to notice how you feel when you come back to normal consciousness after your meditation time. If you feel foggy and slow, you've been sleeping. If you feel refreshed and alert, you've been deep in meditation. Enjoy it.

If you believe you're truly falling asleep during your meditation time, there are a few things that you may want to consider. First, you may genuinely be overly tired. If simply sitting down in a relaxed way is sending you straight to sleep, ask yourself whether you are getting enough sleep. Sad to say, many lawyers spend so much time working they are chronically and severely sleep deprived. If your sleep deficit is paid up but you're still drifting off during meditation, you may want to try sitting in the middle of the room or at the edge of a chair so you have no back support and have to maintain your balance. This added physical challenge may be enough to keep you from drifting off. Some people also find using a mantra (see Week Six of the program) is helpful in maintaining alertness during meditation. If the sleepiness persists, you may try meditating with the eyes slightly open and focused on a spot approximately four feet in front of you.

Distractions

A very disconcerting experience many people have when they first begin to meditate is the sense they are constantly distracted during their sitting time. Many people in classes we have taught come back after the first week reporting that just trying to meditate makes them more distracted than ever. If this is your experience, you're in very good company—but we can assure you meditating isn't making you any more distracted than usual. You're just noticing for the first time how many thoughts flow through your mind and how they veer from one topic to the next, in a surprising tangle of associations. It seems you just sit down to meditate, focus on the breath, and before you know it, you're reliving a conversation you had with your uncle twelve years ago, or mentally measuring the windows in your hallway to see how much fabric you need to order for drapes. You have no idea how you ended up in this train of thought, and it's a far cry from the peace and concentration you were expecting.

While distractions that come up in your practice can be frustrating, the fact that you are experiencing them is actually very good news. You're face to face with your own mind, and that's a great place to be. Getting to know your mind is one of the basic building blocks of any meditation practice. Over time, you'll start to know your mind's patterns and sensibilities. As you get to know your mind and its ways, you'll likely appreciate it more and also take some of its views less seriously.

In terms of how to deal with repeated distractions during your meditation time, patience, kindness, and persistence are the best tools to use. Whenever you notice you're caught up in a train of thought, simply return to your meditation practice; in this case, the body scan. Again, there's no need to berate yourself for having thoughts or having fallen away from your practice. Remember, it's the nature of the mind to produce thoughts, so getting caught up in thoughts periodically is a normal part of meditation practice. Rather than being upset with yourself, appreciate each time you bring your mind back to the meditation method, you're strengthening your "meditation muscles," and building your practice.

50

Boredom

Rather than fighting distraction, some people wish they could find some distraction during their meditation time. They fight a feeling of terrible boredom almost the minute they sit down to meditate. If this is your experience, you may feel each second you sit lasts an eternity; and you're constantly fighting the urge to check the timer to see how much time is left in your sitting period.

Here is where practicing law may give you a leg up on your sitting practice compared with other meditators. Practicing law does require a relatively high tolerance for boredom, so chances are you're familiar with boredom and know how to deal with it. One caveat here is if you're used to powering through boredom and forcing yourself to focus, try to take a more gentle approach in this situation. See if you can, rather than grinding your way through the boredom, gently disengage from it, bringing your focus back to the breath with a sense of ease and appreciation.

If, in spite of your years of legal practice, you find the boredom of a meditation period particularly challenging, it may in part be coming from a feeling you ought to be doing something beyond just sitting quietly. If that's the case for you, see if you can give yourself permission not to be productive for the very short amount of time you are setting aside for meditation. This first week, we're just asking you to sit for ten minutes, but even if you are sitting for half an hour per day, that still leaves you with twenty-three and a half hours to get things done. For this short time, try not to get anything done. Over time, you may be amazed at what happens without any overt effort on your part.

If boredom is persistent, you may use the boredom itself as the object of the meditation. After all, what is boredom if not a set of thoughts, beliefs, and sensations? Boredom, like other thoughts or sensations, will pass with time. Rather than fight the boredom, see if you can pivot toward the boredom. What are the underlying thoughts behind the boredom? How do you know you're experiencing boredom? What thoughts, or physical experiences, do you associate with boredom? Remember, meditation is all about becoming more familiar with our mind. Just like a scientist, we can begin to study our mind rather than be a victim of it.

You may also want to notice whether you're trying to fight your boredom in an active way. Paradoxically, fighting something like boredom can have the effect of making it feel even stronger. Again, patience, kindness, and persistence are key. If you feel bored at every practice session, see what happens if you allow yourself to be completely bored. Continue to follow your breath, but don't try to talk yourself out of your boredom—let it fill your mind. You may find it loses some of its power as you stop wrestling with it.

Surprising Emotions

Almost everyone who meditates experiences, at one point or another, unexpected emotions during their sitting time. Waves of sadness, anger, laughter, or joy may wash over you without any seeming warning or obvious connection to what is going on in your life. When this happens, it can be surprising and disconcerting, especially if you experience some of the more difficult emotions in a strong way early on in your practice.

If you find sitting to meditate immediately brings up strong emotions, it's possible you have some unfinished business to attend to. Perhaps you've pushed something you didn't want to think about or deal with to the back of your mind, and sitting quietly gives that thing a chance to ask for your attention. The busy life of practicing law sometimes gets in the way of engaging with issues or feelings that are uncomfortable. We may not have allowed ourselves the space to feel the discomfort we had about something that took place years ago. Gently allowing that issue to have some space could be healing. Or maybe you never fully processed an old loss, and letting its sadness move through you could be what you need to bring a long-interrupted grieving process to closure.

To be clear, we're not suggesting you use your meditation time to analyze your past or review wrongs you've endured. We're simply suggesting that if emotions arise while you're sitting, you allow yourself to feel them. Later, if you decide you need to better understand what is driving these feelings, you can explore them outside of your meditation time. And, obviously, if you feel overwhelmed by what's coming up, or simply want the support of a counselor or therapist, you shouldn't hesitate to seek help.

It's also possible, while on the cushion, to experience emotions that don't appear to be related to any particular event or issue in your life. They may feel a little like the weather, or the movement of the ocean—tides of feelings that have their own logic. If this happens, you can just allow yourself to feel them and they will very likely pass on their own.

Your Meditation Cushion Is a Place Where There's No Right or Wrong

There is no such thing as right or wrong meditation. Lawyers tend to live in a very binary world, where everything must either be right or wrong. During your meditation, you may notice your inner critic telling you that the practice isn't working, that you're not doing it right or correctly. You may even judge yourself for your worrying mind. Know that these experiences are perfectly normal. Each time your mind gets distracted with thoughts about doing this practice right or wrong, gently guide your mind back to the objection of attention (e.g., your breath). Let go of the idea of right or wrong way of practicing.

—

Give Yourself a Break

Finally, if in dealing with any of these challenges, you realize with horror you've been lambasting yourself for being a poor meditator, relax. As much as we'd like you to be gentle with yourself, we know it's inevitable that lawyers will judge themselves at times. Don't judge yourself for judging yourself. After all, that's just having more thoughts about thoughts! Instead, smile at yourself and connect with the part of yourself that can just be and let the judging part of yourself take a rest.

Practicing On and Off the Cushion

53

At the end of this chapter, and of each of the chapters covering the eight weeks of your meditation program, you'll find meditation instructions to follow during your sitting practice. You can read the instructions before sitting down to meditate, or if you'd prefer, you can visit the website we've set up for the book, www.theanxiouslawyer.com, where you'll find an audio recording of the same instructions.

In addition to the instructions for seated meditation, we'll include a related off-the-cushion practice each week. This week, the off-the-cushion practice is mindful showering. At this point, you haven't had a lot of experience with using mindfulness, so you may feel confused by how to shower mindfully. Don't worry too much about that. For now, the most important thing is to give it a try and have a practical experience of attempting to bring mindfulness into your daily life.

While you're busy getting used to the experience of seated meditation, it may be tempting to skip the off-the-cushion practices, but we strongly recommend you do them. As valuable as sitting practice is, the insights of meditation are of no value if they stay on the cushion—they must be brought into daily life in order to help us, and the off-the-cushion practices help us make that leap. One way to think about this is that meditative practices happen both on and off the cushion, so by doing the off-the-cushion practices, you're giving yourself more opportunity to get the full benefit of your sitting practice.

Your Meditation Journal

Following the practice instructions at the end of the chapter, we've included a worksheet for you to track your meditation practice over the course of the week. As we discussed in the introductory chapter, keeping a record of your meditation practice has a number of benefits, so we encourage you to make use of this worksheet or a journal of your preference. In either case, you should record the date, time of day you sat for meditation and for how long, and the practice you used. Briefly describe the quality of your sitting time and any notable experience you may have had. If, for some reason, you didn't sit on a particular day, note that fact and the reason you didn't sit. Do the same for your off-the-cushion practices.

Keeping the journal is intended to be a simple task. If it takes you more than five minutes per day, you're most likely putting more effort into it than you need to. Of course, if you like to keep a detailed journal, go ahead and do so. There's nothing wrong with longer journal entries but they're not necessary for our purposes. The kind of notes you might make about a typical sitting period could be something like:

> Difficulty settling. A lot of work thoughts. Felt like I must have returned to focusing on the body scan about 100 times! Eventually did settle in and had a few minutes of quiet. Surprised when the bell went off.

Or:

> Today was interesting. Many colors moved across my field of vision. Most of them were shades of blue and purple. When I focused on the colors, they faded away. Then I was looking at a huge gray field. It was endless in every direction. It was cool! My friend knocked at the door (he was early) and interrupted me, so I stopped early.

Or:

I couldn't stop thinking about the conversation I had with my son last night. My heart broke thinking about what a hard time he is having. What I should have said. After a while, I let the conversation go and just let myself feel the sadness I was feeling.

The point here is that there is no right meditation experience. Whatever you experience is fine. Just record it in a simple way, so you can remember what happened later when you come back to it.

Enjoy Yourself!

Now it's time to start. Dive into meditation and don't worry too much about all the advice we've given you. Above all, give yourself the gift of enjoying your meditation time. Meditation time is just for you—think of it as mental vacation time. Just like the body, the mind needs rest, and meditation gives our brain a chance to reboot. You don't have to worry about getting anything done during your meditation period. Just by sitting quietly, you're already doing everything you need to. You don't need to show up to your practice in any particular way or with any mindset. Meditation is a "come as you are" party. Have fun.

Body Scan

I will meditate for _____ minutes, every day.

Our first meditation practice will be the body scan. During the body scan, we bring our attention to all the different parts of our body. This practice allows you to connect with your body, noticing different sensations and feelings. You may notice a lot of different sensations in your body, or perhaps little or no sensations. It's also possible you may notice pain or discomfort in your body. This is very normal. As you bring your attention to the different parts of your body, it may also trigger emotions. Perhaps noticing how your body is different or not as it once was. Whatever your experience, bring a sense of curiosity and kindness to the practice. If, during the body scan, you lose your place, you can pick up where you left off or simply begin again with the left foot.

Instructions for Body Scan—For an audio version of this guided meditation, visit www.theanxiouslawyer.com

1. Find a comfortable seated position. You may also do this practice lying down.
2. Allow your eyes to soften or keep them slightly open and focus on a spot in front of you, approximately four feet ahead.
3. Ground yourself by taking some deep inhales and exhales. Allow your breath to return to normal and then simply be with the breath. With each inhale, you're drawing in fresh energy and with each exhale, you're letting go of anything that is no longer serving you.
4. Bring your attention to your left foot. Notice any sensations or feelings in your left foot. If you don't feel anything, that's okay.
5. Next, bring your attention to your left ankle. Notice the point of connection between your left foot and your left ankle.
6. Moving up the leg, bring your attention to your lower leg—the calf and the shin.
7. Now, bring your attention to your left knee. Notice the position of your knee.

8. Bring your attention to your thigh. If you are sitting, notice the pressure of your body weight against the chair. Feel the contact of your thigh to the chair.

9. Now, bring your attention to your entire left leg—from the toes all the way up the leg to where the leg is connected to your hip socket.

10. Repeat on the right side, starting with the right foot and moving up the leg.

11. Next, bring your attention to your hips, genitals, and your lower torso. See if you can notice any sensations of the organs in this part of your body, responsible for reproduction, digestion, and elimination.

12. Moving up the torso, bring your attention to your stomach and lower back. Notice how your stomach rises and falls as you breathe, as your diaphragm expands and contracts.

13. Now, move up to the chest and upper back. See if you can notice your heart beating or your lungs as it fills and deflates with air.

14. Bring your attention to your shoulders.

15. Next, move your attention to your left hand and move up the left arm, stopping at the wrist, forearm, elbow, and upper arm.

16. Repeat the same instructions with the right arm.

17. Next, bring your attention to your neck. Notice how it connects your head to the rest of the body.

18. Moving up the face, notice the chin, the lips, cheeks, nose, eyes, and forehead. Notice the back of the head. Then the crown of the head.

19. Now, bring your attention to your entire body, feeling how all the different parts of your body are interconnected. Feel your entire body all the way from the toes to the fingertips to the crown of the head.

20. Pause here for as long as you'd like, and simply be with this wondrous instrument that is your body.

~

Mindful Showering

Consider for a moment the last time you showered. What thoughts were going through your mind? Perhaps you were busily running through your to-do list. Or had a moment of panic because you couldn't remember if you filed that motion with the court. Or maybe you were thinking about what you were going to say when you called your opposing counsel.

What if, instead of having your mind busily run in 100 different directions, you simply paid attention to what is happening? What if, when you turned on the shower and put your hand under it to check the temperature, you fully paid attention to that sensation? What if you got into the shower and enjoyed the sensations of the hot water running down your skin? What if you simply enjoyed this luxurious experience with gratitude? How would that change your day?

For this week's off-the-cushion practice, we invite you to practice mindful showering. During the time you're showering, gently keep your focus on the physical sensations you experience as you shower. Similar to the body scan, bring your full attention to your body as you bathe. You can pause and deliberately see and notice all the different parts of your body. As you wash your left foot, pause and really take the time to look, feel, and notice it. As you do this, undoubtedly, your mind will wander. When that happens, do not be distressed by it or judge yourself. Simply bring your attention back to the sensation of the shower—the hot water, the foaming soap, scents of the various products—and how it feels on your body. See if you can turn your shower into a spa experience. After all, queens and kings throughout history have never enjoyed the luxuries we enjoy.

Meditation Log

Day	Time/Length	Notes: Sitting	Notes: Off the Cushion
Mon			
Tue			
Wed			
Thu			
Fri			
Sat			
Sun			

59

Mindfulness

People travel to wonder at the height of mountains.
At the huge waves of the sea; at the long courses of rivers;
at the vast compass of the ocean;
at the circular motion of the stars:
And they pass by themselves
without wondering.

61

—St Augustine (399 A.D.)

YOU'VE NOW COMPLETED YOUR first week of meditation. Congratulations! How did it go? This week you'll have a chance to continue with the practice you started. If you struggled last week, know it will all be a little easier this week, as you're now familiar with the basics of your practice. If there's something you need to change, like the time of day you're sitting or where you do your practice, you'll be able to see the effects of making those changes.

In this chapter, we'll introduce the concept of mindfulness. You've already had a practical experience of mindfulness, since the body scan practice you've been doing is an example of mindfulness-based meditation. Now we'll delve into some of the philosophy and concepts behind mindfulness as well as consider a number of different ways you can bring mindfulness into your daily life and professional world.

Mindfulness, Both Inside and Outside of Meditation

You may have heard the term "mindfulness" being bandied about in popular culture without much to underpin it. You may have heard it associated variously, with spirituality, calmness, or being nice, being a thoughtful person. When we use the word mindfulness in this book, we mean something very specific. For our purposes, mindfulness is a particular state of mind, a way of being, a way to engage with the world. It's often defined as being aware of the present moment without judgment or preference.

Tara Brach in her book *Radical Acceptance* describes mindfulness in this way:

> This is the quality of awareness that recognizes exactly what is happening in our moment-to-moment experience. When we are mindful of fear, for instance, we are aware that our thoughts are racing, that our body feels tight and shaky, that we feel compelled to flee—and we recognize all this without trying to manage our experience in any way, without pulling away. Our attentive presence is unconditional and open—we are willing to be with whatever arises, even if we wish the pain would end or that we could be doing something else. That wish and that thought become part of what we are accepting.

So often, we live in a place far away from this present moment. We may physically be here but our mind is someplace else. This can happen when you're at the office thinking about something that needs to be done at home, thinking about your child, your significant other, or having your mind someplace else. Of course, the opposite can also happen. You may be helping your child with his homework and find your thoughts absorbed in some work situation.

Over the course of our lives, our minds become habituated to a constant stream of thoughts, worries, emotions, and memories that pull us away from being here—noticing the sensation of our feet on the ground, the voice of the person with whom we're speaking, the sunlight on our face. These seemingly ordinary moments are the very ones that make up the fabric of our lives. Mindfulness is the practice of fully engaging and being in our life. Instead of escaping to the past, or the future, mindfulness asks us to take our seat—right here, right now. We may resist being in this moment because it's painful, boring, or for some other reason. With the Internet, social media, e-mail, iPhone, and all the other constant distractions, it's easy to check out and miss precious moments. We can mistake busyness and distraction for productivity, genuine connection, and quality time. In so doing, not only do we disengage from others, we can easily disengage from ourselves. For example, many of us disengage with our physical body until we're faced with physical pain and illness.

It's natural, as we go about our day, to get carried away by all the things we have to accomplish, get carried away by our worries, or get trapped in some past event. When we're mindful, we're in the present moment. This moment, right here; this is all we have. Despite all of our best intentions and efforts, we have very little control over our future. Yet lawyers spend an inordinate amount of time in some other space aside from the now. We try to control what is completely out of our control. Instead of focusing all of our attention on the legal research at hand for the Motion for Summary Judgment, we obsess over what the judge will say at a hearing eight weeks from now. This incessant worry is ineffective and harmful. So much of our own misery is self-induced. This moment—it's here *anyway*. Making peace with this very moment actually reduces suffering and pain. This isn't to say you can't do anything to alleviate future suffering, but in this very second, if there is pain, accepting it instead of wishing it was some other way is the wise choice.

When we practice mindfulness, we're accessing our inner calm. We have all experienced this deep sense of inner calm. Perhaps you experienced it on a hike in the woods, a walk on the beach, in the shower, or during some other moment. As we train our attention, we are better able to access this inner calm "on demand." We can strengthen or even create new neural pathways, making the ability to access this inner calm easier. There are few things that do not become easier with practice and patience.

As you practice mindfulness, you can become more familiar with the habits of your mind. Perhaps you begin to notice your mind's tendency to always label things as being good or bad. For example, you may be enjoying an afternoon with your family at a park but perhaps you'd like it to be a bit

63

cooler or a bit warmer. Perhaps you're dissatisfied with the food choice, or the way your children are behaving. All of this preference—wanting things to be different than the way they are—causes our suffering. What if you can simply accept the temperature just the way it is, enjoy the food choices you've made, or enjoy your children, just the way they are? Wouldn't that open the possibility for increased satisfaction and happiness? With practice, we become more aware of our "judging mind" and we can see it for what it is—simply a flow of thoughts. Then we have the ability to notice our thoughts and allow them to be without reacting. This practice of living without judgment or preference can feel counter to the way we've been trained to do as lawyers. After all, much of our legal practice is about judging right from wrong and catering to our client's preferences.

To clarify, when we say to be mindful means to be without judgment, we are not suggesting you set aside your obligation to use your legal judgment, expertise, or experience in your law practice. What we are suggesting is you become aware of your mind's tendencies to constantly judge other people, their behaviors, as well as judge yourself.

Consider the past twenty-four hours: how many of the 86,400 seconds were you consciously aware of? Mindfulness also means "to remember." Remember what? To remember your priorities, your intentions, the people you love, and to remember to savor these precious moments.

Engaging Mindfulness: Sitting and Off-the-Cushion Practices

This week we'll be practicing mindfulness both on and off the cushion, and it's particularly important to do both your sitting practice and your off-the-cushion practice. Mindfulness is about connecting with what is happening right now, in the present moment. Its greatest power comes from bringing it into play in everyday experience, so it's important to start building the habit of bringing your mindfulness practice into your ordinary life.

Mindfulness Sitting Practice

Using the practice of mindfulness in meditation, we observe ourselves exactly the way we are. We can turn our mindful awareness to our thoughts, emotions, physical sensations, and anything else that may arise. In many ways, when we meditate mindfully, we're taking our internal temperature. We're taking our physical, emotional, psychological, and spiritual temperature. How am I feeling in this moment? What is present? What do I notice? What am I preoccupied with? Mindfulness is becoming aware of all this.

This week, we'll use mindfulness in our sitting practice to focus on the sensations of the breath. As we noted in the introductory chapter, following the breath is a very straightforward and practical meditation technique. It's one of the most practiced meditation methods, and, for many people, the only one they ever use.

In contrast to the diaphragmatic breathing exercise you did in the introductory chapter, when you sit to meditate this week, you don't need to consciously change the rhythm of the breath. Relax completely and allow the breath to do whatever it wants. Your only task is to follow its movements with gentle attention.

65

Preoccupation with Breathing the Right Way

While it's true that focusing on the breath is a simple meditation practice, many people do initially become preoccupied with breathing when they first begin this practice. While this is perfectly normal, as a group, lawyers seem to encounter this issue more than others. This may be because we've put so much time and energy into succeeding, first academically and then professionally, that we're always a little anxious about doing everything right. For the record, breathing is not something you can do wrong! If you find yourself wondering whether you're breathing correctly or not, be assured you are breathing correctly.

If you find yourself obsessing about how you're breathing, or even feeling like you can't breathe naturally while you're sitting to meditate, gently remind yourself that there is no right or wrong way to breathe. Let go of any thoughts or worries about the breath, and bring your attention back to the simple sensations of the breath. Even if you find you're breathing in a stilted or unnatural way, don't try to correct yourself. Just focus your attention on the sensation of the breath moving in and out of the body. It's absolutely fine to breathe in a strange way for your entire meditation period, if that's what happens. Chances are that after refocusing on the sensations of the breath, you'll relax and the natural rhythm of your breathing will take over.

In practicing mindful awareness of the breath, the first step is to bring your attention to the part of the body where you can most notice the breath. This can be in the nostrils, in your chest, or in your belly. Simply observe the air moving in and out of this part of your body. After a while, your mind may wander off. When this happens, simply notice where your mind has gone and then gently escort your attention back to the breath. The moment you return to your breath—this is the practice of mindfulness. Our breath can only exist in this moment.

It's important to note that, as with other meditation practices, the point of mindfulness meditation isn't to clear your mind of thoughts. The thoughts aren't the enemy. In fact, the practice of meditation and mindfulness is the act of becoming a good friend to ourselves, our thoughts, and our emotional state. We're trying to cultivate a sense of kindness, acceptance, and compassion toward ourselves and others. Often, students feel discouraged or frustrated because they can't "clear their mind." It bears repeating the message—meditation is not about clearing your thoughts. It's simply about observing the moment-to-moment experience. This may be thoughts, sounds, feelings, pain, tingling, itching, or whatever may arise.

Celebrate every experience in your practice. See if you can approach your practice with curiosity and child-like playfulness. Again, if you find yourself judging your meditation practice because you think you aren't doing it right, you believe you should feel more calm, you're thinking too much, or whatever your inner dialogue is, please know this too is part of the meditation practice experience. Instead of fighting your judgmental thoughts, try simply allowing them to be. If the thought "you're a bad meditator" arises, acknowledge it as just a thought and return to your breath.

Off-the-Cushion Mindfulness Practice

The off-the-cushion practice of mindfulness includes all of the other time spent during the day aside from meditation. We have given you a specific off-the-cushion practice for the week, but, in reality, each moment of the day presents a new opportunity to practice mindfulness. Consider your typical day. What's the first thing you do or think about when you wake up in the morning? Do you immediately reach for your smartphone and check your e-mail? Is your mind racing off to all the things you have scheduled later that day? Do you immediately go into full worry and anxiety mode? If so, what would it be like to simply notice this busy internal state and take a few deep breaths?

Each day is a new gift, and you get 1,440 minutes to spend. How do you spend those minutes? Do you spend it trapped in your inbox, letting it dictate how you'll focus your attention? When you pause for a moment and connect with your heart, what does your heart truly desire? Is it to take the extra minute to connect with your spouse and embrace him or her before you rush off to work? Is it to connect with nature by taking a walk in the woods? Even the most mundane activity can be done with mindfulness.

67

Off-the-Cushion Mindful Practices to Do at Work

1. Intentionally pause to take three breaths—complete inhalation and exhalation—before you respond to an e-mail.
2. Let the phone ring three times before answering. Spend that time checking in with yourself.
3. If you eat at your desk every day, schedule time to eat your lunch elsewhere. You can find a bench outside, a quiet table at the office kitchen, or someplace else. See what it feels like to eat by yourself where you're intentionally bringing your attention to your food.

As you go about your day, pause to check in with yourself. This doesn't have to be a formal or lengthy activity. Simply take one or more breaths and really pay attention to each one. Can you notice the four distinct parts of a breath? Can you feel the cool air as you inhale, feel the brief pause before you exhale, feel the warm air as you exhale, and, finally, feel the brief pause before your next inhale? You can also simply pause to notice whatever your senses can feel—what are you seeing, hearing, smelling? What physical sensations are arising? Also notice any thoughts or emotions that are present. This continual practice of pausing to be mindful will strengthen over time.

All the basic concepts of mindfulness explained in this book are just as applicable to lawyers as they are to doctors, students, or to any human being. There's no special way to be mindful in legal practice. Just like exercising your muscles will give you an advantage in any physical activity you engage in, practicing mindfulness will help you be more present in each moment both in and out of the office.

Using Mindfulness in Your Legal Practice

There are so many ways in which mindfulness can help lawyers to be more effective, not only at work but also in every aspect of our lives. After all, mindfulness isn't something you *do;* it's a way of *being* in the world.

By practicing mindfulness, you become an expert in the domain of the only thing you have ultimate control over—your view and reaction to situations. We can easily fall into the trap of wanting to fix or control our opposing counsel, change his behavior, get him to stop acting like a jerk. We spend precious mental energy and resources trying to change what we cannot change. What if you can let this go and instead focus your attention on how you're showing up to each situation? What if you can remain in a neutral space when the opposing counsel is screaming on the phone? Would that help you be a more effective lawyer? Absolutely.

~

Mindful Lawyer Example by Jeena

I can feel the heat rising from my chest up to my face when I open the e-mail. "Your client still needs to complete the business questionnaire." My mind begins to race and my thoughts are spiraling out of control. "They're always creating busy, unnecessary work for us. She's completely ridiculous. The questionnaire doesn't apply to my client. He doesn't own a business."

Before I started practicing mindfulness, I would've hit reply and told her exactly why she was wrong to ask for this document from my client. I would have vented all of my anger, frustration, and pounded out an e-mail in haste. I would have signed off the e-mail by finishing with "I'll just file a motion. We can let the judge decide."

I pause to ask myself—what would my most mindful, lawyer self do in this situation? The answer is obvious. Self-care first. I can't be an effective lawyer when I'm physically burning with rage. In addition to the heat radiating throughout my chest and face, I notice I'm holding my breath. I sit back in my chair and take some conscious, diaphragmatic breaths. The tension begins to soften but another thought arises: "Her request is so unreasonable!" I notice the thought, and go back to breathing. It takes awhile but finally, I am at a place where I'm no longer burning with anger and I feel calm.

I turn my attention back to the e-mail and I remind myself she is simply doing her job, she is trying her best (just as I am), and trust she's not doing this with bad intention. I respond to her e-mail by greeting her and calmly explaining my position. I explain that I understand her job is to make sure she has all the information necessary to examine my client's case and I am fully ready to cooperate with her. However, I cannot have my client complete and sign the business questionnaire because my client would be signing under penalty of perjury that everything in the questionnaire is true and accurate. The only problem is my client doesn't own a business.

I save the e-mail in the draft folder, and get up to drink a glass of water. I reopen the e-mail, read it once again, and imagine I was on the receiving end of this e-mail. How would I perceive this e-mail? Would I read it as aggressive? Assertive? Angry? Hostile? Friendly? The underlying message I want to convey is that my relationship with her is important to me.

69

Understanding her reasoning, understanding her needs, is also important to me. And I have to balance this with my client's interest. I have to do my job, which is to represent and protect my client. Finally, I send the e-mail.

A few minutes later, there is a reply. I can feel my stomach clench as I anticipate the worst. "I just know it. She's going to force me to take this to the judge." Again, I take a few breaths, relaxing my stomach and noticing the anticipation. I open the e-mail. It reads: "I understand. Please have your client provide bank statements instead."

The law is a wonderful profession in which to practice mindfulness because we're constantly having to navigate and balance what the law requires, our client's interests, and our own sense of ethics or moral code.

The first step in becoming more mindful is to set your intention to be in the present moment. As you're reading these words, see if you can notice yourself. Tune into your body, the parts of your body in contact with the chair you're sitting on. If you're standing, notice the sensation of your feet on the ground.

As mentioned above, mindfulness is a way of being. We can practice being mindful anywhere and at any time. We don't need to sit in lotus position, on a cushion, or set aside an hour to do this. We can choose to be fully present, to fully listen with our heart and mind to the speaker, whether that is our client, the opposing counsel, the judge, our children, or our spouse. Every second offers us the opportunity to begin again—to be mindful.

When we're mindful, we can also tune into what we are actually paying attention to. In any given moment, there are numerous things we can pay attention to.

For example, in this moment, you can pay attention to the words on the page, the sensation of the clothes against your body, the chair beneath you, the sounds you hear, the light, or the decor in the room. You may notice you have the ability to shift your attention from one thing to the next. So, you want to be mindful of what you set your attention on. You also want to make sure you're paying attention in a way that's reflective of your true nature. Are you paying attention with anger, cruelty, or with kindness? With compassion? Pay attention to the *quality* of your attention.

Mindfulness can't be achieved by brute force. It's not about trying. In fact, it's about letting go of the trying and simply *being*. This method for practicing mindfulness—simply allowing the moment to be exactly the way it is—is simple but that doesn't mean it's easy. However, as with anything, what you practice gets stronger.

Mindfulness and Client Engagement

Without clients, there would be no attorneys. We take an oath to represent our clients with competence and to be zealous advocates. Like all relationships, the attorney-client relationship requires care, attention, and awareness. Being mindful can play a critical role in every aspect of the attorney-client relationship from the initial client meeting to the close-out letter. Each client interaction can be an opportunity to manifest our highest intention as attorneys.

Initial Client Meeting

Consider for a moment your typical first meeting with a client. What type of legal issues do they come in with? What is their emotional state? How do you start the meeting? Do you start by asking an open-ended question such as "What brings you into my office today?" or do you start with a closed-ended question such as "I see you valued the home at $1.1 million. How did you come up with that number?" How often do you interrupt the client? Do you find yourself feeling annoyed when she goes off on a tangent?

Mindfulness Meditation: Initial Client Meeting

1. Find a comfortable seated position. Place both feet firmly on the ground. Feel the weight of your body sink into the chair. Roll your shoulders back, making sure your head, neck, and back are aligned. Allow the eyes to close.
2. Begin to tune into your breath. Simply feel the air as it moves into your body when you inhale and feel the sensation of the exhale.
3. Once your mind feels settled, bring to mind the client you are about to meet. Notice any sensations in your body, thoughts, or feelings that

may arise. Whatever you feel is perfectly okay. Simply allow the sensations or feelings to rise and fade away, without giving them additional energy.

4. Notice any preconceived beliefs or thoughts you have about this person. Allow these thoughts to come and go, knowing they're just thoughts, not facts.

5. Imagine a clean whiteboard or a wall. Walk up to the white space and write the person's name on it. You're about to embark on a journey of getting to hear this person's story, to deepen your relationship, to understand them.

6. Bring a sense of curiosity and wonder to this meeting, similar to the way a scientist would conduct an experiment for the first time.

7. Take three deep breaths. Feel the inhale and exhale. With each breath, you're breathing in fresh energy. With each exhale, you're letting go of anything you no longer need, and anything that is no longer serving you.

End the meditation by gently wiggling the fingers and toes then allow the eyes to open.

72

As you're interacting with the client, are you fully present or is your mind wandering off to the next meeting, the phone call you forgot to make, or thinking about what may await you in your inbox? Are you being mindful of your own internal state as you're interacting with the client? Are you paying attention to your emotions? Noticing potential warning signs?

The initial client meeting is an opportunity to engage in a deeper connection with the client than merely a fact-gathering mission. It can be an opportunity to fully understand the client's motivations, her emotions, and explore what is left unsaid. Often, the client may have a very poor understanding of her own internal state. For example, she may be full of anger or rage but not be able to articulate the pain just beneath the surface. By being mindful both of ourselves and our client, we can begin to co-facilitate the building of the attorney-client relationship.

To be mindful means to fully engage through listening both with your mind and heart. It's to be present to your clients, their pain, as well as whatever may come up for you. You may notice feelings of frustration, anxiety, anger, or impatience as you sit with the client. You may have judgment around what your client did (or didn't do). When we practice mindfulness, we are intentionally bringing spaciousness to *what is* in that moment. This requires making room for pleasant and unpleasant emotions, thoughts, and sensations. We practice making room for not only the client's experience and her emotions but also yours. It's important to make room for you—the attorney—in the attorney-client relationship, too.

Often, as lawyers, we find ourselves in situations where our clients failed to tell us the whole story (or we failed to see it). There are other situations where our clients were less than truthful with us. Practicing mindfulness helps reduce stress and anxiety. As this happens, the way we interact with our clients and the way the clients respond may change. As we ease into each moment and become fully present to our interactions with clients, they may feel more comfortable opening up and sharing those things they otherwise would not. It may mean opening up and sharing something deeply embarrassing, shameful, scary, or angering, just to list a few emotions our clients may face.

When our clients do open up and share their deep, dark place, how do we care for them without getting sucked in and taking on their problem as our own? How do we stay engaged but not lose ourselves in their problem? This is where the foundational practice of mindfulness comes in.

When you're with your client, you can practice being present with her, in that moment, without judgment or preference. For example, you may notice your mind is wandering off to the next meeting. Or perhaps, you're noticing yourself passing judgment on your client. Or you might have a preference—for example, if your client is showing very strong emotions, wishing she would stop being angry, crying, etc. Being mindful means becoming aware of these tendencies in yourself and returning to the present moment.

73

Mindful Client Interview

In Jeena's bankruptcy practice, frequently, clients will go into great detail about how they ended up in financial turmoil. Often, the client also wants Jeena to understand they are responsible people but circumstances beyond their control (illness, death, unemployment, divorce, etc.) led them to this situation. If we can't make space to allow the full story to come out, make space for the client to tell *her story* the way she needs to tell it, it's unlikely the client will be in the frame of mind to hear anything the attorney has to say. It's easy to feel impatient, be dismissive, and go through the list of "*relevant* facts." The fact that the client is a recovering alcoholic and part of turning her life around is being in a bankruptcy lawyer's office may be seen as irrelevant as far as the case is concerned but it's absolutely relevant for cultivating a trusting attorney-client relationship. If the attorney responds dismissively or fails to acknowledge the client's struggle to overcome her addiction and her path to recovery, it's unlikely the client will feel as though she can trust the attorney with her legal issue.

As lawyers, we love to fix problems. We're often looking for just the right words to relieve our clients from their pain and make it all better. However, is this really true or even possible? Think of a time when you experienced a tragedy such as a death or a major illness. Of all the things people said to you in their effort to comfort you, did any of it really help to completely stop the pain? Often, what people say when they're trying to help just makes us feel worse or angry. For example, consider a phrase like "Well, at least he didn't suffer long before passing." Even though it's meant to help, it probably has the opposite effect. Frequently, what we find comforting is the person's presence. A hug, a caring touch, or even holding the pain in silence can help us feel slightly less pain. However, only time will truly heal the pain and no matter how much we'd like to wave our magic wand and make it instantly better, such a cure is unlikely. Sometimes, the best we can say is "Wow. I don't even know what to say."

It is important to understand that as lawyers, we are limited in terms of what we can fix. No amount of money we can get for our client will truly restore her.

Setting Boundaries with Clients

As lawyers, we can often get pulled into our client's problems and get lost or overly involved in their world. There is no exact rule for determining the line between when you're involved enough in your client's case and overly involved. Each attorney must use her own inner barometer to decide where that line is. Some attorneys give out their cell phone number. Other attorneys make home or hospital visits. Often, the attorney-client relationship deepens into friendship.

Sometimes, without meaning to, our clients can become overly dependent on us. The attorney-client relationship can turn dysfunctional if the client requires more emotional energy than we're willing or able to provide. We as attorneys must always remember to put self-care first. If we aren't in a healthy space, if we're running on fumes, if we're giving more than what is available to us, we can't be effective. Understanding our own limitations and setting boundaries requires awareness.

Your client's need for your attention may increase slowly over time and you may miss cues letting you know there is a problem. Seeing issues in the attorney-client relationship early enough so you can make small course corrections rather than letting things deteriorate to a point where you must terminate the relationship is key for having a satisfying legal practice. This means recognizing when your client's tone in her e-mail is starting to get more hostile, she's requiring more attention than you can provide, when there is deterioration in communication or there are unrealistic expectations, just to cite a few examples.

Of course, there are situations where, despite your best efforts, the attorney-client relationship doesn't work out and you must terminate the relationship. This is a difficult challenge for most attorneys. We're invested in the relationship. We don't enjoy telling clients no. We may also fear our client's reaction. Again, mindfulness is useful in these situations. We can notice all the fear, concerns, hesitations, or whatever may be present without reacting to them. We can stay calm and focused without turning away or suppressing the difficulty. Mindfulness also allows us to tap into our innate capability for compassion. When we do have the conversation with the client to terminate the relationship, we can act from a place of kindness and compassion rather than from a place of fear or anger.

The Power Dynamic in the Attorney-Client Relationship

As attorneys, we have a lot of power over our clients. They rely on us to help them navigate through difficult situations. They rely on us to protect them. They rely on us to advise them about complex issues. Striking a balance between caring for our clients and being sensitive to our own needs can be a challenge. In our practice, there are many situations where our own best interest is in direct conflict with the client's best interest. If we aren't self-aware, we can fall into the trap of fear mongering our clients in order to get the client to do what we want. We may emotionally taint our clients.

Jeena's Story of a Difficult Client Situation

I practice bankruptcy law. In bankruptcy, the basic rule is that any property inherited within 180 days of filing bankruptcy becomes the property of the estate. The estate is all property belonging to the client that can be used to pay the debtor's creditors. My client called me shortly after filing her case and said her mother was in the hospital with a terminal illness. No one was certain how long her mother would survive but it was possible that she would pass during the 180 days. I encouraged her to have a conversation with her mother about the situation—that if the estate was left in a will, it would go to the bankruptcy estate and be used to pay her creditors. In short, I was asking my client to speak to her mother about changing her will while she was on her deathbed. A week went by and the client still had not had the conversation with her mother.

I did what I was supposed to. I sent my client a CYA letter, which, in hindsight, was probably not very considerate of her situation. I was doing what I was supposed to do as a lawyer—informing her of her legal obligation and also protecting myself from malpractice claims. What I wasn't doing was looking at the whole picture of what was going on in that moment.

Her mother did pass away within 180 days of my client's bankruptcy and we spent many months litigating the issue. At the end, a significant amount of her mother's estate was spent on attorney's fees and part of the estate was turned over to the trustee. I was feeling frustrated because all of this could have been avoided if my client's mother had changed her will.

Several months after the case concluded, I had an opportunity to speak with my client. During that conversation, my client expressed her deep feeling of shame about being in bankruptcy and about her misman-agement of money. It also became clear that between facing the trustee and bankruptcy court, or the prospect of telling her dying mother about her financial difficulty and bankruptcy, it was less painful to face the court.

Had I been more mindful, I would have seen the extremely painful and difficult situation my client was in. I could understand my client's desire to avoid worrying her dying mother. I was only focused on keeping the inheritance out of the bankruptcy estate and on my frustration with my client for not following my advice. Had I been able to step back and look at the entire situation with mindfulness and compassion, I probably would have approached my client differently.

I would have at least acknowledged my client's difficult dilemma—tell-ing her dying mother that she was having financial difficulty and had filed for bankruptcy. Even more difficult would have been asking her to change the will.

Lawyers may engage in such behaviors not with ill intention but sim-ply as a shortcut to get to the desired results. We may also have learned such strong-arm tactics from our mentors or developed them as a defense mechanism. It's in these challenging moments when we're under extreme pressure and completely focused on the desired result that we may reach for the hammer in our toolbox. As our mindfulness practice deepens, we can begin to see with clarity the truth of the situation and choose our response with full awareness. In other words, we want to cultivate the wisdom to see we are in a challenging situation, we could potentially get the desired outcome by heavy-handed tactics—by pulling out the hammer from our toolbox—or we can choose to reach for a different tool. The key isn't whether we should ever use the hammer but rather having a full tool-box, becoming an expert in understanding the use of each tool and having the discernment to know which tool may work best in a given situation.

Using Mindfulness to Break
Habitual Patterns of Thought

By practicing mindfulness, you begin to know yourself, beyond your thoughts, feelings, or physical body. Knowing yourself doesn't come from thinking or contemplation. You can't *know* yourself only by engaging in logical, intellectual pursuit. It can only come from the mind engaging in simply *being*. From this perspective, perhaps the most compelling reason for meditation is to gain the simple pleasure of knowing one's self.

In our very busy, overfilled, and over-scheduled days, we rarely get a moment to just *be*. Mindfulness meditation calms the body and mind so we can practice nonattachment and not judging. During the normal course of a day, our energy follows our thoughts.

You might be in a meeting but have a thought about a brief that's due in two weeks. Your energy follows that thought and you may think about additional research you need to complete, some angle to an argument you have not considered, or think about an e-mail you have to send to your associate. In that moment, you've disengaged with *being* by not being fully present in the meeting.

We naturally give attention to our thoughts out of habit. We have a tendency to believe every thought is important, crucial in this moment. After all, our thoughts are *our* thoughts. However, our thoughts are biased by our mood, past experience, situation, and, of course, lack of information or lack of *accurate* information.

As you practice meditation, you may begin to notice patterns. You may notice those patterns are often inaccurate and misguided. As you move past those patterns, you may be more open to different points of views or interpretations. This ability to remain open is crucial for good lawyering. Coming to a premature conclusion or being rigid in your ideals limits your ability for creative problem solving. It also limits opportunities and options.

For example, you may notice whenever you engage with a particular opposing counsel, you get irritated. You may feel you're justified in your irritation and probably have a long list of reasons why this person irritates you. This is a pattern. Whenever you interact with this person (or think about this person), you get irritated. What if you set your intention to protect your mind by not allowing this person to irritate you? In this way, you are beginning to recognize and consciously choose a *response* to the pattern. You also begin to recognize you are ultimately in charge of deciding how you allow external triggers to influence your mental state.

Mindfulness as a Way to Cope with Emotional Pain

As lawyers, we're constant witness to human suffering. In many ways, the practice of law is very intimate. Our clients share their deepest, darkest secrets and we're the keeper of these secrets. Holding other people's secrets can take a toll on us. As one woman who does child advocacy work shared, there are certain things you hear or see that you can never un-see or un-learn. Despite this, we are not taught tools for handling the trauma of witnessing the pain of others. We're often told we shouldn't bring our emotions or feelings into any case and there is no room for it in any professional context. If we cannot have a healthy outlet or a way of processing our emotions and caring for ourselves, is it any surprise that as a group we disproportionately use substances to dull the pain?

Mindfulness asks us to look at every situation as it is, without filters, without avoidance, shame, or guilt. To borrow a phrase from the Persian poet Rumi, it asks us to look at the "bandaged places." This idea of looking at pain can feel terrifying. You may ask yourself, "Why would I ever do that?" It can feel as though there will be no end to the pain, that the pit of despair is bottomless. However, when you really *see* the situation for what it is, and look at the pain, it's not all negative, painful, or horrifying. Yes, there will be some terrible parts, but even in the most painful situation, there's opportunity for beauty, healing, something positive.

Practicing mindfulness doesn't mean you'll never feel pain again. It means you'll be able to see the pain and the ways in which your *reaction* to the painful situation compounds or makes the pain worse. With practice, you will learn to react in a more healthy and favorable fashion. In other words, you'll become more *mindful*.

Understanding and Working with Anger and Other Difficult Emotions

As lawyers, we often experience anger. The judge rules against you, opposing counsel is rude or unreasonable, your client goes against your advice and then blames you for the adverse result. Hours, days, or even weeks after the event, you may find yourself stewing over these events and dwelling in anger. This inability to work through or let go of the anger may compound the problem and make you feel even more frustrated or helpless. You may continually feel anger or hostility toward the judge, opposing counsel, or client. How do you cope mindfully in situations where you're seeing red?

What Is Anger?

Let's start by looking at anger. Why do humans experience anger? What is its function? Anger is an essential survival mechanism. It protects us from harm. It serves as an alert system. It lets us know when we are being mistreated, when we're under attack, or when our boundaries have been crossed. It also protects others from harm; for instance, when those we care about are in danger or are being mistreated, it propels us to take action.

Since anger is a necessary emotion for survival, it's important to recognize we don't want to get rid of it. In our mindfulness practice, we're focused on working with anger so it reduces our suffering. Consider the last time you were really angry. The feeling of anger was probably very uncomfortable for you. The purpose of being mindful in moments of anger is to release it when it's no longer serving a necessary function. When you are being mindful, you're seeing the anger for what it is—an emotional state. You aren't trying to suppress the anger or deny its existence. With mindfulness, you practice directing your attention. So, when the event has passed but you're still feeling the anger, you can redirect your attention.

Seeing the Anger

When you experience anger, first, ask yourself what function the anger is serving in this moment. For example, when someone cuts you off on the highway, you may feel angry because the other driver put you in a danger-ous situation. However, if you find yourself driving all the way to work in anger because of the other driver, the anger is no longer useful. The danger has passed, the threat no longer exists. Now, you're simply suffering from *secondary anger*. You may notice yourself feeling angry long after an unfa-vorable ruling; as you consider whether you should appeal the judge's deci-sion or not, you continually feel anger. The anger alerts you to the fact that perhaps you feel the judge's decision was wrong, but anger is probably not a useful emotion when you need to objectively consider the judge's ruling.

Anger can be triggered just by recalling a situation that angered you in the past, even if it's been years since the event has occurred. You can blame or target the person, thing, or event that initially caused the anger but the only thing you can change now is your relationship to anger.

Just because you can recognize that anger isn't serving a useful func-tion doesn't mean it will automatically fade (although, oftentimes, the intensity may decrease). You may need to spend some time observing and releasing the anger. Using a mindfulness practice, you can observe your anger wash over you like waves. Some waves will be fairly smooth and shallow. Others will be tall and violent. You can practice noticing the waves of anger come and go without getting absorbed in the content of the anger. For example, your mind might be saying "I am so angry. That client should have listened to me!" See if you can add some distance between the angry thoughts and words by labeling them. You can note "Ah. There is an angry thought."

Aside from noticing the angry feelings and thoughts, you can also bring kindness and compassion to how you deal with those feelings and thoughts. Regardless of what situation caused you to be angry, it's impor-tant to acknowledge your emotions. Again, this doesn't mean you should act out in anger. Just as you would treat a child who is experiencing anger with gentleness, you can practice this with your own anger. Meeting angry thoughts with anger will only lead to additional anger. You can practice saying a phrase such as "I acknowledge my angry feelings and I treat myself with kindness." You can also visualize holding the anger with gentleness. Imagine a bubble filled with unconditional love and kindness encircling the angry feelings and thoughts. Alternatively, imagine what you'd say to a dear friend or a loved one if he or she was feeling such anger, frustration, and pain.

Acknowledge the common humanity you share with others in the situation that brought up your anger. Anger is a feeling all human beings experience. In this way, feelings bond us to each other. Even the person who caused your anger has his or her own anger. He or she may be feeling angry about the very situation you're angry about. Is there any room to acknowledge this common humanity? Can you wish yourself and the other person well?

Feeling the Anger

When you're feeling angry, it's helpful to work through it and release it by seeing how it's impacting your body. Does your stomach or chest feel tight? Does your heart rate increase? Are you tensing your jaw, shoulders, arms, or curling your fists?

By becoming more familiar with how anger feels in your body, you can get better at recognizing the first signs of anger rising. Tapping into your body is a powerful way to know and work through your emotions. Often, you can get completely trapped in your head as you try to intellectually work through an emotion. This often only serves to further escalate your emotion. When you bring the attention into the body, you shift from trying to reason your way through an emotion to noticing and feeling the contours of your emotion. As you become an observer of the emotion as it exists in your body, you also begin to recognize that sensations in the body are consistently evolving.

You may feel heat rising from the core of your stomach all the way up to the face. You can add fuel to this physiological response by adding a narrative "I can't believe he objected to that Request for Admissions. He's just trying to create more work." Your mind can fuel the fire and further escalate the emotion.

Often, when you are experiencing a very strong emotion, such as anger, fear, hate, or love, you can prematurely jump into action instead of finding a place of calm and clarity first. Resisting the desire to take action can also further provoke our emotion as our mind continues to replay what has occurred. This is the moment where connecting with the breath is crucial. The old adage, "count to ten before you say something when you're angry," works because it forces you to breathe before reacting. This ability to find a place of calm rather than reacting reflexively, understanding your narrative or the story you're telling yourself about the situation, and getting clear about your own motivation allows you to choose a wise course of action.

As you practice being with strong emotions rather than reacting to them, remind yourself you're experiencing a difficult moment. Oftentimes, there may be an additional narrative of self-criticism running through your mind for not being strong enough, for letting this person get under your skin, or for having these emotions in the first place. By reminding yourself this is a moment of difficulty and acknowledging your suffering, you're tapping into your compassion.

Finally, hold anger tenderly. Treat it with kindness. Bring compassion to it. Bring gratitude for its function in protecting you. We'll return to this topic again in Week Seven, where we include an exercise for releasing difficult emotions using mantra practice.

~

Mindfully Following the Breath

Meditation Instructions—
Following the Breath

Visit www.theanxiouslawyer.com for audio guided meditations.

1. Set a timer for the desired length of meditation.
2. Sit with a straight spine, in a comfortable position you can hold for the time you will be meditating. Commit to that posture.
3. Allow your eyes to close or find a spot approximately four feet ahead of you and gently gaze at that place.
4. Take a couple of deep breaths in and out of the nose to help you settle in and make the transition from an outward focus to a more inward one.
5. Notice what is around you and inside you. Spend one cycle of your breath (one in-breath and one out-breath) noticing each of the following:
   a. the temperature of the air;
   b. the sounds around you, both the closer sounds and the sounds that are further away;
   c. the feeling of your body, its solidity;
   d. the feeling of energy in your body, the vitality inside you;
   e. your mood;
   f. the quality of your thoughts.
6. Turn your attention to your breath. If you don't know where you should let your attention rest, you can silently ask yourself the question, "How am I breathing?" Wherever your attention naturally goes is the best place for you. It could be your nose, your chest, your throat, your belly, or anywhere you can easily notice the movement of the breath.
7. Allow yourself to enjoy the physical feeling of the breath in your body.

8. Meditate, keeping your attention gently focused on the breath. If you find you're getting distracted or getting caught up in thoughts, that's fine. It's normal. Just gently return your awareness to the breath.
9. Notice the four parts of the breath. The inhale and the brief pause before exhale, followed by a brief pause before the next inhalation.
10. Continue to observe the breath until the bell rings, indicating the end of the meditation. Slowly begin to wiggle fingers and toes or check in with your body and move in any way that feels good to you.

~

Bringing Mindfulness into Your Daily Life

List five ways you can cultivate mindfulness in your daily life. It can be routine activities such as walking, washing the dishes, brushing your teeth, eating, driving, or answering the phone.

1. _____

_____

2. _____

_____

3. _____

_____

4. _____

_____

5. _____

_____

Choose one activity from the list above and bring mindfulness to that activity this week.

Meditation Log

Day	Time/Length	Notes: Sitting	Notes: Off the Cushion
Mon			
Tue			
Wed			
Thu			
Fri			
Sat			
Sun			

WEEK THREE

Clarity

∞

I know but one freedom, and that is the freedom of the mind.

—Antoine de Saint-Exupery

THE INTELLECT IS A vital tool, and one we rely on almost constantly in our work as lawyers. Yet there are times when trying to cogitate our way through the complex dilemmas of life only pulls us further and further into a cycle of thinking, worrying, and second-guessing ourselves. On the other hand, we've all experienced moments when our over-analyzing mind quiets down, and a solution surfaces in a way that feels effortless. Those moments of insight and inspiration are times of mental clarity.

Meditation increases our access to mental clarity by loosening the hold of preconceptions we bring to bear on the situations we face. As we learn to observe our thoughts and feelings without trying to hang on to the pleasant ones and push away the unpleasant ones, we are more able to experience the world directly, without the filter of our mental concepts, and to allow space for our own wisdom and intuition to show themselves.

This week we'll be working directly with our thoughts to get a view of how they move through our minds. We'll discuss some common mental traps we all have a tendency to fall into as lawyers, and we'll explore an exercise to help us deconstruct troubling or persistent thought patterns that aren't working for us.

Meditation Practice: Following Your Thoughts

This week we will be trying a new variation of mindfulness: following the thoughts. Just as we have been observing the movements of the breath, we will now be focusing our attention on the movement of thoughts: we'll watch thoughts as they arise, inhabit our consciousness, and then fall away. This practice allows us to have a tangible experience of thoughts as phenomena, and helps us gain a concrete understanding that thoughts are something the mind produces. Just as the body is always breathing, the mind is always thinking, and thoughts are the by-product of that natural process.

When you apply the practice of mindfulness to your thoughts, you watch your thoughts from the point of view of an observer. Don't worry about what you're thinking. We're not concerned with the content of your thoughts. Instead, watch how your thoughts flow through your mind. Each has a beginning, a middle, and an end. Some thoughts may sound loud to you, some soft. Your thoughts may cascade, one after another with little noticeable pause between them, or they may feel slower, drifting gently through the space of your mind. You may experience periods of time when your mind is very quiet. As all this happens, simply watch your mind. There is no need to intervene in what is going on. To repeat, this practice does *not* involve thinking. Don't engage with your thoughts, judge your thoughts, or think about your thoughts. And if you notice yourself doing those things, don't be upset with yourself—it's natural to do all of them, especially in the beginning. Just take a moment to thank yourself for noticing your attention has wandered, and gently bring yourself back to the practice.

As you'll notice once you practice this method, following your thoughts can be a little tricky, since you need to be aware of your thoughts without being caught up in them. You've been practicing meditation for a couple of weeks now, so hopefully you've had a chance to experience a sense of your own mind when it's in a relaxed and open state. In that state of relaxed awareness, it's much easier to perceive some spaciousness around your thoughts and to see each thought has a beginning and an end.

90

Nonetheless, most people find it takes some time to develop the skill of observing their thoughts. Don't worry if you find yourself getting caught up in trains of thought quite frequently in the beginning. The mind will always circle back to a moment of awareness eventually, and that's when you can exercise the choice to return to your meditation practice.

Meditation Side Effects

You've now been meditating for several weeks, and may have encountered some of the physical and emotional side effects that can come up during a meditation session. Without an appropriate context, these side effects can be startling or seem strange, but they are quite normal. Side effects that are common enough to be considered "classic" meditation experiences include:

- Movements—Your head or other parts of your body may move spontaneously. These movements can be very subtle and feel almost like tremors, or they may be very strong.
- Feeling "energy"—You may have a sense of energy in your body. This can feel like tingles in your head or heart area, it can be more diffused throughout your body and it also can feel stronger and have a quality of pulling or movement.
- Physical pain—You may feel headachy, particularly in the spot between your eyebrows. Some people report an achiness in their heart area as well. These pains are distinct from any discomfort that may come from your sitting posture. If you're experiencing back, hip, or neck pain from misalignment, see if you can adjust your posture to be more comfortable next time you sit.
- Strong emotions—As we discussed in Week Two, you may experience strong feelings of joy, sadness, anger, or bliss, that appear unconnected to what is going on in your life.
- Colors, visions—You may see colors, that are either solid or that change and move. You may see images. Some people have quite vivid meditation visions that unfold a complex narrative similar to a dream.
- Sounds—You may hear sounds like bells, chimes, or drums.

While it may seem surprising that just sitting quietly can have such wide-ranging secondary effects, meditation is effectively rewiring the brain, so when we sit to meditate we are engaging in a process that affects our entire nervous system to some degree. Seen through that lens, these physical and sensory experiences are unsurprising, and it seems natural that most meditators experience at least one of these kinds of side effects at some point in their practice. If hearing that still worries you, remember no one experiences all of the side effects listed, and relatively few people have strong meditation reactions.

Generally speaking, these side effects to meditation are benign and there's no need to try to stop them. You can engage with your meditation experiences as much as is interesting to you. Some people find visionary experiences to be fascinating, and analyze them as they might a dream. Others consider such experiences to be a distraction and choose to ignore them. Both approaches are fine.

When engaging with meditation experiences, keep in mind the goal of your practice and use your judgment. Assessing what kind of support you need is a basic part of taking responsibility for your practice. Many people decide they want to find a regular meditation teacher if meditation experiences become strong or surprising. And, of course, if serious difficulties arise at any point, you may decide they need more than a meditation practice to address.

To help you maintain the stance of an observer of your thoughts, you can try some variations on observing your thoughts if you like. These variations are entirely optional—just use them if you find them helpful:

- **Noting your thoughts.** In this variation on following the thoughts, you can name each type of thought as it comes into your consciousness. Pick a few very general categories, such as "judging," "wishing," "remembering," and "planning," and then as you notice a thought, gently put a label to it, silently repeating the label in your mind and then returning to an open state, waiting for the next thought to arise.
- **Noticing when a thought arises.** Rather than following the entire arc of watching a thought arise, fill your consciousness, and fall

away, you can focus on just one part of the evolution of a thought. Where exactly does a thought come from? See if you can notice how it starts. Is there a feeling quality you associate with the beginning of a thought? Is there a feeling you have *before* a thought happens, when it is about to arise? Does a thought start as something vague and then crystallize into clarity? Or does it arrive fully formed? Does a thought "sound" quiet in your mind in the beginning? See what you can notice about each thought as it forms, and once the thought forms, let your attention move to an open state, waiting for the beginning of the next thought.

If you find following your thoughts to be extremely challenging, we suggest you spend at least three consecutive days trying it, and then assess how things are going. Even if you feel you're still struggling, ask yourself whether things have gotten a little easier. Are you able to come back to the practice more frequently than you were on the first day? Are you thinking the entire time, or do you have periods of time where you are noticing the movement of thoughts? If you genuinely feel the answer to these questions is "no," then if you like, you can return to the practice of following the breath for the remainder of the week.

93

Thinking and Clarity

As our mindfulness practice for this week should make clear, meditation can't and won't "take you away from your thoughts." Escaping one's thoughts is a fantasy about meditation often portrayed in popular culture, but not one based in reality. As we've seen, the mind generates thoughts naturally; that is one of its primary functions. Just as you can stop yourself from breathing by consciously holding your breath, it is possible through various concentration practices to briefly cause the mind to stop thinking. Many people also experience periods of time during their meditation practice when their minds are naturally very quiet. And, just as the breath will naturally restart as soon as you stop holding your breath, thoughts will naturally start again, no matter how much you manage to quiet your mind.

Less Mind Wandering, More Focus

One effect of meditation that may be of particular interest to lawyers is that the brains of experienced meditators appear to wander less, are more disciplined, and better able to stay on task than the brains of people who don't meditate. While better concentration has obvious application for maintaining a busy professional life, the seemingly simple ability to stay more focused also has powerful implications for mental health and happiness that go far beyond increased efficiency at the office.

Most of us experience a wandering mind about half the time—and this is not good news. Besides the obvious problems of poor focus and difficulty in completing tasks, we feel unhappy when our minds wander. Paradoxically, this is true even when our minds wander to pleasant subjects. A study conducted by Harvard psychologists in 2010 revealed participants were less happy when their minds were wandering than when they were focused on the task at hand, regardless of what they were thinking about, and even when they were doing something they didn't enjoy.[8]

Mind wandering not only impacts our day-to-day sense of well-being but also has significance for overall mental health. Those who daydream more often are more likely to be depressed, perhaps because getting caught in a cycle of rumination pulls the mind into depression, or because depression erodes concentration (the causal mechanism isn't clear). An overly wandering mind is also associated with attention deficit disorder and other, more serious mental health problems, such as autism and schizophrenia.[9] The good news is meditation appears to help with mental focus. In a series of studies conducted at Yale University's medical school, researchers found meditators are better able to bring their minds back on task and rein in wandering thoughts.[10]

Through our meditation practice we change our relationship with thoughts. This shift in perspective manifests in a host of ways, both subtle and obvious, over time. A few very significant changes that can result from observing our thoughts include:

- **More spaciousness, more clarity.** Prior to taking the time to consciously observe our thoughts, we may not realize we are separate from them at all. Operating in a culture that values logic and reason, we naturally spend a great deal of time thinking. In fact, practicing law may have trained us to be comfortable thinking continuously and we may unconsciously feel uncomfortable allowing our thoughts to slow down, or to allow any space between our thoughts. We may not realize we have a choice about whether to get caught up in specific thoughts or even to focus on them at all.

  Observing our thoughts allows us to see directly that the mind has a natural clarity, and this clarity is relatively easy to notice in the moments between our thoughts. As we discussed in Week One, the mind's activity has a circular quality to it: while the mind produces thoughts that tend to carry us away into trains of related ideas, it also naturally circles back to awareness of the present. Learning to recognize and appreciate these moments of clarity has the effect of creating more spaciousness in our minds. This isn't about forcing out thoughts or wrestling our minds into a state of artificial and uncomfortable silence, but rather allowing the natural moments of open, relaxed awareness to be.

  As we become more familiar with the mind's natural rhythms, we are less likely to shy away from the moments of open awareness that allow our mind to rejuvenate, give us an opportunity to exercise choice about where to put our focus, and make space for our own natural wisdom to surface. The more comfortable we become resting in the clarity of the mind's quiet moments, the more frequently we are likely to experience such moments.

- **Realizing that thoughts aren't reality.** Many people live their lives believing all their thoughts are real. Their clients are all helpless; judges' rulings are always arbitrary; that opposing counsel is diabolical; changing jobs will inevitably lead to financial disaster. This is a profoundly disempowering stance, which can lead to feelings of helplessness and being at the receiving end of life.

  Thoughts are wonderful tools we can use to help us solve problems and gain insights, but allowing our thoughts to run our lives is like putting our computers in charge of important life decisions—they just weren't designed for that. Once we see thoughts are simply something the mind creates, we can choose which ones to believe and which to leave aside and, in doing so, put ourselves back in the driver's seat.

- **Taking our patterns less seriously.** As your meditation practice develops, over time you will have a chance to see the patterns of your thoughts. You'll very likely start to notice you always think certain thoughts in reaction to certain types of events. Whenever a deadline looms, you always begin to feel let down by others. Or whenever you get recognition, you immediately worry that there are unstated strings attached. After you see this play out for some time, you realize, *whenever x happens, I always think y.* Be alert for these patterns. For example, if every time you have to work late, you think, *I'm a bad parent*, you can start to notice this thought comes up automatically, regardless of what is going on at home. Since "I'm a bad parent" is just a thought, not necessarily reality, you can begin to take that snap judgment less seriously, and have much more freedom to evaluate how you're handling this particular situation.

Getting Back to Reality

Allowing more clarity into our lives allows us to live with more freedom from the beliefs and other mental constructs we may have built up over time. These beliefs can limit our perspective and, consequently, the choices we feel we have in life. Far too many of us in the legal profession feel trapped: we think we can't put boundaries around our clients' demands, can't take time out for teaching, can't drop off partnership track, can't put the kind of time into that *pro bono* project it really deserves. If we can step back and look more objectively at the maze of barriers our minds have created for us, we may see we have much more practical and mental freedom than we ever guessed. In reality, we've been holding the keys to the door we thought was locked this whole time.

Our legal practice, which emphasizes rule-based thinking, the winner-take-all ethos of our society, and perhaps our own psychology that drew us to the profession in the first place, can lead to a very binary way of thinking: either you win your point or you lose it; either you're right or you're wrong. We want to boil things down to black or white, and, in doing so, we can miss important details about the world around us, about the people we deal with, and even about ourselves.

Jeena's Story: Getting Real About What We Can Control

When I speak to groups of lawyers, one question I often ask is "What is your role as a lawyer?" Often, the answer will be something along the lines of "to win" or "to get the outcome the client desires." I then ask the group what percentage of any given case they believe they have control over. Frequently, the lawyers will say they have control over 60%–80% of the case.

How much control do *you* think you have over the outcome of your cases? If you agree with the lawyers in my groups, ask yourself the following questions:

Do you have control over the law?

Do you have control over the facts?

Do you have control over the witnesses?

Do you have control over the opposing counsel?

Do you have control over the opposing client?

How about your own client?

How about the judge?

Is it really true you have *that* much control over the ultimate outcome of any given case? Isn't it more realistic to admit the percentage of what you control is substantially less than what you often think? If you believe you have control over 70% of the case but, in reality, you only have control over, let's say, 5%–7%, is it really fair to expect to win every case?

This isn't to suggest that knowledge, experience, dedication, hard work, and preparation aren't important. Of course, they are. However, using an unrealistic yardstick to measure ourselves contributes to negative self-image, which can lead to stress, anxiety, depression, and other problems.

Clarity is stepping away from the black and white, and permitting ourselves to see the world in all its glorious and confounding profusion of color. Getting away from black and white thinking brings us much more fully in contact with reality. Seeing reality more clearly can be disconcerting at times because it requires us to look at details we may have been happy to gloss over. But acknowledging even uncomfortable truths lets us approach our professional and personal challenges from a sane and open perspective, and that can ultimately allow us to feel much more comfortable in our own skin. Below are a couple of examples of mental constructs many lawyers hold. Consider whether you buy in to them, and whether stepping away from them, even provisionally, might bring some useful perspective.

The Role of Luck in Our Lives

As a group, we lawyers are a bunch of control freaks. Let's face it, just to get through the amount of higher education you need to practice law, it's likely you're at least a little obsessive by temperament. Add to that the degree to which winning is lionized in our profession, how much our clients expect from us, how much we genuinely care about them, and the ever-shifting set of very crucial details we must attend to on a daily basis in order to be effective in our work, and you're well down the road to neurosis.

Now, add the reality that we truly can't control the outcome of the work we do: sometimes the witness says unexpected things, sometimes the economics of the business deal we've been negotiating change, sometimes the client has unexpected financial reversals unrelated to any legal issue. When you consider the many factors that directly affect the outcome of legal work that no lawyer can control, it's easy to see why so many lawyers are completely wound up, compulsive people. We are literally trying to do the impossible: consistently delivering outcomes that can't be guaranteed, and judging ourselves whenever we fail.

Our meditation practice can help us break out of this crazy-making bind, first and most simply by helping us find our way back to reality. Movies, novels, and even news stories may depict successful lawyers as brilliant heroes who always manage to win a case or a negotiation in the face of impossible odds. Those stories are compelling narratives—who wouldn't want to be an invincible champion, always delivering great outcomes to grateful clients? But we all know that in reality legal success comes about from a combination of hard work, focus, and luck.

Reading the paragraph above, you may have had some trouble with that last word, "luck." Lawyers often have a hard time owning up to the uncomfortable truth that we, along with our clients, are at the mercy of a highly irrational and uncontrollable force—the thing we call luck. We experience this every day of our working lives, although our training and our temperament are such that few of us openly admit it. But regardless of our attitude toward luck, it affects the results of our work, occasionally in dramatic ways.

Sometimes we win when we know in our hearts we deserved to lose. Ironically, those unwarranted successes can feel particularly sweet! We thank our lucky stars, look over our shoulders to make sure no one saw what really happened, and revel in our victory. Other times we lose when, by all rights, we should have won. We were completely prepared, the facts were on our side, but something totally outside our control ended up turning the situation against us. Maybe the judge was in a bad mood, maybe the client arrived at the meeting wanting something totally new and different, maybe a witness refused to testify. Whatever the specific reason, we've all found ourselves unexpectedly on the losing side of a case or a negotiation, and we know it can be totally crushing. We can spend years mulling over these kinds of events, retrying cases in our heads, imagining what exactly we could have said or done differently.

Meditation can help us find enough detachment to look clearly and honestly at the role luck plays in our work. By loosening the grip of our thoughts—including the mental images we have of lawyer-heroes who always beat the odds—meditation helps us stay connected to the reality that the effort and skill we bring to our cases is only one part of the picture. Openly acknowledging we don't have absolute control over the results of our work can be enormously freeing and can help us be kinder to ourselves when we have reversals. We can begin to stop holding ourselves to a standard that, however attractive, is impossible to meet.

Seeing Each Other for Who We Are

Lawyers learn early how to construct straw men—and then level them to the ground. If we can make our opponents' positions look foolish and simplistic, it's that much easier to score a victory, in the courtroom or in the boardroom. Boiling our opponents' views down to simplistic and easily refuted positions can be a useful tactic. But how often does this become our default stance toward others? Negotiations may feel simpler if we deal with people as categories—aggrieved widows, corrupt politicians, brilliant innovators—rather than fellow human beings, who are unique, complex, and, to some degree, mysterious. But, again, what potential for agreement do we miss entirely if we put our counterparty in a box?

Oversimplifying the people we interact with often serves another, more subtle purpose for us. Our profession constantly puts us into situations where we are dealing with conflict. It can feel simpler to manage the discomfort of conflict if we filter that conflict through black and white thinking. If our opponents are bad, unreasonable people, we can find it easier to take the aggressive positions we may feel are required to do our jobs as advocates. In fact, many lawyers are trained to see their opposing counsel as bad people. Both of us have been in situations as young lawyers when we were told not to shake our opposing counsel's hand. As unprofessional and petty as that sounds, a surprisingly large number of attorneys have either been told the same thing or been witness to it.

100

Karen's Story "Are You Talking to Me or Your Idea of Me?"

Quite a few years ago, I was in a heated argument with my husband. I no longer even remember what exactly we were fighting about, but I do remember he said something that surprised me. In the middle of our exchange, he suddenly looked directly at me and said: "Are you talking to me? Or are you talking to your idea of me? Or is your idea of you talking to your idea of me?"

What my husband said made me laugh and ended the argument, but afterwards I kept coming back to his questions. I couldn't help but admit they were pointing out a very real dynamic. I wasn't talking to him as if he was a real person, but a caricature of himself, someone who wanted to thwart me and undermine my ideas. And, just as I was reducing him down to a caricature, I was doing the same thing to myself, making myself into a perfect embodiment of my best qualities, pure, sweet, giving, and absolutely right. There was no way the imaginary conversation I was engaged in could ever lead to a good outcome, and by insisting on framing the dialogue the way I was, I was reducing the two of us down to uninteresting parodies of the people we are.

Since that conversation, I'm better able to recognize my tendency to try to make myself right by reducing anyone opposing me to a cardboard cutout, someone who is so patently unreasonable my views have to carry the day. When I see myself doing that, I remember my husband's questions, which always make me smile inwardly. I try to back off and see the other person for who he or she is, in all their complexity—and I try to do the same for myself, to acknowledge I may not be the perfect person I wish I were. I remind myself to see the entire situation in full. I believe even trying to do that, with whatever limited success, has reduced the amount of unnecessary strife in my life and helped me arrive at better outcomes in my dealings with others.

Unfortunately for those of us who've made a regular strategy of putting others in a box, over time this habit takes a professional and personal toll that far outweighs its benefits. It limits what we can get out of any interaction, since once we've pegged another person as being a certain type, we're likely to miss any information that contradicts this oversimplified view. So we miss opportunities. We never see the strength that needy client might have, or even push away a generous gesture from an opposing counsel we *know* is obnoxious. Worse, when we commit ourselves to ignoring the details of the people we are engaging with, we lose the benefit of human connection in our day-to-day interactions. How many lawyers end up stressed, isolated, and lonely even as they spend most of their days in meetings, on the phone, or in court, surrounded by people? But it's very hard to experience any sort of fellowship with others when you can't or won't go past your preconceived notion of who you're dealing with.

Our meditation practice can help us get back to the details of human interaction. As we break through the grip of our thoughts, we make space for reality to peek through. This doesn't mean we have to give up our role as strong advocates, but rather that we take on that role more consciously, and don't sacrifice our relationship with the complexity of the world when we do so. Simply allowing yourself to be surprised by others brings possibility and pleasure with it. You may take up your obtuse partner's strange suggestion and find it's actually brilliant. Or find your way through a stalled negotiation by listening more carefully to what the person on the other side is asking for. Seeing more clearly doesn't have to be limited to others. Getting past your preconceptions about yourself and more comfortable with the reality of who you are can help you find flexibility and creativity you didn't know you had. You may surprise yourself by finding you are actually a better advocate when you allow yourself and others more authenticity.

Loosening the Grip of Our Narratives

These two examples of how we can limit ourselves through black-and-white thinking also illustrate another limiting form of mental construct: the narrative. As lawyers, we are expected to have facility with narrative: we can and do tell our clients' stories to their best effect, knowing how we shape those stories can have a stronger bearing on the outcome we are seeking than the technicalities of the law involved. Yet, as facile as we may be with other people's narratives, we often fail to see how we allow ourselves to be trapped by our own. Too often, we limit our own options by buying in to deep-seated narratives we can't seem to step away from.

The good news here is that the natural clarity of our minds can see right through even the most deeply entrenched story lines. As we meditate and connect with that clarity more and more strongly, we are doing something akin to washing the windows of our minds. The more we sit, the more light shines in. This is significant, because we are most deeply in the grip of limiting narratives when we don't see them at all. If you're drawn to exploring meditation, it may be because one or more of your core narratives are beginning to lose their power over you.

Questioning Our Narratives

Begin to question thoughts that appear to force you into an unpleasant situation, or otherwise limit your options in some way (e.g., "My opposing counsel always acts like a jerk," "I can't be a good parent and a good lawyer," "I'm only happy on vacation."). When you notice such a thought, take a moment to connect with sensory experience: notice the feeling of your feet on the ground, look around yourself, or take a few slow breaths. Then spend one to two minutes asking yourself:

- Is this thought always true, or are there times when it could be false?
- What if the opposite were true?
- If the thought is true, does it *matter*?
- Think of a hypothetical situation, no matter how silly, when the thought would be obviously untrue.
- Can you think of any time you acted as if that thought weren't true, and yet things were fine?
- Would you force this thought on someone you cared about?

The point here isn't to disprove this thought, but simply call into question your mind's determination that the thought is absolutely true.

As you begin to free yourself of the narratives that don't serve you well, you will likely experience moments of great freedom and possibility, when you suddenly see potential in yourself and your life you never knew was there. At the same time, there can be awkward phases that are quite uncomfortable. You may be aware of one of your narratives, but feel unable to step away from it. "Leaving my job would be a betrayal of my parent's hopes for me." "If I don't make partner, I'm worthless." "I need to work this hard, I have to support my family." "If I don't do it, it won't be done right." In these moments, it's important to remember to bring gentleness as well as clarity to your situation.

You may find it helpful to write down the narrative—without censorship or worrying about whether the narrative is rational. Once complete, ask yourself what function the narrative is serving. For example, using the example above, if you believe you are worthless if you do not make partner, what function is that belief serving? Perhaps it's motivating you to be excellent and has served you to be successful up until this point. Recognizing the usefulness of the narrative is very important since there may be lessons that can be gleaned from it. Finally, ask yourself if the narrative is still useful and serving its purpose *now*. Perhaps, as you've been climbing the ranks at the firm, your values have changed and making partner is no longer a top priority. Another possibility is you've been using the belief to push yourself so hard your life feels out of balance.

Meditation practice can help us bring perspective to uncomfortable transitions. Everything has a beginning, a middle, and an end, and this can include our fascination with unhelpful story lines. The good news is the clarity we build through our meditation practice can help us step out of canned narratives and into a world where we experience more agency, expansiveness, and possibility.

~

Following Your Thoughts

I will meditate for _____ minutes, every day.

Meditation Instructions—
Following the Thoughts

Visit www.theanxiouslawyer.com for audio guided meditations.

1. Set a timer for the desired length of meditation.
2. Sit with a straight spine, in a comfortable position you can hold for the time you will be meditating. Commit to that posture.
3. Allow your eyes to close or find a spot approximately four feet ahead of you and gently gaze at that place.
4. Take a couple of deep breaths in and out of the nose to help you settle in and make the transition from an outward focus to a more inward one.
5. Notice what is around you and inside you. Spend one cycle of your breath (one in-breath and one out-breath) noticing each of the following.
   a. the temperature of the air;
   b. the sounds around you, both the closer sounds and the sounds that are further away;
   c. the feeling of your body, its solidity;
   d. the feeling of energy in your body; the vitality inside you;
   e. your mood.
6. Turn your attention gently to your thoughts. Rather than thinking about the content of your thoughts, notice the quality of your thoughts:
   a. Are your thoughts coming quickly, one right after the other, or more slowly?
   b. Do your thoughts sound loud to you, or more quiet?
   c. Do your thoughts feel rough? Do they feel smooth, or gentle? Fuzzy?
7. Allow yourself to enjoy the feeling of your thoughts as they run through your mind.

8. See if you can follow a thought as it arises, fills your consciousness, and falls away.

   a. Where does the thought come from? Is there a feeling that lets you know a thought is starting? Does it start quietly and then become louder in your mind?

   b. What does it feel like when the thought is fully in your consciousness? Are there words associated with it? Does it echo? Is there a feeling quality to it?

   c. What happens when the thought falls away? Does it fade, or stop abruptly? Is there a feeling you have when it stops?

9. As each thought falls away, allow yourself to rest in an open state until the next thought arises.

10. Meditate, keeping your attention gently focused on the flow of thoughts. If you realize that you've begun to think about the content of those thoughts, don't worry about it. Just gently bring your attention back to an open state and wait for the next thought to start.

11. If you have difficulty and are getting caught up in the content of your thoughts, you can follow the movement of the breath for a breath or two, then return to following the thoughts.

12. Continue to observe the flow of your thoughts until the end of your meditation time. Slowly begin to wiggle your fingers and toes or check in with your body and move in any way that feels good to you.

Noticing Transitional Moments

As attorneys, the workdays we routinely face are so full of competing demands we can easily lose touch with what is going on in the current moment. We can be so busy trying to juggle commitments and anticipating problems that we continuously project our thoughts into the future, without fully focusing on what is happening right in front of us. Ironically, only in the present moment can anything actually be accomplished!

This week, make a point to come back into the present during your moments of transition from one task to the next. When you finish a phone call, before immediately jumping into answering e-mail, take a few seconds to reconnect with your surroundings. Look around your office. Feel your feet on the floor or your breath in your body. Notice the sunlight playing across your desk. Say to yourself, "I am here." Then move to your next task from that place of connection with the present.

Meditation Log

Day	Time/Length	Notes: Sitting	Notes: Off the Cushion
Mon			
Tue			
Wed			
Thu			
Fri			
Sat			
Sun			

Compassion Toward Others

It may be that when we no longer know what to do,
we have come to our real work,
and that when we no longer know which way to go,
we have begun our real journey.

—Wendell Berry

IN THIS CHAPTER, WE'LL begin to explore loving-kindness or *Metta* practice. This practice involves connecting with our innate ability to be compassionate in the face of difficulty. Before we move into talking about this practice, we want to acknowledge it's not an easy one. In our experience, compassion is challenging for most attorneys. We tend to be perfectionists and expect nothing but perfection from others and ourselves.

You can start to explore compassion practice in this chapter—where we'll practice loving-kindness toward others—or, if it feels easier, you can skip to the next chapter and start with self-compassion. While we are covering loving-kindness practice in two separate chapters, it's important to understand these chapters are related and build on each other. We can't express compassion toward others without first experiencing it ourselves. If you struggle with this practice or notice resistance to it, be patient and kind with yourself and know this is a difficult practice.

When we've taught eight-week classes on meditation for lawyers, the topic of compassion is one of the most difficult for lawyers to grasp. Especially for the litigators among us, we're often taught to see the opposing side as enemies and to adopt an unnecessarily aggressive mindset. Our work can make us overly cynical, skeptical, and view the world as a warzone where we must always be on guard. We may walk through life with a sword in our hand, always ready for battle. In the compassion practice, we invite you to open yourself up to the possibility of walking through life with a different lens—the lens of compassion.

There are many reasons why it's difficult for lawyers to tap into their innate ability to be compassionate. First, lawyers are trained to see compassion as weakness. True compassion involves a certain degree of vulnerability, and as a society we are simply uncomfortable with being vulnerable. In order for us to acknowledge the suffering of others we must acknowledge our common connection to humanity. Second, lawyers fear that being compassionate means we're required to condone unacceptable behavior. We'll explore these misconceptions further in this chapter.

Nothing Is Happening!

Now that you're several weeks into the program, you have concrete experience of what it's like to meditate. It's probably somewhat different from the idealized image you held before you actually started meditating, and it's useful to acknowledge that. For example, you may have begun your meditation practice thinking you'll be free of stress within a few weeks and feel disappointed or perhaps even feel like a failure because you're still experiencing stress.

As lawyers, we have high expectations of ourselves and we're achievement-driven. These attitudes can be useful, but it's also important to remember to take a posture of gentleness and compassion for yourself as you build your meditation practice. Meditation will transform and unfold for you in its own unique way. Part of the practice is to bear witness to how your own practice unfolds without criticism or expectation. Your practice will be different from everyone else's. While there are certain predictable stages of how a meditation practice will likely evolve over time, there's no set schedule for that evolution or predictable way in which it will happen. That's part of its beauty.

A common experience for many meditators is that for days or weeks, you'll feel as though the practice is going well, then you may hit a setback where your mind is racing like a car at NASCAR or you experience intense boredom, pain, or some other undesirable experience. When you hit these obstacles, it's important to recognize this too is an expected experience. Your meditation practice is not linear. It will have lots of twists, turns, and unexpected surprises. Allow yourself to be present with whatever may come up both in your formal and informal practice. No two sitting practices will ever be the same because you're never in the exact same state. Stay curious. Allow yourself to take the attitude of a scientist toward your own practice, and wonder, what will happen next?

111

For the two of us, compassion practice has profoundly affected the way we relate to others, including our clients, opposing counsel, and those in our personal lives. Compassion is a doorway for finding common ground with others. After all, every human shares life's ups and downs. To practice compassion, a person acknowledges: just like me, you have good days and bad days; just like me, you love some people and have difficulties with others.

What Is Compassion?

When we introduce the concept of having compassion for others in the classes we teach, we often find that lawyers react with fear and hesitation. Lawyers fear that when we ask them to be open to the possibility of bringing compassion into their lives (and their law practices), we're asking them to surrender advocacy or quit being good attorneys. That's not what we're suggesting. When we discuss compassion, we are not advocating submission, becoming a doormat, or suggesting that you give in to weakness. That would obviously be a disservice to yourself as well as your clients.

So, what do we mean when we say "compassion?" We define the practice of compassion as having four components:

1. Recognizing difficulties or suffering (either our own or others)
2. Noticing our innate desire to help those who are experiencing difficulties
3. Recognizing that difficulties, suffering, and pain are part of the human condition
4. Taking some step to alleviate or help

Practicing compassion toward ourselves and others is an ancient practice, also known as loving-kindness. In this practice, we cultivate our own ability to be compassionate by sending good wishes to people in the following categories:

1. People we love
2. A stranger
3. People we're having difficulties with
4. All beings
5. Ourselves (This final practice is the focus of Week Five.)

It's important to note this practice is merely strengthening our innate, compassionate nature. You don't need to be taught compassion, since you already have that capacity inside you. This practice is all about cultivating, strengthening, and flexing the compassion muscle.

In the context of our discussion, offering compassion to another is not:

- condoning;
- forgiving;
- agreeing with the other person;
- altruism;
- liking or loving the other person;
- letting the other person off the hook;
- pity;
- feeling sorry;
- heroism;
- self-sacrifice;

- giving in or allowing the person to have his or her way.

You may be wondering, "Why compassion? What does compassion have to do with understanding my mind?" Compassion is a vehicle to understanding our own suffering. It's a way to feel our way through the painful experiences that exist for every living being.

When you practice compassion toward others, you practice *knowing* why another person is suffering and consider how you may alleviate that suffering. As you engage in this practice, you may notice it helps *decrease your own suffering.* One could argue you practice compassion toward others because it's *good for you.* This is because you are always the immediate recipients of your own feelings. Before you can express anger toward another person, you experience the anger first. Similarly, before you can be compassionate toward others, you get to experience it first.

Meditation, Compassion, and Well-Being

Besides helping us cope with the challenges and stresses of life, there is increasing scientific evidence that meditation actively improves our quality of life. Meditation has been shown to increase our sense of compassion for ourselves and others, as well as how we act in the world. More generally, over time meditation does something that can be difficult to describe but is highly valued by most people who meditate: meditation helps us appreciate and savor life more fully.

One recent study sponsored by the Mind and Life Institute, a research institute dedicated to the scientific understanding of contemplative practice and established at the behest of the Dalai Lama, found that people who had completed a meditation training course were more than three times more likely to offer their seat to a disabled person than non-meditators.[11] This research is the first documented evidence that meditation may make us more aware and responsive to others and more willing to take action to help others. The study authors are now pursuing research to understand what it is about meditation practice that may lead people to act more compassionately.

Another intriguing line of meditation research is investigating the question of whether meditation may affect our level of happiness. Western psychology suggests that each person has a "set point" or default level of happiness. While life events like falling in love or experiencing a life crisis may temporarily make us uncharacteristically joyful or melancholy, according to this view, eventually we will return to our emotional set point. At the University of Wisconsin, professor of psychology and psychiatry Richard Davidson found in his research that meditation may actually be able to shift our set point so our base level of happiness increases.[12] In one study he conducted, one group of participants took a meditation course while a control group did not do any meditation. Not only did the meditators report feeling happier but they also showed lasting changes in the way their brains functioned, with increased activity in the left frontal region associated with feelings of happiness, well-being, and alertness.

We intuitively practice compassion. Someone we love, our spouse, parent, sibling, child, suffers from an injury or an illness, and our natural capacity for compassion kicks in. We recognize the pain and feel our innate desire to help and take action. Compassion also underlies much of what we do in our work. Lawyers tend to be heartful people who want to be of service to others. We'll continue to explore this often unrecognized side of our profession later in this program, but for now consider whether your innate compassion and empathy hides behind a veneer of fierceness as you advocate for your clients.

Practicing Compassion Toward Others

Each of us has the capacity to love and the capacity to hate. At any given moment, we have a choice as to how we'll respond. Will you respond through the lens of love or hate? To be clear, we are using the word "hate" in its broadest sense of the word. This includes aggression, negativity, and general feelings of disliking the other person. As lawyers, we're frequently taught to be overly aggressive, never give an inch, never show weakness, or the worst offense of all—show any emotion. One lawyer shared that the managing partner at her firm would regularly say, "We're lawyers. We don't have feelings." This same partner insisted she continue working on due diligence as the World Trade Center towers fell after the 9/11 attack. It's difficult to imagine this partner had a peaceful inner world.

We'll now turn to the mechanics of loving-kindness practice. While the practice itself follows specific, defined steps and may initially feel a little artificial, remember that in going through these steps we are simply building on a natural capacity. During each stage of the practice, we imagine a person (or group of people) and practice wishing that person well.

As we've said, this isn't an easy practice and you should be very gentle with yourself through this exercise. It's possible you may have strong feelings arise during this practice. If you notice this, give yourself permission to stop the practice or change the person you're offering compassion toward in your sit. For example, if you choose your mother to offer compassion to and it triggers a painful memory or other reaction, you can go back to your breath or choose another person. Who you choose as the object of your compassion practice is unimportant. What's important is to practice extending compassion toward another, thereby harnessing your innate ability to extend compassion toward someone who is suffering. As you do this practice, you may sense your heart opening and you may feel life more deeply. This is also a normal part of practice.

In compassion practice, we move our focus from one category of person to another, starting with someone we deeply care about, to a stranger, to someone we are experiencing difficulties with, to groups of people. We cultivate compassion by sending good wishes, care, and concern to each person or group of people (see Week Four exercise below for more details). What follows is an overview of the practice. We will return to each of the steps and go over the practice in more detail later in the chapter.

- The practice begins by choosing someone you care about. This can be a dear childhood friend who you see each year. It can be your spouse, your parent, your sibling, your significant other, or your friend. You may also choose a pet. You can choose a different person with each sit or you may always choose the same person.
- The next group is someone you don't know very well, a stranger. It can be the teller at your local bank, the clerk at the grocery store, the bus driver, or the new intern at your office. Although you may not know them personally, they have offered benefit to you in some way, whether a simple smile, or a service, like delivering your mail.
- The third category is someone you're experiencing difficulties with. This can be an opposing counsel, a client, an estranged friend,

115

or a family member. Again, who you choose for the practice is unimportant. What is important is that you engage in this practice willing to acknowledge the suffering of others and to cultivate the natural capacity for compassion—even toward those you have difficulties with.

- Next, we practice bringing compassion toward all living beings. This can sound lofty or even impossible. There is no need to hurry through this practice. You may spend weeks, months, or even years with the first stage by offering compassion to someone you care about. When you are ready, begin by selecting a group of people. This can be everyone in your office, everyone who lives in your building, everyone on your block, everyone in your city, and so on. Through this practice, you are gradually expanding your field of compassion. You may find that your ability to be compassionate expands far beyond what you imagined to be possible.

- The final step is to practice compassion toward yourself. Because self-compassion can be especially challenging for lawyers, we'll devote all of next week to focusing on this important practice. For now, you can practice self-compassion by taking a gentle stance toward yourself as you engage with compassion practice. Remember there's no need to judge yourself if you find this practice very challenging. You can engage with it one small step at a time.

116

Compassion Toward Our Clients

Compassion, in the context of working with clients, means we acknowledge our clients' suffering. Before we jump into pumping our clients for all the relevant facts so we can apply the applicable law and analyze it, we can practice taking the time for the client to tell his or her story. We can allow the client to tell the story in the way he or she needs to tell the story, not the way we need it so we can write it into concise statements of facts in the Complaint. Often, what our clients need the most is to simply be heard.

The truth is that the law is very limited in terms of the relief it can offer our clients. Rarely can monetary damages restore our clients and adequately compensate them for the pain they've suffered. Money is often what the parties fight over but it's only a symbolic representation of something deeper. For example, many estate planning attorneys have told us that while siblings may be fighting over their deceased parent's estate, underlying the dispute is a question of who the parent loved more. Similarly, in family law, spouses may fight over money but underneath is a lot of unprocessed emotional baggage, and money symbolizes those unresolved issues. When we take the time to understand our clients, we often find the clients aren't fighting over money at all—what they want is an acknowledgment of the wrong that has been committed, an apology, or restoration of a broken relationship.

When lawyers can look beyond the dollars and cents and compassionately engage with the psychology of our clients, we may be able to come up with creative solutions. Often, we view our client's problem as a zero sum game: he is fighting over a pie and we have to get him the biggest piece possible. By becoming more attuned to our client and looking at the problem holistically, we will be able to make the pie bigger or redefine it all together.

For example, if you're an estate planning attorney representing a sibling seeking legal action because she's resentful of the other sibling who the deceased parent always favored, you can skillfully find a way to bring peace between your client and her sibling instead of further tearing apart their relationship. Similarly, when your client in a divorce proceeding insists on taking a matter to the judge because she wants the judge to tell the husband he is responsible for causing the divorce, you can bring compassion into the picture and facilitate your client's healing process.

It feels important to emphasize at this point that we cannot be an agent for facilitating healing or bringing compassion toward our clients until we can fully acknowledge our own difficulties. Many family lawyers go into this profession because they either experienced a painful divorce themselves or their parents have. Compassion toward others necessarily starts with compassion toward self, something we'll explore in greater detail in Week Five.

Compassion Practice—Tuning In

Practicing compassion requires courage. At the core of this practice, we return to the basic premise that we all share a common thread—a common humanity. We can connect with the truth of this commonality by saying to ourselves: just like me, my opposing counsel has good days and bad days; just like me, my client experiences a full range of emotions from love to hate; just like me, the judge is trying her best. The practice of compassion asks us to step into our vulnerable space, acknowledge our humanity, and be with what is difficult. Instead of denying or turning away from what is painful, we face it. As we begin to explore this space, we begin to recognize that in being with what is—this human experience—we are not alone in our experience. We begin to explore what we can do and, as importantly, accept what is beyond our control. There are so many circumstances where we may feel utterly helpless because we can't fix it or make it better. The practice of compassion gives us something we can do in the spaces of powerlessness.

Jeena's Story of Facing What's Painful

I grew up poor in Queens, New York. I remember as a child, I'd avoid looking at homeless people on the street—partly out of fear that I too could be homeless and partly out of helplessness. There was *nothing* I could do to help this person. This continued into adulthood. In fact, when I moved to San Francisco, the avoidance became worse. I'd cross the street, walk in the opposite direction, or look away, just so I wouldn't have to see this person's suffering.

Then I signed up for a class at Stanford called Compassion Cultivation Training. In this class, we were encouraged to *be with* and gently approach the pain and suffering of others. As I began to unpack the pain of even looking at a homeless person, what I noticed was my own deep fear and insecurity around money and being poor. There was also the feeling of injustice about the fact that we can live in one of the richest cities in the world and still have so many homeless people.

Over the weeks, as we worked through bringing compassion for friends, loved ones, strangers, enemies, and ourselves, I made a conscious decision to stop avoiding homeless people. I decided even if there was nothing material I could offer this person, I could offer him good wishes. So I began my experiment. Whenever I saw a homeless person, I'd pause, look at this fellow human being and silently repeat the phrase "I wish you happiness. I wish you freedom from suffering." This practice continued for many weeks.

One day, I was walking through the subway station and I saw a homeless person. As usual, I looked at the person and silently wished him well. He asked if I had any spare change. I told him I was sorry but I couldn't offer him money. He then asked if he could have a donut. I happened to be carrying an entire box of cream-filled pastries. I happily obliged. I reached into my box and offered him one. He smiled and thanked me. In that moment, I saw that while being homeless certainly has its pain I wasn't always helpless. There are moments where I can help. Even if it's just in some tiny way.

Several weeks later, I was walking through the streets of San Francisco. It was raining. I saw a homeless man, standing on the sidewalk. He had on at least three layers of jackets. Over the layers, he was struggling to put on a rain jacket. He had one arm in the sleeve and was swinging the other arm in an awkward position to find the other sleeve. I walked up to him and helped him find the other sleeve. He looked at me and said, "Thank you."

I read somewhere that one of the most painful parts of being homeless is you don't feel seen. People look right through you. When I connect by making eye contact with a homeless person, or simply look at him or her and send good wishes, I hope I am helping him or her feel less isolated, that I am acknowledging our common humanity.

119

We invite you to gently explore this space. As with all the practices described in this book, the benefit is the practice itself. This practice, like all others, is not about getting to any certain outcome or result. Do as much or as little as you are able to. There is no need to rush. Recognize thoughts or beliefs around having to do the practice perfectly or do it correctly. Engaging with this practice—that is enough. This isn't something you can will yourself to do but, rather, it's a practice in opening yourself up to the full range of your experience.

Loving-Kindness Practice for Someone You Love

As mentioned previously, humans are innately compassionate. We can cultivate our ability to tap into this natural tendency and strengthen our ability to lead with compassion through practice. To begin, bring to mind someone you love and care for. Who you choose isn't as important as tapping into the *feeling* of compassion. Find someone who is easy to love. Someone who you don't have a complicated relationship with. Someone who immediately gives you that feeling of warmth and love. Imagine yourself in this person's presence. Notice any sensations in your body. Gently begin exploring this feeling as you think about this person.

Next, recall a time when your loved one was in pain or was suffering. Again, the exact details of the event are unimportant. The practice is about exploring the feelings that are triggered when you imagine your loved one in pain. Notice if there are any shifts in what you can feel in your body. Is there tension, pain, discomfort, or other sensations? As you imagine this person you love in pain, or suffering in some way, repeat the following phrases:

— May you be happy.
— May you be healthy.
— May you know ease and joy.
— May you be free from suffering.

If these phrases don't feel quite right, feel free to substitute other phrases. Bring your attention to your physical heart. Notice any sensations or feelings in that area. Perhaps there's an opening or expansion from your heart center. If you don't notice any physical sensation, that's okay too. This practice may feel strange, challenging, difficult, or artificial at first. Allow yourself to notice and be with whatever your experience may be. Not that it's not enough to read these words, and gain an intellectual understanding of the practice. The key lies in the *practice*. You must *do* the practice, this meditation, with persistent effort in order to see the benefits.

Loving-Kindness Practice for a Stranger

Once you've practiced loving-kindness for a loved one long enough that you feel ready for the next step, you can move into extending the practice to a stranger—someone you do not know well. You may feel ready to do this within a few minutes of practice, or it may take you days, weeks, or longer to do so. Your judgment is the best guide here. The stranger you choose can be the cashier at your local supermarket, the coworker you occasionally say hello to, or some other person you recognize but don't have a relationship with. Again, who you choose isn't as important as engaging in the practice of sending well wishes to someone who is a stranger to you. If this practice feels difficult, return to practicing with someone you love as described above.

The invitation is to tap into the same feelings and emotions you noticed when thinking of the person you love and now expand that out to others. Bring to mind this person. Imagine this person in your presence. Notice any feelings, sensations, experiences, or emotions. Now, as you imagine this person, think about the person suffering in some way. You do not need to know the details of this person's life, nor the difficulties he or she may be facing. You can make up the details of this person's difficulty, being as detailed or as general as you'd like. As you imagine this person suffering, repeat the phrases:

— May you be happy.
— May you be healthy.
— May you know ease and joy.
— May you be free from suffering.

121

Feel free to substitute or add other well wishes. Notice any changes from this practice.

Working with Difficult People

You've practiced loving-kindness toward people you love, to a stranger, and now you're ready to move onto difficult people. Your relationship may be strained or challenging with certain people for many different reasons. Perhaps the person has wronged you in some way. They've betrayed your trust. Caused annoyance. The person may have caused you harm, or even committed a crime against you or someone you care about. It's worth mentioning again that compassion does not mean you must forgive the person or condone the action.

When we practice loving-kindness, we're tapping into our natural ability to feel compassion, to acknowledge each person is more than any single action he or she has taken. To use an extreme example, a person may commit murder but he's not just a murderer. He's still a human being capable of feeling, expressing different emotions, including compassion, and capable of change. Despite his actions, there is a common thread binding us. We can know that just like us, he too has experienced pain in his life.

The practice of loving-kindness for difficult people is identical to the practice toward loved ones and strangers, as described above. While the practice itself is the same, your experience, how you feel as you're doing the practice, will likely be very different. The thought of wishing your opposing counsel well may literally make you cringe. You may believe she isn't deserving of your good wishes or that there is absolutely no room for such thought. We encourage you to give this practice a try. There is no need to jump to the most difficult person in your life. You can find someone who doesn't trigger such strong or painful emotions. As mentioned previously, who you choose isn't as important as your willingness to engage in this practice. Remember to always take care of yourself first. As you engage in this practice, you may gain more clarity as discussed in Week Three. Perhaps if you send good wishes to people you have difficulties with, you may begin to see the narratives you've been carrying around toward them.

Jeena's Experience of the Law of Natural Consequences

A few years into my mindfulness practice, I had a case where the client was caught trying to conceal an asset from her bankruptcy petition. After she was found out, she raised the advice-of-counsel defense. I was both furious and devastated. I had to obtain my own counsel to defend myself against my own client. The United States Trustee called me as a witness against my own client. In my more than twelve years of law practice, this was probably the most traumatizing experience.

For months, I replayed every interaction I ever had with my client trying to see if I could've been somehow "more mindful" or looked for signs that I wasn't "mindful enough." While logically, I knew the client was at fault, emotionally, I wanted to protect her. I certainly never wished this upon her (or myself). It's never a pleasant feeling to have to break the sanctity of the attorney-client privilege and engage in a battle of "he said, she said." It felt very personal and it was deeply painful. I was looking for something I could've said or done to prevent this from happening. In many ways, having to testify against my own client felt like proof that I had failed as a lawyer.

Years later, I shared this experience with a group of lawyers at a meditation retreat for lawyers. I noticed the compassion I felt toward my client and the compassion I felt toward myself. And I realized, no matter how good our intention, how deeply we desire the best outcome for our clients, how hard we try to protect our clients (from themselves and others), ultimately, clients have to face the natural consequences of their own actions. As much as we would like to, oftentimes, we simply cannot shelter our clients from these consequences.

We should also remember that mindfulness isn't a cure-all and notice when our mind goes into judgment mode in terms of whether we were mindful enough or could've been more mindful.

Holding Compassion and Assertiveness Together

123

One common concern attorneys express in doing this practice is that it will make them go soft, lose their edge, or otherwise not be zealous advocates. This is certainly understandable. Our ability to be effective as lawyers feeds our sense of purpose, and, of course, directly impacts our livelihood. In approaching this practice, we both had similar questions and concerns. However, we have both found the practice of compassion doesn't make us weak—quite the contrary, it makes us more aware of the fullness of each situation. It allows us to hold different perspectives, including those of others with whom we deeply disagree. It gives us greater access to wisdom, so we feel more able to let things go, to move forward; or to sense where we should draw a line, dig in our heels. It allows us to get out of the us versus them mentality and see all the different players in a case as part of the puzzle. Everyone has a role to play. It allows us to see everyone is doing their best given their resources, including us. It gives us the room to forgive ourselves for mistakes, make room for imperfection, and truly be our own best friends.

With that as background, we'll explore how compassion fits into the legal practice, especially when we're supposed to be adversaries and we're in a zero sum game. How does a lofty ideal such as compassion fit into our profession?

First, let's examine the relationship between self-compassion (discussed in Week Five) and compassion toward others. When we're being cruel toward others, does that only harm the other person? Or does it also harm us?

Now, you may argue that by taking every opportunity to flex your muscle and to be adversarial, you're advocating for your client. And perhaps it's true that with behaviors such as not shaking the opposing counsel's hand or not offering water, you're gaining some minuscule advantage. But at what cost? What's the cost to you for always keeping on your warrior armor? Hostility is usually met with more hostility. The old adage "you catch more flies with honey" is often true.

Perhaps it's this win-at-every-cost, cause-as-much-pain-to-the-opposing-side-as-possible attitude that has led our legal profession to the state it's in today. There are often discussions of lack of civility in the profession, and many states are now implementing rules for professionalism. Part of the incivility comes from not seeing opposing counsel as a fellow human being who deserves a certain level of respect and acknowledgement—not because she said or did anything to earn your respect, but simply because, like you, she's a person. Just like you, she experiences all the facets of the human condition and this can be the basis for offering her compassion. In its core, the legal profession is about humanity.

Jeena's Experience of Toxic Mentoring

I recall, as a young lawyer, sitting in on a deposition for the first time. The opposing counsel and his client were waiting for us in the conference room. When I walked into the room, I asked if they would like some water and if they were comfortable. The partner (who was taking the deposition) pulled me aside after and said he better not ever catch me trying to make the opposing side comfortable. In fact, it was my job to make the opposing side as uncomfortable as possible. When I've told this story to other attorneys, what's surprising is that this type of behavior is expected and tolerated. I've had lawyers tell me their boss instructed them to never shake the opposing counsel's hand. One attorney said his boss never spoke at CLEs because he was afraid of "training the competition."

This type of "toxic mentoring" is rampant in our profession. It often starts in law school where all of a sudden, you realize you are no longer one of the smartest kids in class. Now, you're surrounded by other students who are just as smart as you, if not smarter, and you are being graded on a curve. I recall students ripping pages out of the books in the library in an effort to prevent other students from completing their research and writing assignment. Even the Socratic method, which is supposed to help lawyers think on their feet, often only promotes the extreme fear and intimidation law students experience in school. We're put into these very challenging, intimidating, and difficult situations but no one is allowed to admit fear, or show any type of emotions, except perhaps aggression.

In Torts class, students are taught only to analyze the facts, apply the applicable law, and come up with the conclusion. There's never a pause or consideration for the horrible tragedy the person in the case suffered. We gloss over the fact that the plaintiff in the case lost his arms, his wife, his child, because of the defendant's negligence. We don't consider how the defendant may feel for causing this horrible tragedy to occur.

What we fail to teach, and what we fail to learn in law school, is humanity. When a client comes into our office, often, it's because they are facing an unbearable pain or suffering they cannot fix on their own. Of course, not all areas of law are so emotionally charged, but lawyers often fail to see and understand that humans are driven by emotions.

125

Compassion, as mentioned previously, does not mean not advocating for your clients or not doing your due diligence. It *does* mean you draw boundaries and express where the line is and if your boundaries have been crossed. Clients come to us because someone has wronged them, or violated a basic social contract. A client comes to us because she's suffering and seeks our assistance in finding ways to end that suffering. The role we play as attorneys is far more than our ability to pull the facts from our client, conduct legal research, run the analysis, come to a legal conclusion, and calculate the damages. Lawyering also involves understanding the role emotions play in our client's decisions, understanding what motivates their behavior. More importantly, lawyering involves understanding our own inner world and our inner state.

Connecting with your purpose, your reason for practicing law, can guide you in navigating the relationship between compassion and your law practice. For a moment, take off your lawyer hat and ask yourself "Who am I?" Does the answer to that question include "I'm a person who inflicts as much harm on my adversary as possible?" Or is the answer something closer to "I believe in the legal system and doing meaningful work?"

There are two reasons for why being compassionate may, in fact, lead you to be a better lawyer. First, by practicing compassion you can better understand the other side, their point of view, their strategy, their grievance. By gaining a fuller understanding of each side, you are in a better position to more skillfully think through your client's case. It also serves to reduce your own bias in the case, from seeing the case only from your own perspective.

Second, as you become more compassionate toward yourself and others, you become able to more fully engage with the case and all involved. You'll feel less overwhelmed with difficult or negative emotions. You can become more emotionally independent. Your emotions will not be at the mercy of what happens in your external world. When your opposing counsel unreasonably refuses to turn over documents to your discovery request, you won't feel flooded with frustration and anger. This isn't to say you will never feel negative feelings. However, you can catch the rise of frustration and anger within yourself and more quickly defuse it by recognizing those feelings for what they are—passing feelings.

Recognizing Common Humanity

Compassion doesn't mean you're living in a delusion. You don't need to pretend to like your opponents. You don't need to give in. It does mean you begin to examine your deeply held beliefs about others and your relationship to them.

For example, think about someone you're having difficulties with. This can be a family member, friend, your neighbor, opposing counsel, your client, etc. What are some of the thoughts that come up when you think

126

about this person? What do you feel? Is it annoyance, frustration, anger, sadness, or some other feeling? Can you notice any sensations in your body as you think about this person you're having difficulties with?

Now, see if you can find some common denominator—some commonality between you and this person by completing the sentence "Just like me . . . s/he also . . ." This can be very broad, for example, "Just like me, he also has good days and bad days." It can also be very specific. "Just like me, he too is angry about our argument last week." This recognition of your common humanity is the essence of the compassion practice. Despite your differences, the conflict, the intense feelings, you can acknowledge his or her difficulties. Your common human experiences—both positive and negative—unite you, and you can use that commonality as fuel to feed your practice.

There are times where lawyers may need to be harsh or be perceived as being harsh. This can happen when you're cross-examining a witness, in discovery disputes, or in other circumstances. You may have strategic or ethical reasons for doing this. There's no easy rule of thumb for when you should be harsh. Again, we are not advocating that you give up being assertive or that you never be harsh. We are encouraging you to evaluate your higher purpose, your commitment to the type of attorney you'd like to be, your commitment to your own ethical values and align your behavior to that. In other words, gain clarity around *why* you are engaging in certain behavior. Is it truly because you're advocating for your client or is it to get even with your opposing counsel?

127

Finally, there's no singular mold for how compassion looks or may be experienced. You can be stern, yet compassionate. You can be assertive and compassionate. You can zealously advocate for your client and be compassionate. The aspiration is to be the most skillful attorney, which includes conducting yourself with dignity, courtesy, respect, and compassion, and standing by your personal ethics.

The Importance of Forgiveness

Forgiveness is closely tied to compassion. When you practice sending good wishes to those you're having difficulties with, it will often trigger memories of misgivings toward that other person. It's likely you're having difficulties with that person due to a conflict—something she did, or something you did, or a combination of the two. Forgiveness and compassion are intertwined. When you extend compassion toward those who have wronged you, it may organically move you toward the path of forgiveness. However, you may practice compassion without forgiveness.

Practicing forgiveness, moving toward letting go of the emotional boulder, benefits us even more than those we seek to forgive. As mentioned previously, we cannot express toward others what we don't first feel. We can't express hate toward others without first feeling the emotion of hate ourselves. Similarly, we can't forgive others without experiencing the benefits ourselves. Forgiveness can be a difficult thing to practice because it requires vulnerability. We must face the painful parts of our past and gently work toward letting go. It's an emotional clearing.

Forgiveness, like practicing compassion, isn't something we can force or do only with our intellect. It requires involvement of our mind, body, and spirit. We must explore the full range of emotions, feelings, and sensations. It's not something we can rush. We can tell ourselves "I forgive that person," but saying it and feeling it are not the same. Just as healing from a physical wound can't be rushed, we also can't rush healing from emotional wounds. However, there are certain things we can do to facilitate healing.

128

The first step is to open to the possibility of forgiveness and healing. Not that you must forgive in this moment but consider the possibility that in the future, you will be able to truly forgive. The second step is to recognize forgiveness isn't a linear process. You may feel as though you've fully forgiven a person and then, the next day, feel another wave of anger. Forgiveness, like all the other exercises described in this book, isn't about getting to a destination but rather being fully committed to each step of the journey.

When we discuss forgiveness, what we're talking about is an emotional clearing, letting go of the hostility, pain, feeling of betrayal, or other negative emotions. Forgiveness isn't about condoning the other person's actions, allowing the person back into your life, or even expressing your forgiveness to the other person. It's not about apologizing. If you're estranged from the person, you do not need to reengage or reestablish a relationship with this person for forgiveness to take place. You may emotionally come to a place of forgiveness, yet not want to reengage contact with this person. This doesn't need to be a permanent state. You don't need to come to any decisions about how you're going to engage with this person now. Remember, the process of forgiveness is all about you and taking good care of your emotional needs.

Ask yourself why it feels important to forgive this person. Getting clear on your intention for moving toward forgiveness is crucial for propelling you toward this direction of forgiveness. There are many exercises you can do to facilitate the healing process. Here are some suggestions. Additional resources are provided at the end of the book.

Forgiveness Meditation

Find a comfortable position. You can practice lying down or sitting upright. Close your eyes and begin to tune into your breath. Observe your breath for as long as you need in order to feel centered. If you notice your mind wandering, gently bring it back to the breath. Gently bring to mind the person you'd like to forgive. Approach your experience with curiosity and gentleness. Notice any physiological experiences as you think about this person. If, at any point, the sensations become overwhelming, return to the breath. Be very kind to yourself, as this is a difficult practice.

Your mind may replay the experience when you bring this person to mind. Without judging yourself or the person, ask yourself if there's a different interpretation or some other view you may not have considered. Consider the fact that she tried her best, despite the outcome of her efforts. You may notice judgment, sadness, anger, frustration, and other emotions.

Make room for whatever your experience may be. You may also have regrets toward how you acted or for not acting in a certain way. Give yourself credit for also trying your best, despite the end result and what has transpired. As you continue to be with this experience and this person, see if there is a shape or some description for what you're holding onto that prevents you from forgiving this person. Does it feel light or heavy? Does it have a color? Does it have a shape? Does it have a sensation or a feeling? What is the emotional tone? What function is it serving? Imagine creating a feeling of spaciousness around this experience. Give yourself the permission to fully feel whatever your experience is, without forcing or rushing it. If it feels right, you can say the words "I forgive you" or "I forgive myself."

When you feel ready, bring yourself back to the breath. Take three breaths, paying attention to the four parts of the breath—the feeling of inhalation, and the brief pause; the feeling of exhalation and the brief pause before the next inhalation.

129

Forgiveness Letter

Another powerful exercise in facilitating forgiveness is to write a letter. The goal isn't to draft a letter you'll send to the person (although you certainly can). The point of the exercise is to get your thoughts down on a piece of paper so you can view the experience with a bit of distance. This may help you gain a different perspective and give you a bit of spaciousness around the experience. Instead of holding tightly to the experience, you can create a sense of ease.

You can start the letter in any way that makes sense to you. It doesn't have to be linear, or even well thought out. This isn't a brief or research paper. There is no right or wrong way to write the answer. This exercise may come naturally to you, or it may be a struggle. Whatever your experience may be, give yourself credit for engaging with this practice. This is a difficult practice. You may notice your inner critic chiming in. Welcome him or her to this practice as well. As you engage in this letter writing exercise, you may find you not only want to forgive this person but you may also need to forgive yourself.

There may be some parts of this past experience that are simply too difficult or painful to think of or write about. This is also okay. The practice is all about making an effort. Give yourself the permission to do as much or as little as you are able. You do not need to complete this letter in one sitting. You may take days, weeks, or even months to complete it. You may also write multiple letters. As you write each letter, you may notice your views, your tone, how you interpret the situation may shift.

Some prompts that you may find to be helpful:

- What happened? Without censoring or editing, simply write down what happened from your perspective. You may find it helpful to set the timer for ten minutes and write without stopping to read what you wrote.
- What is the other person's narrative? There are always multiple ways of viewing a situation. Consider the experience from the other person's perspective and write the narrative from her perspective.
- What is the impact of her actions? Was there something she did or failed to do that wounded you? Consider whether she intended to cause the impact she's had on you. Oftentimes, people don't intentionally do things to hurt us.

- How do I feel about her? How do I feel about her behavior? Can you separate out the behavior from the person? For example, the person may have lied to you, which caused you harm. However, can you see the person for who she is outside of her action? Recognize your own cognitive shortcuts and tendency to label. There is a difference between saying "she lied to me" and "she's a liar."
- If you assume she did the best she could, given the resources she has, and under the circumstances, does that change how you view the situation?
- If you assume you did the best you could, does that change how you view yourself or the situation?
- Recognize your common humanity with the other person. Despite her act, what reality do you share? Are there some common human bonds you share? Complete this phrase "Just like me . . ." For example, "Just like me, this experience also caused her pain."
- If it feels appropriate, you may find it helpful to write the words (I forgive you" or "I forgive myself."

~

Offering Compassion to Others

I will meditate for _____ minutes, every day.

Meditation Instructions

Visit www.theanxiouslawyer.com for audio guided meditations.

1. Find a comfortable seated position. Feel your feet firmly on the ground. Allow your body to rest. Feel your body sink into the chair below you.
2. Bring your attention to the breath. Breathe in and out. Notice the air as it moves in and out of your body. Continue to breathe in and out until your mind settles in the natural rhythm of the breath.
3. Next, bring an image to mind that represents unconditional love or acceptance. This can be the sun, which shines its light on everyone without discrimination, the ocean, a tree, or any other place in nature you resonate with. It can also be a person you view as having unconditional regard, love, and acceptance. It can also be an animal such as a pet. Spend some time bringing this image into your mind's focus. Imagine being in the presence of this loving person, place, or object.
4. Bring to mind someone you care about. It can be your friend, spouse, significant other, child, parent, sibling, or anyone you can easily extend care, attention, and warmth toward.
5. As you think about this person, notice any feelings of tenderness or warmth that arises inside of you. Imagine this person sitting in front of you.
6. Now, imagine this person you care about is experiencing some difficulty. This may be a difficulty known or unknown to you. As you imagine this person suffering, notice any feelings of tenderness arise in you. Notice any desire to help.

7. As you imagine your loved one suffering, repeat these phrases. You are welcome to use other expressions of good wishes that feel right to you.
   - "May you be happy."
   - "May you be healthy."
   - "May you know peace and joy."
   - "May you be free from suffering."
8. Repeat these phrases for as long as you'd like. Notice any feelings that arise as you do this practice. It may be feelings of tenderness, care, and concern for this other person. You may also become aware of your own difficulties in life. Allow your awareness to simply be with whatever feelings or thoughts arises for you.

Continue with this meditation for as long as you'd like. Once you are familiar with the practice and ready to proceed, you can extend this meditation practice to a stranger, to someone you're having difficulties with, then to groups of people (e.g., everyone who works in your building).

~

Sending Good Wishes to Others

This week, practice sending good wishes to a stranger. You can practice by silently repeating good wishes such as "May you be happy" or "May you know peace and joy." Who you send the good wishes to isn't important. The practice is just about cultivating a sense of understanding and feeling our common humanity. You can send good wishes to the random stranger you walk by on the street, the person standing behind you in the grocery line, or the driver in front of you who is also stuck in morning traffic. As you send good wishes to strangers, see if you notice any shifts or feelings arise.

List three people you'll send good wishes to this week:

1. _____

2. _____

3. _____

Meditation Log

Day	Time/Length	Notes: Sitting	Notes: Off the Cushion
Mon			
Tue			
Wed			
Thu			
Fri			
Sat			
Sun			

Self-Compassion

Opening to my loss,
Willing to experience aloneness,
I discover connection everywhere;
Turning to face my fear,
I meet the warrior who lives within;
I gain the embrace of the universe;
Surrendering into emptiness,
I find fullness without end.

—Jennifer Welwood, *Unconditional*

WHEN WE INTRODUCE THE concept of self-compassion, frequently students will say those two words *self* and *compassion* shouldn't go together. Compassion is our innate response to suffering and our desire to help. We think about compassion as something reserved for people very close to us, such as our friends and family. When we use the term self-compassion, we are talking about the ability to extend compassion to ourselves.

Think back to a time when a friend or a colleague shared with you a difficulty in her life. Perhaps she lost a month-long trial she spent years working and preparing for. Or maybe your friend told you he was having difficulty in his marriage. When you think back to when your friend shared his or her difficulty, how did you feel? What did you do or say to comfort your friend? Did you empathize with what she or he was going through? Did you feel that sense of compassion welling inside?

Now, think back to a similar difficulty you had in your own life. Maybe when you lost a hearing, a motion, or a trial. Were you able to extend a similar feeling of kindness, empathy, and compassion toward yourself? Probably not. Chances are you were filled with self-criticism, self-doubt, or even self-hate. It's also possible you felt angry at the judge or the opposing side.

We can cultivate self-compassion, a sense of unconditional positive regard for ourselves in times of difficulty instead of being overly harsh or critical. When we practice self-compassion, we're recognizing our own difficulty, pain, anger, or other suffering in that moment. Perhaps you lost a hearing on an important issue you spent months preparing for. In that moment, you can recognize what you're going through and say, "This is a moment of difficulty." You can then acknowledge these events are a part of life. Suffering is a part of the human condition. You can begin to offer yourself self-compassion, perhaps by saying, "All lawyers lose hearings from time to time." You can then practice being kind to yourself by saying, "I know I worked really hard on this. I know that really hurts." By acknowledging your pain, accepting this pain is common to many others, and offering kindness toward yourself, you are practicing self-compassion.

138

Importance and Benefits of Having Compassion for Oneself

When we're working with clients who suffer great tragedy or experience unbearable emotional pain, we may attempt to embody the idea of a tough, emotionless attorney by shutting down our feelings or try to protect ourselves by emotionally distancing ourselves. We may even say things like "What you're telling me isn't relevant to your case" and dismiss the client. This isn't because we're heartless or uncaring. Just the opposite is true. We fear that if we allow the pains of our clients into our heart, it will completely consume us.

Self-Compassion Versus Self-Esteem and Selfishness

Frequently, when we say "self-compassion," people think of self-esteem or selfishness. While these words all may sound similar, they're very different. In fact, one could argue that being compassionate toward self or self-compassion is the *opposite* of self-esteem and selfishness.

Self-esteem is related to worth and externally achieved. It comes from measuring ourselves against a particular yardstick, and we only experience self-esteem when we achieve what we strive for. We impose that yardstick on ourselves as we try to achieve the goal that will allow us to feel self-esteem; for example, being the best in our softball league or being the "best" lawyer. If we only feel good from achievements, it can also feed insecurities.

If you are motivated principally by self-esteem, you may also find that you struggle with self worth. Do you ask yourself questions such as "Am I good enough?" or "Do I deserve _____?"

Selfishness is being concerned with only one's own well-being. It lacks consideration for others. When we're being selfish, we are *taking* something from others, purely for our own benefit.

With self-compassion, we practice being kind, accepting, and loving toward ourselves. This is done *without* condition or question. Unlike self-esteem, there's nothing we must do in order to be deserving of our own kindness to ourselves.

When we practice self-compassion, we become more aware of our own difficulties. When we're compassionate toward ourselves, it allows us to more fully open to the experience of our own as well as others' suffering. We're better able to help those who are in pain because we have the emotional capacity, the resilience to do so. Hence, it's completely the opposite of being selfish.

However, ignoring or refusing to hear our client's pain doesn't protect us from absorbing it. Consider the fact that so many lawyers suffer from alcohol and drug abuse or suffer from mental illness such as depression, which is probably an indication that as a profession we aren't managing our difficulties very well. Instead of denying the realities of our job—that there is suffering inherent in our work—we need to find a way to process the pain in a healthy way that doesn't lead to abusive, self-destructive behaviors.

In our experience, extending compassion toward oneself is perhaps one of the most challenging practices described in this book. We've both struggled with this practice. As with any new skill, what you practice becomes easier. Practicing self-compassion is no exception. Despite the challenges, this practice has been one of the most rewarding and enriching for both of us. As we learn to approach ourselves with more kindness and gentleness, we begin to approach others with the same attitude. As mentioned in Week Four, we can't express any emotions toward others without first experiencing those emotions ourselves. As we engage in self-compassion practice, we may recognize we can only extend as much compassion toward others as we have toward ourselves.

Self-Compassion and Understanding Our Mind

Part of the practice of cultivating self-compassion is to understand our mind and how it works. Humans have the ability to direct the mind. As an experiment, bring your attention to your right foot. You can direct your mind to make your right foot move. Next, move your attention to your right hand. Notice how you can use your mind to direct your attention. How you direct the mind is important because your mind is an incredible instrument that finds answers. The question you pose to your mind is important because it will answer that *specific* question. For example, if you lose a hearing and ask your mind, "Why are you such a loser?" the mind will happily come up with a list of answers.

Imagine your mind files events of your life in filing cabinets. When you criticize yourself by saying, "You're a terrible lawyer" after losing a hearing, your mind will file away that event in the cabinet labeled "Terrible lawyer." And the next time you ask yourself, "Why are you such a terrible lawyer?" your mind will go into that filing cabinet and give you a very long list of examples or reasons. As mentioned previously, humans have a negativity bias. Therefore, chances are you probably have a very large filing cabinet for all the things you perceive as being negative about yourself and you may lack a positive filing cabinet. We all carry around views about ourselves and others. Therefore, if you only see yourself as angry, you'll always look for behaviors or actions that validate this view. Similarly, if you see your opposing counsel as a "jerk" or difficult, you'll only look for actions that validate this perception.

As you become more familiar with your mind, you can begin to see your thoughts and challenge them. Instead of having the mind automatically find the answer to the question, "Why are you such a loser?" you can notice the flaw in the question itself. The assumption is that you are a "loser." In these moments, instead of allowing your mind to be self-critical, you can direct it toward compassion.

When you observe your inner chatter, see if you ask "why" questions—which look backwards (e.g., Why am I always so angry?)—as well as "how" questions—which direct the attention forward (e.g., How can I avoid getting angry?). Both questions can clue us in on our mind's habits. Remember the pattern, *when x happens, I always think y*? Maybe every time you have to give a talk, you always think "I'm going to be terrible at this" or "I'm going to forget everything I'm supposed to say and make a fool of myself." You can examine the underlying thought patterns and ask yourself, "Why do I believe this? What evidence do I have to show that my thoughts are true? How can I show up as my best self?" or "Can I simply allow this anxiety to pass?"

141

Working with Difficult Opposing Counsel

Your phone rings and the Caller ID shows the familiar name of an opposing counsel you loathe. You can feel the blood rush to your face, the muscles in your arms and legs tense. Your heart starts beating faster. Your body's fight or flight response is triggered and you cringe wondering why he's calling. All of this happens within a second or two and you may not even notice the physiological response. The only thing you know is how much you dislike this person, the list of annoying things he's done to you and your client.

Our legal system often requires us to be adversarial, but rarely are we taught how to cope with our own discomfort and pain when navigating this system. What's worse, the lack of frank conversations about our own difficulties of being in an adversarial system only compounds our pain because it can feel as though we're the only ones who can't hack it. The mildly annoying to rude, abrasive, discourteous behaviors are rampant in our legal system, particularly in litigation settings.

Often, when we speak to attorneys about the most difficult part of their job, the list consists of opposing counsel, judges, clients, lack of time, deadlines, and financial pressure. The attorneys who register for our classes often want a solution for fixing the bad behaviors of others. Get the opposing counsel to stop being a jerk, get the judge to see things from our perspective, or get the client to follow instructions.

The other common reason attorneys join our class is because they want to be completely resistant to the bad behavior of others. Wouldn't it be much easier if all these behaviors of others didn't affect you—at all? If you could respond to your opposing counsel's denial for your request for an extension with robotic precision so you can always get the desired outcome? Wouldn't it be great if you could, in fact, leave your emotions at home so you never experienced anger, frustration, sadness, annoyance, or any other feelings at the workplace?

Many lawyers spend a great deal of time severing their emotional selves from the office. However, by doing this, we're stopping ourselves from being fully present to our lives! Most of us spend more than half of our waking hours at the office. Is it ideal or desirable to spend so much of our lives disconnected from ourselves and others? We firmly believe that while it may be possible to convince yourself you don't care or are immune from your feelings, suppression of your emotional self will manifest itself in other toxic ways—for example, using or abusing drugs or alcohol to numb the pain. What if, instead of disengaging from yourself, you can bring mindfulness into the picture? What would that practice look like?

Let's pause for a moment and consider the scenario above. You're in litigation and there's a long history of resentment, hostility, and other negative feelings toward your opposing counsel. When the phone rings, and you see his name come up on your Caller ID, what do you feel? What thoughts are going through your head? Can you identify what parts of your body are reacting to this event? Can you slow down your thoughts and the physiological response so you can take a moment to pause and notice what is happening? Can you give yourself a moment of reprieve and spend a few seconds practicing diaphragmatic breathing?

Often, when your fight or flight response is activated, all you know is you're experiencing an intense feeling and your mind says, "I don't like this feeling. I want it to stop." Then your mind begins looking for a reason for why you're feeling this way. Once it identifies it as this person you loathe who is calling you, your mind might go into judging mode by saying "You shouldn't feel this way. Stop being so weak!" You may also go into full fight mode and your body goes into battle-ready mode. "That jerk! I'm going to show him!" All of this is happening and you may not even be fully aware of it. You may feel helpless, unable to moderate your physical or emotional response.

Through the years, you may have developed strategies for dealing with such situations. You may disassociate from what is happening, react with aggression, or avoid in-person confrontation by getting into drawn-out e-mail wars. You may also have your favorite strategies for getting under this person's skin, further provoking her and tearing apart your relationship.

As much as we wish there was a magic wand that could change the behaviors of those who cause us grief, what we often fail to recognize is that the only person whose behavior we have control over is ourselves. While this may feel restrictive or lacking at first glance, it's actually a liberating realization. Instead of wasting precious energy and effort trying to control or change other people's behavior, we can redirect that energy toward moderating our own behavior. We can focus on being present to each moment and doing our best instead of obsessing over the outcome (which we often do not have control over). The invitation is to show up to each situation as our best self and do our best given the tools and resources available to us—in that moment. With a combination of self-compassion and mindfulness practice, we can access our inner resilience so we can respond in a healthy and appropriate way.

143

Going back to our example, you see the Caller ID, your mind starts to race, and you can feel the adrenaline pumping throughout your body. Instead of using your typical habitual reaction (ignoring the call, answering in anger, suppressing your feeling), can you make room to give yourself a moment of reprieve by taking a few deep breaths? Can you give your nervous system a chance to recover?

Before going into an explanation on tools you can use to cope with difficult opposing counsel, it's important to know that while the practices are *simple*, they are not *easy*. To use them, practice and patience are required. In addition, this is an ongoing, lifelong practice. Just as in your meditation practice, your ability to use these tools will be different from day to day, from moment to moment. If there's a single message we could convey, it is this: be kind to yourself. Being a lawyer is difficult.

There are two main tools for working with difficult opposing counsel—cultivating compassion toward self and cultivating compassion for others. When we use the word compassion, we are not suggesting you condone or accept the opposing counsel's behavior. We're also not talking about sympathy or feeling sorry for yourself. In the context of mindfulness practice, compassion has a very specific definition, as described earlier.

First step is recognizing what is happening. This means noticing the anger, frustration, or annoyance you feel toward this person. This willingness to look at and acknowledge your inner state, how you are feeling, can itself feel scary and you may notice a lot of resistance around it. This makes sense given that you may have spent years ignoring or suppressing your feelings. You may fear that if you allowed yourself to *feel*, you may lose yourself in your emotions, like jumping into a pit of despair. With continued meditation practice, you cultivate the ability to observe all of your emotional states—positive, negative, those that feel like blazing hot steel, and those that feel a giant block of ice. As you practice noticing your emotional states as simply passing moments without reaction or judgment, your reaction to people who trigger you may lessen. Show up with curiosity. Can you be a scientist of your own mind, whose job it is to examine your thoughts and reactions?

After you allow yourself to see how and what you are feeling, the next step is to acknowledge that moment as a moment of suffering. The work you do as a lawyer is difficult work. This does not mean dwelling in your difficulty or feeling sorry for yourself. You're simply acknowledging as a fact that, in this moment, having your opposing counsel call is triggering an emotional reaction and this is a difficult moment for you.

Our mindfulness practice can help us access the compassion, for ourselves and for our opposing counsel, which we need in order to move through this situation in a skillful way. Mindfulness is all about awakening to *what is* and *responding* in a thoughtful, considered manner with compassion. This isn't possible until we fully allow ourselves to be with our own difficulty, emotions, and reaction. This doesn't need to be a labored process (although it may be). It may be as simple as acknowledging and saying "John's calling and I'm noticing my reaction. My heart's beating faster, my mouth feels dry, and I can feel anger rising." You can then acknowledge your difficulty. For example, "John and I have a long history of having a very difficult and adversarial relationship. This is a painful moment. I feel extremely frustrated thinking about our last conversation." As you do this, notice your breath. This isn't an intellectual practice. This practice requires you to connect with your mind and body. The way to connect with both is through the breath.

By acknowledging what is instead of resisting, denying, or ignoring, you can begin to move through and process what is happening. Suppressing your emotion is akin to pushing a beach ball under the water in a swimming pool. It takes a lot of effort and, sooner or later, it will pop back up with more force.

The mindful way of processing described here won't happen overnight. Also, if you use meditation only when you're triggered, it likely won't be very effective. Like long distance running, we can give you all the strategies and tools—proper running form, breathing techniques, clothing, shoes, diet, etc. However, you can't master all of these strategies on the morning of the marathon. You need practice. You can practice being mindful when you're walking down the street, washing your hands, talking to your spouse, or other times when you are not triggered. With continued practice, you'll get better at observing your thoughts, your default reaction, and your triggers. You can become more familiar with the patterns of your mind.

By taking a stance of compassion toward yourself, you may notice you can take more ownership and responsibility over your own reactions. Instead of saying "John *made* me angry," your inner dialogue may change to "When John refused to give me an extension, I felt angry." This can be incredibly empowering because you're no longer constantly a slave to your reactions. You may also begin to notice there are times where you can talk to John and not feel triggered. You can even see a possibility for having a completely different response to John. Instead of immediately lashing out at John, you may approach the situation with curiosity and inquire as to why he's refusing to give you an extension after you've given him three extensions previously. You may ask yourself how others might respond to John in similar circumstances. This isn't to suggest your default reaction will change overnight. It probably took many years, even decades for your brain to wire itself with this reaction and it may take many years before you can develop different neural pathways and responses. However, in the meantime, you can practice being very gentle, kind, patient, and compassionate with yourself.

In addition to acknowledging your own emotional and physiological response, you can practice noticing additional thoughts. One common

145

thought pattern is judgment around your reaction. When you see John's name pop up on the Caller ID and you feel yourself get triggered, your inner critic may chime in. Your inner critic may say, "Stand up to him! Stop being so weak!" or berate you for the way you're feeling. Again, practice recognizing it as a pattern and make room for a different response.

Softening self-judgments is an organic process that happens through practice. Perhaps one of the first steps in loosening the grip of always needing to be perfect or constantly using the whip is recognizing that how you are in this moment isn't permanent. Each of us is constantly evolving and changing. Research shows our brain can be changed, due to changes in behavior, environment, neural processes, thinking, emotions, as well as changes in the body. This process is known as neuroplasticity. Therefore, you can influence how you think, experience, and perceive the world. You can soften your identification with your current self.

146

Practicing Self-Compassion

There are specific steps we can use to practice compassion toward ourselves.

1. Acknowledge this is a painful moment or moment of suffering

When we use the word "suffering," we don't necessarily mean huge tragedies such as a severe illness or death. We simply mean any event in our life that causes pain, discomfort, uncomfortable feelings, or anguish. It's important to acknowledge how we feel, because unless we do so we can't begin the process of understanding what's happening or thinking about a way to respond.

This simple act of acknowledging you are in a difficult, painful situation—a moment of suffering —is the first step in cultivating self-compassion. Without first acknowledging our own pain in the situation, we cannot effectively acknowledge or help those in pain. As repeated in every safety instruction on every flight, "Secure your own oxygen mask before helping others."

2. Notice how this moment feels

The next step is to notice how this moment feels. You can notice the emotions, anger, fear, frustration, or any number of other feelings that may arise. You can also notice how it feels in your body. Do you notice yourself curling your shoulders in, as if you're trying to protect yourself from a blow? Do you feel your stomach tie into knots? Do you notice tensing in your arms or legs? Do you notice pain around your heart? All of these give you information about how you're feeling in this moment. By simply noticing and acknowledging how you feel, you can then make a decision to respond. The response will, of course, depend on the specific circumstances but until you can tune into how you feel, you can't begin to formulate a response.

As you practice *being with* how you are in this moment, without clinging or rejecting, and without judging your emotions, you may find it helpful to name your emotions. For example, when you can feel the heat rise to your face when your client blames you for an outcome after he specifically refused to follow your advice, you can name the emotion by saying to yourself, "I feel anger."

Ever have an experience of being so completely overtaken by your emotions you can't even begin to put words around how you feel, or you simply snap? By regularly practicing and tuning into how you're feeling, especially in moments of difficulties, you'll be better able to modulate your response to a given situation.

147

3. Tune into your natural tendency to feel compassion

As human beings, we're hardwired to feel compassion. When we see someone in pain, we feel compassion—there's a natural desire to help, to see that the person not suffer. For most of us, it's much easier to extend compassion to others than it is to ourselves. If this is true for you and you have difficulty extending compassion to yourself, imagine seeing yourself as you would a loved one, a good friend, or a child. If this person you deeply cared about was in a situation where she was faced with working with a difficult client or case, wouldn't you feel and express compassion? Can you extend this care toward yourself? As you engage with this practice, remember to treat yourself as you would someone who is dear to you, someone who you love. Afford yourself the same compassion, kindness, empathy, and love you'd extend to a loved one.

4. You are not alone

The next step in being compassionate toward ourselves is to remind ourselves that suffering is a human condition. No human is free from pain, uncomfortable experiences, anger, frustration, disappointment, shame, and thousands of other feelings and emotions that make up the fabric of being human. This fabric can be said to bind us together. In fact, all living beings experience suffering of one form or another. It's part of life. Of course, life isn't all about suffering. The opposite is also true. We also experience joy, happiness, delight, satisfaction, and all the positive emotions that make up being human as well. The invitation of this practice is to recognize the common bond—this condition of being human and show up for each experience.

Recognizing this interconnectedness among all human beings and recognizing that we all feel negative and positive emotions can help us feel less isolated and alone when it feels like life is crashing around us.

5. This is temporary

When we're in the midst of whatever life event we're struggling with, it's hard to see the light at the end of the tunnel. It may feel like this situation, this painful moment, this suffering will last forever—that there will be no end. Of course, this isn't true. Everything is transitional and nothing is permanent.

This includes how you're feeling in this moment. Even when you're experiencing unbearable pain, if you pay attention, you'll notice the intensity of the pain shifts from moment to moment. Remembering "this too shall pass" may be one of the most difficult but perhaps one of the most powerful reminders when you're in the thick of suffering.

Selfishness Versus Self-Care

Often, when we teach self-compassion and self-care, students express concerns about becoming selfish or self-centered. These concepts, while sounding similar, are completely opposite from each other. As we noted earlier, *selfishness* means lacking consideration for others and having concern only for one's own gain. *Self-care* means caring for ourselves so we can maintain optimal physical, emotional, psychological, spiritual, and mental health. Self-care allows us to care better for others. There's no diminishing others or their values in self-care.

Karen's Story of Learning to Relax Between the Stressful Moments

When I was preparing for labor with my second child, my childbirth coach gave me advice that turned out to be key for getting through this classically challenging experience in a pretty wonderful way. The labor coach said, "Your labor is likely to last for a long time—certainly several hours. So for hours, you'll be having contractions, and then there will be time between the contractions. I'm going to give you some techniques for how to manage the contractions, but you also have to pay attention during the time between the contractions."

My coach told me it was very, very important to relax completely between each contraction. She explained it like this: if, the minute your contraction is over, you start to worry about the next one, you'll tense up and tire yourself out so you have very little energy when that next contraction actually comes. If instead you focus on what is happening—no contraction—and enjoy that break completely, you'll get a real break and be ready for the next contraction.

I was lucky with this second labor; it was a relatively easy one. On the other hand, it was long—more than twenty-four hours—and the advice my coach gave me turned out to be crucial for getting through it. I was amazed that simply relaxing when I had the opportunity to do so could make such a big difference, but it did. When I remembered to relax, I was fine when the next contraction started; if I forgot or was distracted during my "downtime" between contractions, the next contraction almost overwhelmed me. Needless to say, I became a very motivated relaxation expert in short order!

After I returned to work, my coach's advice stayed with me. The deadline-oriented work I did as a litigator was characterized by periods of intense activity, and stretches of time when there was little going on. It certainly wasn't as intense as labor, but I began to consciously take time to relax when I could. Rather than fill all my extra time with busy work, I might see a friend for a long lunch, go for a walk, or leave the office early to spend an extra hour with my children in the evening. The busy times always returned, and I found I was enjoying them more and had more energy for them when I'd taken a real break from the frenetic pace litigation sometimes requires.

Once I began meditating, I began to better understand why resting the mind is so important. I could also see how easy it was for me to continue to fall into the trap of needing to feel busy, even when busyness was not necessary to doing my work effectively. Once I got into busy mode, I could easily fill all my spare moments with extra phone calls, making lists, double-checking and reediting prose that didn't need changing—work that was entirely optional, left me depleted, and didn't necessarily lead to better results for my client.

To counter this tendency, I extended the idea of taking time off by making a daily practice of relaxing completely. Even on very full days I tried to take note of the little breaks when it was possible to stop and take a breath. In my case, these moments often happened on the bus going to or from work, or in my office between meetings. I might take a few minutes to follow my own breath, consciously relax my shoulders and upper back, and look at something beautiful or let a pleasant image fill my mind. Just taking those little mental vacations was surprisingly rejuvenating, even in the midst of a very challenging day.

Self-care is something we can only do for ourselves. No one else can consume healthy, nutritious meals for us. No one else can spend five minutes walking around the block during lunch. No one else can meditate for us. By zealously guarding our well-being, we will better be able to prepare for any challenges that will arise in our life. By being more mindful, we can tune into our own needs and desires. The more sensitized we become to this, the more we are able to attend to our inner world.

Lawyers are outward facing—we're constantly focused on others, our clients, our coworkers, law partners, and so forth. Lawyers like to be responsible. We like to be responsible for others. We spend a lot of time trying to deliver the right results. We're people pleasers. This is precisely the reason why being mindful is so critical. We have to carefully monitor our inner state, our emotional fuel tank. If we're constantly giving to others without ever stopping to refill out own tank, sooner or later, we'll start running on fumes. We may be able to operate from this state temporarily but, sooner or later, we'll have nothing more to give.

Give Yourself a Break: Mindful Eating

How often do you eat lunch at your desk, eating bite after bite while staring at your screen only to realize you've finished your meal without having enjoyed a single bite? If you regularly eat lunch at your desk, commit to breaking this habit and practice mindful eating. Get out of your office and go to the break room, to a nearby park, or to your favorite restaurant. Instead of eating your food on autopilot, take a moment to bring a sense of gratitude for this meal. Pay attention to each bite. Notice the sensation of having food in your mouth. Notice all the flavors. When your mind gets distracted with thoughts, worries, or goes into planning mode, simply guide your mind back to the food you're eating.

In practicing self-care, the specific act you choose isn't as important as the intention you bring to the act. For example, you can approach something as simple as hand washing as an act of self-care. As you turn on the water, consider how you're taking better care of yourself by washing your hands. Take an extra moment to adjust the water temperature to your liking. Feel the luxurious sensation of soap against your hands. Take a moment to notice your hands—see the incredible instrument they are. How much you rely on them, how dependable they are, how hard they work for you. Just as helping your child wash his hand can be an act of kindness and love, so can washing your own hands.

Being Kind to Ourselves

"It's your birthright to have your own mind be kind to itself." This was a statement one of our meditation teachers repeated weekly in class. Consider for a moment the truth of this statement. If you can't be kind to yourself, who will? If you can't unconditionally stand by yourself, accept yourself, with kindness and compassion, who will?

Many lawyers are driven by fear. Fear of failure. Fear of criticism. Fear of not getting the right outcome. And when things don't go as expected, we punish ourselves harshly. What is your motivation tool? Is it the carrot or the stick? Your internal source for motivating yourself, is it kind or cruel? When you mess up, do you berate yourself? How loud is your inner critic? Do you hold yourself to an impossible standard? Is anything less than perfection unacceptable? What if you can be just a bit gentler with yourself? When you consider that possibility, how does it feel? Do you feel excited by that idea or do you feel fear? Perhaps you fear that if you were kinder to yourself, you'd lose your edge; that you'd become a failure.

It may seem counterintuitive, but being more compassionate with ourselves, letting go of constantly pushing yourself using the "negativity stick" can help us be better lawyers. As we let go of the harsh narrative and holding ourselves to an impossible standard, we may be more inclined to take risks. When we aren't so fear-driven and engaged in avoiding failure, we can access creative thinking. When we let go of the idea of perfection, we are better able to rebound from mistakes.

As we explore this concept of self-compassion, ask yourself what yard-sticks you use to measure yourself. We have the tendency to hold ourselves to an impossible standard or to someone else's standard. It can feel scary to even consider this line of inquiry. We've had students ask, "What will stop me from eating gallons of ice cream if I let myself do what I want?" This is certainly a valid concern. However, doing what you *want* is probably very different from merely giving in to passion if you think of your task as taking very good care of yourself. Would eating a gallon of ice cream be practicing self-compassion? Would you feed a gallon of ice cream to someone you deeply cared about? Probably not.

The Importance of Rest

Lawyers struggle, perhaps even more than other professionals, with constant demands on time. The billable hours system with which most of us work means we are under continuous pressure to be productive, literally in every minute. Consciously taking time to allow ourselves to rest is a simple act of self-compassion we can give ourselves. When we practice meditation, we are allowing our mind to rest. We learn to use our mind not just for thinking but to simply observe and notice our mind. In a world where we're constantly bombarded by external distractions, it's becoming more crucial to give ourselves the gift of rest. Frequently, we think about rest and relaxation as something that happens only on vacations. Perhaps you've had the experience of going on vacation only to have your mind still at the office, unable to unwind, unable to let go.

New research is showing what all of us intuitively know. More work does not result in increased output. The human body is simply not designed to sit at a desk for eight hours straight. The most productive people tend to balance focused time where all attention is put on a task followed by a period of rest.

Giving yourself permission to have downtime and unplug can feel scary. You may notice internal resistance to the idea of taking a break during lunch and going for a leisurely walk instead of mindlessly scarfing down your lunch in front of the computer. If you notice resistance to the idea of rest, see what internal dialogue is playing in your mind. Perhaps you believe you can't take time for yourself because you have too much to do, or you're being selfish. Perhaps you fear you'll fall behind. These thoughts are perfectly understandable. In this ever increasingly connected world where technology is speeding up at an astonishing rate, you may feel as though you must work harder and faster to keep up. Consider for a moment that the computing power in the technology we use doubles every eighteen months to two years. Is it possible for you to double your work output every couple of years? How much faster can you work while producing *quality* work? What is the cost of continually demanding more?

There is no easy solution to finding a work-life balance. There is no convenient time to rest, to unplug. We must value our downtime as much as we value our work time. We intuitively know there is a point at which working more results in diminishing returns but we continue to work. Even when we are not at the office, we constantly check our work e-mail on our smartphone. Many students in our class describe a sensation of feeling addicted to their e-mail. In fact, each time we check our e-mail, Twitter, Facebook, or other social media, we are triggering our dopamine system. The dopamine system is responsible for pleasure-seeking behaviors. We check e-mail because we're seeking pleasure. When we get an e-mail, it triggers the opioid or "liking" system, which makes us feel satisfied.

There is no shortage of tips for unplugging and taking time to rest. However, no amount of tips is going to work unless there is a fundamental shift in thinking. We must examine our underlying beliefs and thoughts around rest and taking time for ourselves.

It's best to find ways to unplug that work for you and your schedule. Here are some suggestions to get you started.

153

Schedule breaks into your day. If your calendar tends to get jam-packed with meetings and other commitments, schedule regular breaks and put them on your calendar. This doesn't need to be a long break. It's not about quantity, but quality. Aim for short 5-minute breaks to stretch and move your body. If you can't manage that, pause and take three conscious breaths.

Reduce distractions. Turn off auto-notifications on your smartphone device and your computer. The constant alerts for e-mails, Facebook "likes," and Twitter notifications are distractions and they keep you from fully focusing.

No screen time. Have a regularly scheduled "no screen" time. For example, no screens after 10:00 p.m., at the dinner table, during meals, or first thing in the morning.

No e-mail mornings. Use your morning hours for the most important work of the day. Do not give your best hours to your Inbox. Don't let other people set your daily agenda by checking your e-mail.

Get an alarm clock. Do you check e-mail first thing when you get up in the morning? Get the smartphone out of the bedroom! If you use your smartphone as an alarm clock, invest in a standalone alarm clock. Similarly, if you use your smartphone to check the time (only to get distracted in Twitter vortex), invest in a wrist watch.

Leave it at home. Do you notice your anxiety level rising when you accidently leave your smartphone at home? Start to break the cycle of addiction by intentionally leaving it behind. Alternatively, leave it behind in your car.

Digital Sabbath. Choose one day out of the week where you completely unplug for a twenty-four hour period. Before you go to bed, intentionally power down all of your digital devices and commit to staying unplugged until the next night. If this isn't possible, start with a shorter block of time.

Understand your intention. When you are reaching for your smartphone while waiting at the checkout line at the grocery store, ask yourself, "What is my intention or reason for checking my phone?" Is it because you're bored? Fear of missing out? Is it habitual? Are you overcommitted to work? Understanding your intention for *why* you are checking your e-mail again may help you see your patterns with the digital device more clearly.

Exercise

Why is it important to rest and unplug?

_____

_____

_____

_____

_____

One thing I will do to rest and unplug this week:

_____

_____

_____

Being kind to ourselves isn't an intellectual exercise. It's not about making a list of good things you *should* do for yourself. It's not about spoiling yourself. The benefits of being kind to ourselves come from *living* the question. As you begin to pose questions such as these,

— How can I be kind to myself?
— How do I care for myself?
— How can I nurture myself?
— How can I nourish myself?
— What do I truly desire?

the brain develops a different way of thinking. Instead of forcing yourself to be chained to the desk until a task is completed, perhaps you'll get up to stretch your legs and get a glass of water.

Working with Your Inner Critic

Many of us walk around life with the constant chatter of the inner critic. The inner critic is that voice, the broken record in your mind that says you're not good enough, smart enough, and asks questions such as "Who do you think you are?" The inner critic never misses an opportunity to point out your imperfections, your shortcomings, and all the things you dislike about yourself. This week as part of our practice of self-compassion, we'll tune into this inner dialogue and begin to work with it.

Jeena's Experience: Making Change with Gentleness

That part of you—that part that experiences fear—deserves your gentle attention. It's easy to want to shun that weak or even embarrassing part of yourself, deny its existence or push it away. However, if you pay attention to it with gentleness instead of rejecting it, you may find the tender part of yourself actually serves a purpose. Perhaps it's there to protect and guide you through difficult situations.

During the time I was working to overcome a debilitating case of social anxiety, part of me was deeply committed to seeing my own success. That part of me also knew I had to succeed in my own unique way. Once I felt the power of this part of myself, the sensation shifted from fear and anxiety to power and skillfulness. When we're struggling with difficulties, we can feel a deep sense of despair, as though the pain, discomfort, the challenge will never end. Mindfulness practice is helpful during these challenging times because mindfulness practice simply asks us is to be fully committed to being with the challenge in this moment.

You don't have to sit with the challenge forever, for the next year, for the next month, or even for the next hour. You just have to recommit to noticing the experience of the challenge—here and now. There's a sense of trusting in the process of the struggle. Once you commit to simply being in the challenge, moment by moment, you may notice each moment is slightly different. That the challenge has an organic shape, which is fluid and transforms as you observe it.

This is the beauty of mindfulness practice. The tool is the same, but how you use the tool in your own life will be different from others. Once you master how to do this, you have a gift you can bring to the world. This space of your own mastery contains tremendous amounts of power and taps into the core of who you are. It is your birthright to tap into this source of strength and power. The more you can access this part of yourself, the more resilient you'll become.

Living through your own suffering, without avoiding it or denying it allows you to create space for examining it and then learning something from it. These sufferings, once you've experienced them, survived them, learned from them, become an area of service. What better way is there to support someone who is suffering than to have gone through that exact same suffering yourself? This is why support groups for those suffering from illness such as cancer or alcoholism are so powerful.

Note that you have this inner critic because it serves some function (either currently or has in the past). We cannot get rid of the inner critic but, rather, we can redirect it so it's useful. You may pose a question to your inner critic such as "What is your purpose for showing up" or "What are you afraid of?" By looking at the inner critic head-on, you are able to look at the underlying beliefs or concerns and rationally choose your response.

To begin, let's start by acknowledging we are imperfect beings. Yet, there is perfection in our imperfection. We can't have the parts of ourselves we like without the parts of ourselves we dislike. You come as a whole package. As you practice, notice when the inner critic comes up. Instead of becoming critical of the inner critic, bring a sense of gentleness to yourself.

In the box below, write five positive traits about yourself that are easy to accept. If your friend said, "You're smart," for example, is that easy or difficult to accept about yourself? How about "You're attractive?" Next, write five negative traits about yourself that are also easy to accept. For example, you might be bad at math or lousy at golf.

Now, consider five positive traits that are difficult to accept. For example, if someone said, "You're very generous," is that easy or difficult to accept? Try to allow yourself to be honest without judgment about these traits.

Finally, write five negative traits that are difficult to accept. Could it be that you're short tempered and can't admit it? That you're disorganized? Include whatever negative qualities you want to deny about yourself in this last column.

Pay attention to your inner dialogues that use the words such as *should or never*. For example, "A good lawyer *should* always . . ." or "A good lawyer would *never* . . ."

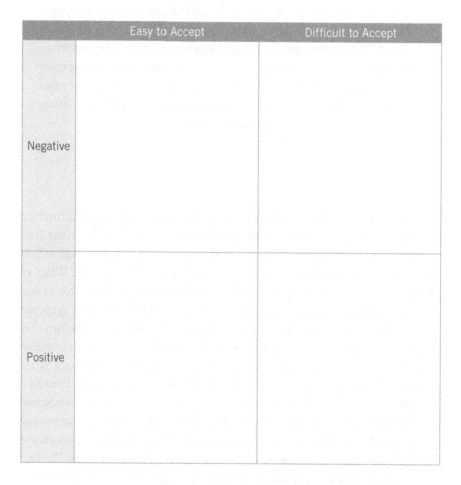

	Easy to Accept	Difficult to Accept
Negative		
Positive		

Now, imagine all the lines in the chart have been erased and you didn't label anything positive or negative. See if you can bring your mindfulness practice into play here and simply look at the list as being representative of who you are as a whole human being, with flaws, imperfections, struggling to do your best—just like everyone else. Remember, the practice of mindfulness is to *accept* what is (including yourself) without preference or judgment. This doesn't close the door to change, improvements, or internal shifts. The invitation is to see yourself and the limiting beliefs you have about yourself—in this moment.

After you've completed this exercise, ask yourself: How does that make me feel? Does that change how I view myself?

It's important to remember that this box—list of positive and negative traits—is dynamic. It can expand or shrink; however, you can't do this selectively. The entire box must expand or contract. You can't only choose to accept the positive traits, while rejecting the negative. Be open to all life experience and bring a sense of non-judgmental awareness to it.

Offering Compassion to Yourself

I will meditate for _____ minutes, every day.

Meditation Instructions

Visit www.theanxiouslawyer.com for audio guided meditations.

1. Find a comfortable seated position. Feel your feet firmly on the ground. Allow your body to rest. Feel your body sink into the chair below you.

2. Bring your attention to the breath. Breathe in and out. Notice the air as it moves in and out of your body. Continue to breathe in and out until your mind settles in the natural rhythm of the breath.
3. Next, bring an image to mind that represents unconditional love or acceptance. This can be the sun, which shines its light on everyone without discrimination, the ocean, a tree, or any other place in nature you resonate with. It can also be a person who you view as having unconditional regard, love, and acceptance. It can also be an animal such as a pet. Spend some time bringing this image into your mind's focus. Imagine yourself in the presence of this loving person, place, or object.
4. Next, repeat these phrases silently to yourself. You are welcome to use other expressions of good wishes that feel right for you.
   - "May I be happy."
   - "May I be healthy."
   - "May I know peace and joy."
   - "May I be free from suffering."
5. Repeat these phrases for as long as you'd like. Notice any feelings that arise as you do this practice. You might have feelings of tenderness toward yourself. Allow your awareness to simply be with whatever feelings or thoughts arise for you.

~~~

"How Can I Be Kind to Myself?"

For this week, ask yourself the question, "How can I be kind to myself." You don't need to find any answers to the question. The assignment is to simply pose the question and let it go. As the question percolates through your mind, you may notice you naturally come up with a list of answers. This exercise isn't about *doing* any of the things to be kinder to yourself. It's simply to open the possibility of being kind in order to cultivate self-compassion.

Put a reminder on your calendar to do this practice. You can also use other cues to practice. For example, you might do this exercise each time you wash your hands, brush your teeth, or stop at a red light.

It's important to remember that the purpose of this exercise isn't to come up with the "right answer" or any answers at all. The reason for not answering the question is twofold. First, it's too easy to fall into the trap of "I should be kinder to myself and I'm failing at that because I'm not doing x, y, and z." The practice of self-compassion isn't doing anything to be kinder to ourselves. It's not about taking ourselves shopping or getting an extra large scoop of ice cream. (Although all of these actions may be part of your self-compassion practice.) It's about cultivating an attitude of kindness and compassion. Second, the practice is to build up the muscle of self-compassion. We want to dial down the inner critic that's constantly at work. By asking the question without any pressure to come up with the answer, we're trying to reduce the tendency of the inner critic to take charge by coming up with "the right answers." Pay careful attention to any answers that have the word *should*, for example, "I *should* be exercising everyday and I *should* be eating more vegetables."

Meditation Log

Day	Time/Length	Notes: Sitting	Notes: Off the Cushion
Mon			
Tue			
Wed			
Thu			
Fri			
Sat			
Sun			

Mantra Repetition

What are words worth?
What are words worth? Words

—Wordy Rappinghood, *Tom Tom Club*

If we repeat something that has meaning for us, over and over, it serves to protect the mind . . . Mantras are the ancient answer to the modern problem "you are your own worst enemy."

—Lisa Dawn *Agerame*

REPEATING A MANTRA IS one of the oldest and simplest of all meditation practices. Every meditation tradition includes some form of this easy and straightforward practice: silently repeating a word or phrase in harmony with the breath. Mantra repetition calms the mind, making it easier to enter into a meditative state. It also promotes concentration, which feels good to our minds. Mantra repetition can also evoke feelings of contentment, love, and joy that give us a window into the fundamental nature of reality.

In Week Six, we'll introduce mantra repetition as a meditation practice. We'll provide some simple mantras you can use, and discuss some considerations you may want to keep in mind in choosing a mantra. We'll also practice using the mantra off the cushion to help settle the mind and improve concentration in day-to-day life. Finally, we'll discuss joy. Mantra repetition can bring up joy, and, ironically, this emotion can be particularly difficult for lawyers to accept, so we'll discuss some of the benefits of allowing yourself to feel joyous.

Resistance

Resistance is a very normal part of meditation practice. You've now been meditating for six weeks, so perhaps you've encountered it already. At various times, you may have great difficulty simply getting yourself to sit down and meditate, to try a specific practice you're interested in, or to be consistent with a practice you've committed to. It happens to all of us, and can surface unexpectedly even after many years of meditating.

Resistance can manifest in obvious or very subtle ways. It could be quite clear you're letting your meditation time slip by without ever sitting down, or maybe you feel uneasy or fearful at just the thought of sitting to meditate. On the other hand, your problem with sitting might be harder to identify as resistance. Maybe you suddenly find yourself getting busy with new projects just when you've decided to commit yourself to meditation. You might suddenly feel restless or dissatisfied with something about your practice: you need a new cushion, a new timer, a quieter spot, a new book, a new teacher. Or maybe you just forget to sit. Resistance can be at the root of all of these issues.

Something Is Happening

Resistance can be particularly baffling to professionals who are accustomed to setting goals for themselves and working toward them. This is normally a straightforward process, so the experience of struggling to sit can be confusing and even a little unnerving. After all, you're just trying to sit quietly for a little while—why should that be so difficult, when you've done so many truly challenging things in your life?

The thing to keep in mind when resistance comes up is that resistance arises only when there is something to resist. Meditation is a transformative process—it changes us. When we begin to change, part of us automatically tries to stop that change from happening. This very conservative part of ourselves is doing its best to protect us. It knows we can get through the day exactly the way we are, even if "the way we are" is stressed out, exhausted, and angry all the time. So it throws up roadblocks, to see if it can stop us from changing.

All of this means that, in a funny way, resistance is good news. It is a very palpable indication that change is ready to happen

Honey Works Better than Vinegar!

When dealing with resistance, the old expression "you catch more flies with honey than with vinegar" is a good guide. Your resistant mind can feel like a buzzing fly: restless, unsettled, and impossible to catch or pin down. Just like putting vinegar out for a fly, getting angry with yourself isn't the best way to help your mind through a patch of resistance. Self-judgment creates an unpleasant atmosphere for your mind; it will be harder to settle down in that kind of environment.

Instead of trying to fight your way through resistance, think about putting out honey for your mind—in this case, offering it gentleness and patience. Rather than focusing on what you haven't done, notice every time you succeed in doing your practice and give yourself positive reinforcement. Take a look at the goals you've set for yourself: are they too stringent? Could you pare them down and still make progress? Taking a gentle approach when your mind is fighting you will serve you best in the long run.

Staying positive and patient with yourself may be quite challenging if you tend to be a hard-charging, goal-oriented person. Again, be gentle with yourself about your attitude! When you notice you're falling into self-judgment about what you see as your lack of progress, try not to add fuel to the fire by judging yourself for judging. As gently as you can, drop the judgment—and congratulate yourself for that.

Keep an Open Mind

One of the pitfalls of dealing with resistance is allowing yourself to feel defeated by it, and giving up on your practice all together. Even if you try but still fail to sit for days or even weeks, keep an open mind. Don't assume the resistance will last forever.

Remember the part of you that is interfering with your practice is just trying to protect you. Once it has a chance to see meditation is leading you in a good direction and get comfortable with what you are doing, it may stop fighting the process. You may even be surprised to find that one day it becomes easy to practice.

Meditation Practice: Mantra Repetition

The meditation practice we will be working with this week is mantra repetition. Repeating a mantra during our meditation time is a little different from the practices we have been using up to this point, particularly the mindfulness based practices we began with. While mindfulness meditation always involves observation, with mantra repetition we direct the mind to silently repeat a word or phrase in combination with the breath. This practice, in which we take a more active stance toward the mind, can give your meditation time a somewhat different feeling-tone than you may have experienced with our previous meditation methods.

The word mantra comes from the Sanskrit words *man* meaning "mind," and *tra* meaning "protection," so a mantra is something that protects the mind. Repeating a mantra gives the mind something to do rather than engage in its usual patterns, which often involve repetitive and unhelpful cycles of thought. Some qualities of mantra repetition include:

- **Improving concentration.** While all meditation practices help improve concentration, mantra repetition is especially well-suited to doing so. In fact, mantra repetition is referred to as a concentration practice in certain meditation traditions. One reason mantra repetition may be so helpful in building concentration is that the mind is usually engaged with words and sounds. Using a word-based practice like mantra repetition to ground and settle the mind may be better suited to building control over the mind than other meditation practices.
- **Evoking joy.** Mantra repetition has a tendency to produce joy and feelings of happiness. Again, joyful feelings naturally arise in any

meditation practice from time to time, but mantra repetition is particularly strongly associated with feelings of happiness. By giving our thoughts something to settle on, we aren't distracted by our normal preoccupations and can see the peacefulness and contentment that is our natural state. Even a tiny glimpse of that natural, contented state can give rise to joy, so mantra repetition can make us feel happy.

- **Helping us process difficulty.** By providing our mind with something to do when it is restless or obsessing over negative thoughts, mantra repetition calms us and helps us center when we are experiencing difficulty. It is a very powerful tool that can help us process and let go of strong emotions like anger, fear, and worry.

A key aspect of mantra repetition is maintaining a light touch. It can be tempting, especially in the beginning, to mentally hold on to the mantra with an intense grip, but over time this will feel tiring and isn't at all necessary. One of our meditation teachers used to use the phrase "sweet effort" to describe how best to engage with a mantra practice. While you want to notice the moment of choice and gently bring yourself back to the mantra when you see your mind is wandering, the feeling tone of the meditation should be quite relaxed.

Once you are settled into your meditation, there may be periods of time when the mantra naturally falls away. This is very common and there is no need to fight it. The mind may be very silent during those times, or you may find yourself absorbed in a deeper state of meditation. All of this is fine and you shouldn't force yourself to repeat the mantra during these natural breaks. At some point, you'll likely notice your mind has started to wander, and you can reengage with the mantra again.

Part of the magic of mantra practice is that it does its work without you having to work hard at it. For example, you don't need to make an effort to concentrate forcefully during your meditation time in order to get the benefit of improved concentration off the cushion. The act of repeating a simple word or phrase can calm and clear the thoughts without a conscious effort on your part. This can be very counterintuitive for accomplished professionals, who are used to working hard to achieve their goals! If you find the idea of making easy progress a challenging one, we encourage you to give it a try: settle into the practice, and then relax and let the mantra do its work. There's no need to analyze, work at, or perfect what you're doing.

Notice how mantra repetition feels to you as compared with the mindfulness and compassion practices you've been using in the earlier weeks of this program. One of our goals in introducing a number of different meditation practices is to allow you to get a sense of the range of choices you have for establishing a meditation practice. Our hope is you'll find one of these practices works well for you and build your practice around it. Depending on your temperament, different meditation practices will feel more or less appealing, so it's nice to have familiarity with a few different practices. How easily does your mind settle into each of these practices? Is there one that feels particularly compelling or enjoyable to you? At the end of this program, you will want to choose one of these practices and practice it daily for some time, so begin to consider which one works the best for you.

Meditation and Physical Health

Establishing a meditation practice brings with it a wide range of physical benefits. One of the most recognized of these is meditation's ability to lower blood pressure and improve heart health, something that has been the subject of numerous scientific studies.[13] Meditation's effect on blood pressure is so well-accepted the American Heart Association endorses meditation as an effective alternative therapy for controlling blood pressure.[14] Its beneficial effects on the cardiac system also appear to extend beyond regulating blood pressure. A 5-year study of patients with coronary artery disease showed that those with a regular meditation practice cut their risk of heart attack and stroke by half compared with a similar group of non-meditators.[15] Recently, a clinical trial conducted with patients who have coronary heart disease showed that a regular meditation practice not only lowered blood pressure but also significantly reduced mortality rates from heart attack and stroke.[16]

Meditation has been used effectively to treat a variety of other disorders, including insomnia, social anxiety disorder, depression, chronic pain, eating disorders, and addiction.[17] It has been shown to be helpful in the treatment of asthma.[18] Meditation may help counteract many of the effects of aging: a study conducted on residents of homes for the elderly showed improved mental function and mental health for meditators than a control group; three years later, the meditators had significantly higher survival rates than their non-meditating peers.[19] Newer and more preliminary studies have identified positive effects on the body's immune function as a result of meditation training, and clinical trials have shown that meditators suffer less from acute respiratory infections associated with colds and flu than those without a meditation practice.[20]

After reading this litany of physical benefits, you may be asking: How can something as simple as sitting quietly on a regular basis create such wide-ranging effects in our bodies? The short answer is we don't understand precisely how meditation works to change the body; scientific inquiry is just beginning to turn to that question. For now, perhaps the best practical answer to this question comes from a simple and common sense perspective articulated by Zen teacher Thich Nhat Hanh: "Healing is possible through resting."[21]

On the scientific front, an intriguing recent study conducted at the University of Wisconsin's Laboratory for Affective Neuroscience points to a possible mechanism behind the health effects of meditation: changes in gene expression appear to be tied to meditative practice. In the study, after a day of mindfulness practice, experienced meditators showed a number of genetic changes, including reduced levels of pro-inflammatory genes.[22] Not surprisingly, the meditators also showed faster physical recovery from a stressful situation. Whether or not this study ultimately leads to the line of inquiry that makes clear how meditation changes the body, it does demonstrate that meditation's effects are much further reaching than we might ever have guessed. Far from simply changing our perceptions, we literally change our cells when we sit to meditate.

169

Choosing a Mantra

Deciding on what mantra to use in your practice can be as simple or as complex a process as you like. Fundamentally, a mantra serves the purpose of helping your mind settle by giving it something to do; from this perspective, it really doesn't matter what word or phrase you use to do this. On the other hand, as a practical matter, you will be repeating your mantra during most or all of your meditation time, so it's worth picking a word or phrase that is pleasant for you to work with. Some people enjoy doing extensive research on different mantras, their meanings, and history before settling on the one they will use, but this is not necessary. If you just want to get going and try mantra repetition, we've included a few here you can use; all of them are good ones.

Mantra repetition originated in India, and mantra repetition remains widely used in a number of Asian traditions, so many traditional mantras are words or phrases in Sanskrit or Pali. If you like the idea of using a Sanskrit or Pali mantra, you can certainly do so. Many people like to repeat a phrase they know has been used in meditation for centuries, and if that is meaningful for you, it can give your practice more resonance. There are many beautiful mantras in these ancient Asian languages. "*Om mani padme hum*" (in the heart of the lotus, a jewel) is a beloved mantra in Tibetan Buddhism; "*So ham*" (I am that) is a widely used mantra from the Vedanta tradition of India. You can find other traditional mantras and learn about their meaning and history by visiting a meditation center from an Asian tradition, from meditation books, or doing research on the Internet.

If you would prefer to use an English language mantra, you should feel free to do so, knowing your practice will be just as effective as using a mantra from another language. An English mantra we like is "Let go." If you choose another mantra in English, be sure to pick something simple enough to repeat in combination with the breath. Whether you choose a mantra in English or any other language, the meaning of it should be something positive and you find appealing. At the same time, it shouldn't have such a strong emotional association for you that you become distracted when you repeat it.

In the Indian tradition, there is a belief that a mantra received from a teacher holds all of that teacher's good wishes in it, and repeating it is a connection with that person's benevolence and support. Whether or not this belief appeals to you, you can enjoy the fact that by engaging in mantra repetition, you are connecting with a practice shared by millions of people over thousands of years.

Using Your Mantra Off the Cushion

Mantra repetition need not be confined to formal meditation time. You can repeat your mantra at any time, and just as with mantra repetition in seated meditation, using a mantra to help settle the thoughts in ordinary life is a time-honored practice that continues to be widely used. In many parts of the world, people traditionally use rosaries or prayer beads as an aid to mantra repetition. You may have seen someone using these beads, perhaps when you were traveling, and wondered what they were doing. They are simply using the beads as a physical cue to remember their mantra practice—as each bead passes through their fingers, they silently repeat the mantra they have chosen.

This week's off-the-cushion activity is to use a mantra while engaging in some part of your daily activities. This may feel strange when you first try it. We encourage you to keep at it long enough to get past the initial awkwardness, and get a sense of how it can clear and calm the mind.

Repeating a mantra in the midst of daily activities enables us to take a more proactive and engaged relationship with our minds. Rather than following your thoughts wherever they may lead, you can actively choose to refocus your mind on your mantra, thereby directing your mind to a calmer and quieter activity. From this quieter place, you are free to notice your surroundings more fully, focus on the activity at hand, or—surprisingly—even listen more closely to the person with whom you are speaking. Mantra repetition is like taking a scrub brush to the mind; it clears out the swirl of thoughts and associations that generally preoccupy us and gives us a single, simple activity to absorb the mind's restlessness.

The benefits of giving the mind something to do *besides* thinking can be counterintuitive for lawyers. As a group, we tend to be very invested in the idea that thinking is important and valuable. Wait a minute, you may be saying to yourself as you read this section of the book. First the authors told us to sit quietly for half an hour a day and calm our minds. Now they're telling us we can stop thinking so much during the rest of the day, too? When do we do our work? We're happy to tell you there's no cause for alarm. You can be assured you have plenty of time to do mantra repetition during your daily activities and also be a very effective advocate and problem-solver for your clients.

One of the primary reasons mantra repetition is unlikely to interfere with your important thinking time is you probably do less of it than you believe. Heretical as it may sound in the face of your legal training, most lawyers can and should spend less time thinking. In general, we don't need to spend as much time thinking through problems as we do. Much of the time we invest in the so-called problem-solving is really time we spend ruminating, or simply repeating the same thoughts over and over again in our minds. If you doubt this, devote a day to noticing what you spend your time thinking about. How much of your thinking is actually related to working out the answers to questions you must solve, and how much is spent remembering past conversations, going over and over the same idea in your head, mentally reviewing others' mistakes, or worrying about what might go wrong in the future? If you are honest with yourself, chances are you'll recognize a great deal of your mental activity is simply unnecessary.

All the unnecessary mental activity most of us engage in can be quite fatiguing, particularly when the focus of our thoughts is negative. We may replay a single unpleasant conversation over and over in our minds dozens or even hundreds of times. That conversation may have lasted less than two minutes in real life, but in our minds it goes on for hours, wearing us down to the point where we have little energy for the next challenging situation we must face. One reason mantra repetition can feel as rejuvenating as it does is because we get a break from the endless and unneeded review of past mistakes, wrongs, and worry that tends to absorb so much of our thoughts. When we choose to break the cycle of repetitive and often negative thoughts we so often unconsciously allow ourselves to slip into, we are exercising agency over how we spend our mental energy.

Mantra repetition can help us change our relationship with our thoughts in another way as well. It gives us a chance to see in a very concrete way that thoughts aren't real. The minute you begin to repeat a mantra, whatever was in your mind disappears, revealing it has no existence separate from your thoughts. You can try this by bringing up a mental image, focusing on it for a little while, and then repeating your mantra. Whatever image you've been holding in your mind will simply fall away. That dog or tree or car is simply a creation of your thoughts—it has no physical existence. In the same way, the irritable partner or unruly witness you've been obsessing over is literally a figment of your imagination. You have created the mental image you have of that person, conjured it up, and, whether you know it or not, have chosen to spend time with it. Repeating a mantra can not only give you relief from the unpleasant images you may hold of certain people but also help you have more awareness of the fact that your idea of them is simply that—an idea that you can set aside if it is unhelpful.

When we exercise choice over what we think, we not only have more agency over what we are doing with our minds in the moment, we also begin to have more control over our mental state generally. After all, whatever we choose to fill our mind with is what determines our mental state. By practicing mantra repetition regularly, you are spending less time unconsciously at the mercy of your thoughts and more time in a settled and quieter state. Over time this begins to build a reservoir of greater calm and resiliency we can draw on in both our personal and professional lives.

If you make a habit of mantra repetition, it can become a great way to focus your energy when you need to concentrate or face a difficult situation. Mantra repetition can be particularly effective for dealing with strong distractions or difficult emotions, helping you settle and face the task at hand in a calm and centered way. To be clear, we're not suggesting you use mantra repetition as a means of evading dealing with painful feelings or unresolved issues. That would be an inappropriate and, ultimately, ineffective way to engage with this practice. Rather, mantra repetition can help you focus on the right thing at the right time.

Repeating Your Mantra When You Can't Sleep

Virtually every lawyer has had a sleepless night or two: Maybe you wake up worried about a case, realize you left something undone at the office, can't let go of a distressing conversation, or just find yourself awake, for reasons you can't pinpoint. This is a time when some people find mantra repetition to be particularly helpful. Mantra repetition is a simple, soothing practice when your mind is tired, irritable, and difficult to control. It can function a little bit like a "lullaby for adults," helping you settle enough to drift into sleep. Even if you remain awake, your mantra can give you relief from your own cycles of thought, which can be restful in its own way. Since there's usually nothing to be done about a work problem in the middle of the night, you can take comfort in the fact that you're doing something worthwhile—taking care of your own mind.

Try repeating your mantra during your daily activities every day this week. In addition to noting your experience with it in your journal during the week, see how you feel at the end of a week of this practice. If you notice your mind feels a little clearer and more settled, this may be a helpful practice for you.

Experiencing the Natural Joy within Us

The joyful feelings that can come up in meditation are particularly common during mantra repetition. Seen correctly, these joyous experiences are not mere side effects, but windows into a very real part of ourselves.

Before elaborating on the benefits of joy and the insights it can bring, we feel we should come to its defense. Joy has a bad reputation in some—mostly professional—circles, with lawyers at the forefront of the joy skeptics. Reading this section, you may well be thinking, joy? Really? You've *got* to be kidding me. If only my client had been less joyful when she signed that loan agreement, or got behind the wheel of that car, we'd all be better off. I'm not getting too joyful. To be clear, we're not talking about spacing out the details of life or withdrawing into a happy bubble. As with anything, a person can engage with joy at a shallow level, and, of course, that's not productive.

You may also have a stereotype of meditation as something very serious that can't easily accommodate feelings of happiness or delight. After all the time and effort we've put into recognizing the reality of suffering, that's understandable, but the goal of meditation is to embrace all of life, the highs as well as the lows. Even so, you may well have seen meditation depicted as a sober practice where joy has no place. That is an unfortunate distortion. Some Asian meditation traditions do teach that we should be wary of joy and not get too addicted to it—this dovetails with American Puritanism in a way that is not so useful, and can lead to a deformed view of meditation practice as extremely austere, heady, and disengaged from the everyday pleasures of life. Seen in appropriate context, those traditional teachings are merely intended to steer practitioners away from obsession with the more superficial aspects of the joyous feelings that can arise in meditation.

People in modern, Western society can have a hard time being open to joy, in part because of a feeling that joyousness is a little frivolous. One of the many concepts we buy into in this society is that difficulty and suffering are very interesting. We obsess about our wounds, and perhaps feel they give us our depth. We may even feel what we have suffered has come to define us. If this is your view, we'd like to challenge it. We're not advocating you ignore your own suffering or that of others. We'd just like to gently call into question the idea of suffering as inherently interesting or deep.

Meditation can offer a different perspective on joy and suffering. While meditation gives us important tools to help us find the strength not to push painful experience away, equally important is that it helps us learn to let our suffering go. In fact, one of the things we learn once we can look at our suffering without fighting it is that ultimately it's just not that interesting.

So even if the idea of feeling joyous seems a little uncomfortable to you, we ask you at least to try to keep an open mind about joy and not automatically push it away. Rather than being suspicious of joy, you can step back a little from the pleasure of it and notice what it is showing you.

Another way of framing the experiences of joy that come up from time to time in any meditation practice comes from the yoga tradition. That tradition teaches joy and bliss are simply part of the nature of reality. Yoga teaches that reality is *non-dual*, meaning everything has the same fundamental nature. Put more simply, this teaching posits we are deeply connected with each other and with the world. According to this tradition, when we experience joy in meditation, we get a glimpse of our true nature, and we also get a glimpse of the nature of everything else and our connectedness. From this standpoint joy is not just a pleasant experience, but an opportunity to deepen our understanding of ourselves and the world.

If you're drawn to exploring the joyful experiences you have in meditation, it's a focus with some major strong points:

- **Joy is very motivating!** If you have strong resistance to sitting for meditation or have some fear about getting to know your own mind better, feeling joyous tends to get you past those things.
- **Joy is experiential.** When we are joyful, we feel a natural connection with others and the world around us. Joy shows us the oneness of being directly, so it takes us past concepts. Most meditation traditions come with their own fairly complex philosophies and teachings. These can be beautiful and interesting to learn, but one potential downfall for heady types—which we lawyers tend to be—is it's easy to become distracted by theories and philosophies, and miss the truth they are trying to convey.
- **Joy is relatively easy to experience.** Compared with many of the other deeper states and insights of meditation, joy is something many meditators experience fairly early on in their practice. This accessibility is a good thing. Unlike many, many other things in life, there are no points for effort in a meditation practice. Insight that comes easily is just as good as hard-won understanding.

What does it mean to engage with joy in a meditation practice? The first step is to develop your ability to look beyond the pure pleasure of joy and see what it's telling you. Joy often marks new experience. When we touch new depths in our practice, that new level of clarity or insight often comes with a wave of joy. So joy is a great indicator that something useful is probably happening. With just a little discipline, you can learn to step back and examine joyful experiences: When I was feeling so joyful, what did I notice about myself, my mind, my relations with others? How did my thoughts appear? Asking these kinds of questions rather than brushing off joyful experiences as fun but inconsequential can help cement new realization.

Joy can also be a much-needed tonic when you're experiencing difficulty. Later in the book we'll be using heart-centered mantra repetition to help process difficult emotions. That exercise explicitly draws on the sweetness and comfort of heart-centered practice to balance the challenge of facing troubling feelings. We know from our own experiences that being able to go inside and experience calm, sweetness, and even joy in times of difficulty is heartening.

Stay Open

This week, enjoy experimenting with mantra practice. See what you notice about how this practice differs from the mindfulness and loving-kindness practices we've been doing so far. You are the expert of yourself, so only you will know how each of these practices dovetails with your unique perspective and temperament. Be open to whatever comes up, be it joy, sorrow, or whatever else this practice evokes for you. And if you do notice more joy and happiness in your practice, remember to enjoy the joy!

~

Using Mantra Repetition

I will meditate for _____ minutes, every day.

Mantra meditation instructions

Visit www.theanxiouslawyer.com for audio guided meditations.

Meditate with the awareness that there is a center of deep contentment and even joy within you. You can allow that contentment to fill your consciousness if you just let go and let it happen.

Should feelings of defeat or self-doubt arise while you are meditating, permit yourself the confidence to know these feelings aren't real—they're just something your mind is creating in the moment. Let them pass.

177

1. Sit with a straight spine, in a comfortable position you can hold for the time you will be meditating. Commit to that posture.
2. Notice the internal and external landscape: the sounds in the room, the feel of your body, any emotions you may be feeling, the quality of your thoughts. Allow these to be exactly as they are.
3. Turn your attention to your breath. You may want to take a couple of deeper breaths to help yourself settle, breathing in deep and breathing out long through the nose. Allow your breath to return to normal.
4. Now add a mantra to your breathing. If you have a mantra you'd like to work with, you can use that. Otherwise, use the mantra, "let go." Repeat "let" on the in-breath and "go" on the out-breath.
5. Meditate, repeating the mantra in coordination with the breath. You may find after some time, the mantra naturally falls away, and that's fine. If you feel you are distracted or are getting caught up in thoughts, return to the mantra.

Repeating Your Mantra while Walking
or Having a Conversation

This week, experiment with repeating your mantra. You can do this while you are walking, driving, or on public transportation, or when you're doing household tasks like cooking or cleaning. At first, this may feel awkward or artificial, but over time you may begin to find your mantra can easily "run in the background," adding its flavor to your actions without taking over your attention.

If you find mantra repetition easy to do, see if you can continue to repeat your mantra while speaking to someone. You may find it actually makes it easier to concentrate fully on the conversation!

Notice how repeating your mantra affects how you experience your daily activities. Does mantra repetition during the day make it easier to settle into your sitting practice? Note any effects of the practice in your meditation journal.

Meditation Log

Day	Time/Length	Notes: Sitting	Notes: Off the Cushion
Mon			
Tue			
Wed			
Thu			
Fri			
Sat			
Sun			

Heartfulness

Nothing is so strong as gentleness, nothing so gentle as real strength.

—St Francis de Sales

The greatest challenge of the day is: how to bring about a revolution of the heart, a revolution which has to start with each one of us?

—Dorothy Day

THIS WEEK WE'RE GOING to explore a topic that may initially seem foreign, but ultimately is something many practicing attorneys strongly relate to: heartfulness. What do we mean by this term heartfulness? We use this word as shorthand for a constellation of attributes: courage, strength, compassion, kindness, gratitude, and generosity. These may initially appear to be a hodgepodge of qualities, but the connection between these qualities and the heart has been recognized across cultures and eras. For example, the French word "coeur," which means heart, has the same root as courage. Similarly, the word *snying* in Tibetan means heart and feelings as well as courage and strength of mind.

This week we'll explore heartfulness through a variety of lenses and practical exercises. Our off-the-cushion practices are designed to complement the heartful quality of our mantra repetition practice and maintain a more conscious connection with the heart as we move through the day. We'll examine our view of legal practice and consider whether acknowledging the role of our hearts in our working lives can bring us to a deeper understanding of our relationship to legal practice. We'll also look at the qualities of the heart and see whether by acknowledging their full range we can arrive at a more realistic attitude toward our own advocacy. We'll also introduce a heart-based practice that employs mantra repetition and can be used to help process difficult emotions.

Rebalancing Head Versus Heart

It may be tempting to shy away from the topic of heartfulness, to cast it as a messy thing, something that doesn't have a place in our professional lives. Most of us prefer to stay in the world of our heads, and like to look at the work we do exclusively through the lens of logic and reason. But denying the role that heartfulness plays in legal practice diminishes us and our actions—without it, we can appear harsh, destructive, and narrow. And we ourselves can buy into that view, allowing ourselves to become caricature lawyers rather than human beings who practice law.

The heart-based exercises are designed to strengthen your engagement with the qualities of your heart, or perhaps rekindle your relationship with your heartful side if you've grown distant from it. One way to look at these exercises is as a means of building our professional competence. You've invested a great deal of time, effort, and resources in sharpening your intellectual skills; spending a week working to better understand your capacity for generosity, kindness, and strength of purpose can begin to balance that effort, so you'll be an even better advocate. In one sense, connecting with the heart is a variation on the practice of self-compassion, since compassion is one of the qualities of the heart. And just as we've seen with compassion, we can't offer kindness, strength, and support to others if we are unable to offer it to ourselves.

If the idea of exploring the heart feels uncomfortable to you, we would like to challenge you to be courageous for the short period of a week, and see how it goes. You may be surprised to find consciously connecting with your own heart even a little can give you a better view into your own strength and help you become more grounded in it. Bringing your own heartfulness out in the open can let you see yourself and your own actions in a more realistic and nuanced way, and acknowledging the full range of qualities of your heart can give you access to greater groundedness, authenticity, and the natural authority we exude when we are comfortable in our own skin.

The Space of the Heart

The meditation exercises this week refer to the heartspace or the heart center. These may be confusing terms if you haven't heard them before. What they refer to is the energetic center in the middle of the chest. The heartspace is not the physical heart—it is in the middle of the body, to the right of the physical heart. Both Indian and Chinese traditional medicine hold that the heart center is a powerful energetic center in the body, and this view is also reflected in many Asian meditation traditions. While we aren't aware of specific modern scientific corroboration of the existence of the heart center, the traditional location of the heart center does roughly correspond to a concentration of nerves in the center of the chest.

183

Observing the Breath with Heartful Attention

It can be challenging to connect with the heart and experience all of its qualities when we're not used to doing so. This exercise uses the breath to help us shift our focus toward the heart:

Settle yourself. Focus on the flow of your breath for a few minutes. Allow your eyes to close. Notice the sounds around you, first the louder and then the quieter sounds.

Once you feel settled, let your attention move to your heart center. The "heart center" is not the physical heart, but the energetic center in the middle of your chest, slightly to the right of where your heart is. Let your attention rest there a few moments.

Turn your attention to the breath. Allow yourself to appreciate the breath, that has so much vitality, that is always moving, always present, constantly taking care of you and keeping you alive without your ever having to ask it to do so. Feel the sweetness of fresh air coming into your body with each inhale, and feel the pleasure in releasing the toxins leaving your body with each exhale. Let yourself relax completely, enjoying the refreshing quality of simply breathing.

Now, allow yourself to hold awareness of both the heart center and the breath at the same time. Feel the benign, nurturing quality of the breath, and feel the appreciation for the breath in your heart. Enjoy both of those feelings—the gentle movements of the breath, and the gratitude you have for this easy, natural process. As you follow the movements of the breath, try to watch it as you would a loved one: a sleeping child or a romantic partner you are deeply in love with. Observe the breath in this way—as if you can't take your eyes off it, as opposed to trying to analyze it. Follow the breath from the space of your heart for a few more minutes, enjoying its movements as you do so.

We use the heart center as a focal point in these exercises to consciously bring our attention away from the head and redirect it toward our feeling side. Connecting with the heart center is also a physical anchor that can help us connect with the very real center of contentment, peace, and joy all of us have inside ourselves and can access. While focusing on the heart center may initially feel strange or even alien if it's something you're not used to, you can do so with the confidence that there is a source of strength and joy within you that is supporting you. With some patience and persistence, you will be able to consciously connect with it and draw on that support.

184

Reframing Our Views

In Week Five, we discussed how compassion is consonant with assertiveness and advocating forcefully for our clients. Now we'd like to turn that discussion around and consider how we see ourselves, and perhaps judge ourselves, when we advocate strongly. Those of us who fight hard on behalf of our clients may be accustomed to seeing our actions and attitudes denigrated as destructive. We hear lawyer jokes predicated on the idea that we are a corrosive influence on human relations (e.g., How many lawyer jokes are there? *Only three. The rest are true stories.*). We also hear our fellow lawyers praised—even if it may be in a back-handed way—for taking advocacy to extremes: the "bull-dog" or "street fighting" lawyer who uses "scorched earth" tactics is the one many clients seek out. Then when we find ourselves facing over-the-top tactics from another lawyer, we may be at a loss as to how to respond, other than to return the aggression in kind. Under these circumstances, we can begin to feel that advocacy itself is destructive, and see ourselves as forces for misery in the lives of others. We've heard many lawyers speak wistfully of wishing they could do something positive in the world, even if it was just being a barista at a coffee shop. After spending months and years focused on crushing your opponents and wreaking havoc in their clients' lives, handing hot, caffeinated drinks to people all day long can begin to sound like an alluring alternative.

Connecting with the heart helps us recognize the positive good we do when we take strong action. It can also help us temper our actions so they don't spill over into destructiveness. As a first step, we can acknowledge one of the heart's qualities is fierceness, and fierceness, in and of itself, is neither good nor bad. Far from demonizing its strength or intensity, meditation traditions recognize the power of the heart, and seek to channel its force for the benefit of practitioners and society.

Some meditation paths, like the yoga and Zen practices, draw explicitly on martial traditions or metaphors. Zen practice, with its emphasis on discipline and austerity, is closely linked with the samurai tradition of Japan. The samurai were warriors in dangerous times, and faced death as a matter of course. When they encountered Zen monks who were not intimidated by death or violence, the samurai were greatly impressed and many adopted Zen practice themselves. Zen's emphasis on fearlessness, freedom, and spontaneity of action harmonized well with samurai traditions, while the samurai emphasis on simple, hard training for its own sake can still be seen in the way Zen is taught and practiced today.

185

Along similar lines, the *Bhagavad Gita*, the principal text in Hinduism and a core document in yoga philosophy, tells the story of a warrior facing a difficult battle and conveys important truths about action, engagement, detachment, and the state of mind we bring to our engagement with the world. The story is, of course, metaphorical—no teacher of yoga would ever advocate violence—but its strong imagery can help cut through an unconscious misconception we may harbor that a powerful, active stance is inconsistent with inner peace or constructive engagement with the world.

Seeing ourselves and our work through the lens of the heart can help us reclaim the narrative of who we are and what we do. Forceful, even oppositional, action can be necessary at times and plays a valuable role in a harmonious whole. Indeed, we need only think of Martin Luther King or Mahatma Gandhi (a lawyer himself) for practical examples of fierce and effective engagement that came from a profoundly heartful stance toward the world.

At the same time, building a stronger connection with our hearts through our meditation practice can help us keep our advocacy strong without letting it tip over into destructiveness. This doesn't mean we let our clients down or concede to our opponents. Meditation does not lead to passivity, or make a person weak or timid. Reality is quite the opposite: one of the great benefits of a meditation practice is experiencing the truth that peace is on the inside, not the outside, and there's no need to shrink from confrontation where it's necessary. What we don't need to do in order to be strong advocates is become vindictive and personal. In fact, demonizing our opponents, refusing to consider their point of view, can harm our advocacy by making us miss potential creative solutions or even blinding us to how we may look to third parties or decision makers. Keeping our focus on our hearts and the strength that lies there can help us find the detachment to stay focused on our goal rather than getting caught up in useless and demoralizing tit-for-tat.

186

Coming to Terms with Vulnerability

As lawyers, we often take a schizophrenic attitude toward our hearts: we can be very comfortable with our courageousness and strength, but may have difficulty accepting the softer side of the heart. As we noted in our discussions on loving-kindness practice, one reason why we may shy away from this powerful practice is that the qualities of kindness and empathy connect us with our vulnerable side. Many of us perceive our own vulnerability as weakness, so try as best we can to stay away from anything that implicates the heart's tenderness. This is an unfortunate mistake, however; rather than making ourselves stronger, we limit and weaken ourselves when we turn away from the full range of the heart's qualities. If we allow it, forging a better connection with the heart can help us engage more effectively with our own vulnerability.

While vulnerability is part of the human condition, most people in our success-obsessed society struggle to accept this. Vulnerability can be particularly difficult for lawyers to engage with, or even admit to. Yet we are face to face with vulnerability every day: we see our clients in painful situations; we see the limits of the law to solve difficult problems; we deal with aggression and discourtesy; we get bad rulings, have frustrating negotiations, lose cases. We also have internal struggles, self-doubt, fear, the inner-critic, and other hindrances.

Finding our way to a degree of comfort with vulnerability, daunting as it may seem, does create the possibility for greater satisfaction in our professional lives. For many of us, a great deal of our frustration and dissatisfaction with legal practice comes from our own discomfort with witnessing our clients' vulnerability. If we can allow our clients to be surprised, upset, or heartbroken without feeling like we need to fix it all or run away, we make room for more authentic human interactions. The truth is that many problems aren't exclusively legal problems; our clients come to us as whole human beings, often in crisis. They haven't had a chance to sort out the legal problems from the others—they just have a divorce, a startup, a bankruptcy, or a nonprofit on their minds. When we feel comfortable owning up to what we can't fix, and can sit with our clients' unsolved problems, we create the basis for more respectful and meaningful relationships with the people who walk through our doors.

187

Even more challenging than tolerating vulnerability in others is learning to allow ourselves to be vulnerable—and the rewards of doing so are commensurate with the challenge. We intuitively understand the truth of this, and as a society we hunger for a better relationship with vulnerability. A dramatic example of our desire to better engage with vulnerability is what happened when social scientist Brené Brown gave a TEDx talk in 2010 before a small audience in Houston, Texas, on the topic.[23] In her talk, Brown pointed out the truth that as uncomfortable as we are with vulnerability, it is necessary for authenticity and connection. Brown's talk went viral—it now has over twenty million views—and catapulted her into the national spotlight.

Knowing this, and with so much exposure to the reality and universality of human weakness, why are we so conflicted about admitting to the reality of our own vulnerability? Unfortunately, we face a host of pressures, both external and internal, to deny all weakness. The mythology around lawyers as heroes we noted in Week Three puts great external pressure on us to cultivate an aura of invincibility. Our clients, our colleagues, our opposing counsel, and others who share our professional environment expect us to be pillars of strength, and, as a result, we may not feel comfortable allowing cracks to show in our armor.

There are also internal pressures to avoid acknowledging that, just like everyone else, we lawyers are vulnerable human beings. We generally are called to take a protective stance toward our clients, anticipate problems for them, and advocate on their behalf, sometimes aggressively. We may not want to admit, even to ourselves, that we can't always be the all-powerful protective force for our clients we would like to be.

For all these reasons and more, we may feel that admitting to any vulnerability is weakness and consequently have spent years or even decades cultivating a tough facade in an attempt to appear strong and competent at all times. The problem with this strategy is we can't effectively cover up vulnerability in all circumstances—no one can. No one can win every case, anticipate every judge's questions, say the right thing in every situation, or stay cool under all circumstances.

Too often, our attempts to cover up our moments of vulnerability fool no one, and instead we end up trying to bluster our way through uncomfortable situations, lowering the level of civility with our colleagues, making ourselves less effective advocates, or even personally looking foolish. Not only do we lose important credibility when this happens, but failing to acknowledge what we are doing diminishes us as human beings. Chances are we realize we're acting badly in order to cover up something that makes us feel exposed, but we numb out and ignore the awkwardness rather than admit to ourselves what we've done. After a while, numbing out can become a habit, and we end up being ill at ease with any emotion, pleasant or not.

Karen's Story: Vulnerability and Scorched-Earth Tactics

After law school, I clerked for Judge Robert J. Ward in the Southern District of New York. One of Judge Ward's notable cases was Wilder v. Bernstein, which involved the alleged failure of New York City's foster case system to provide adequate services to minority children. That case, started in 1973, was still going on during my clerkship in the early 1990s.

After years of failed negotiations and discovery, the Wilder case was set to go to trial. The Thursday before the Monday trial was scheduled to start, the lead attorney for the plaintiffs, Marcia Lowry, got a call at her office with terrible news: her baby sitter had dropped dead of what was probably a sudden heart attack, while she was alone with Lowry's child. Lowry's husband discovered the sitter collapsed on the floor of their kitchen when he returned home from work. Their baby was in tears, hysterical. Doctors later estimated the sitter had died around five hours before.

Lowry called our chambers. She had no back-up baby sitter, her child was traumatized, and there was no way of starting trial on Monday. Although Judge Ward had a reputation for being strict about deadlines, he was a very warm-hearted man with a close family. His initial response to Lowry was to ask whether her baby was okay. He granted her a continuance, to the extreme displeasure of the city's attorneys. Soon after the continuance was granted, settlement discussions began, ultimately resulting in a consent decree. (This story, and the larger story of the *Wilder* case, is documented in Nina Bernstein's excellent book, The *Lost Children of Wilder*, Vintage Books, 2001.)

While I can't prove it, I've always believed the city attorneys' ill-considered, angry reaction to the continuance played a big role in the parties reaching settlement. The lawyers for the city must have realized they were going to have to appear before a judge who had been witness to their callous reaction to their opposing counsel's crisis around caring for her child. At a trial that turned on the issue of the city's practices toward children, this very public and personal callousness was hardly good advocacy. I wonder whether the city attorneys began to rethink their recalcitrant attitude toward settlement when they considered what it would be like to appear before Judge Ward under those circumstances. If so, it's a great example of how scorched-earth, vindictive tactics can work to a lawyer's disadvantage.

189

Connecting with the qualities of the heart can help us find the strength to allow ourselves to be vulnerable and to allow others to be vulnerable. That sounds good, you may say, but how do I do it? Getting even a little bit closer to my heart feels like a tall order. The beauty of meditation practice is that it will always bring you into deeper contact with your heart, whether or not you actively set out to accomplish that. Jon Kabat-Zinn, the Harvard-trained physician and American meditation practitioner who coined the word mindfulness, pointed out not too long ago that in many Asian languages the word for mind and the word for heart are the same, so *mindfulness* could easily be called *heartfulness*. So while even the headiest forms of mindfulness will bring you into relationship with your heart, placing your attention and intention on building a stronger connection to the heart can be beneficial, particularly if you struggle to accept your own softer side.

While vulnerability may never feel wonderful to us, we can come to terms with it, so we don't need to block ourselves from reacting naturally to others and to the situations we find ourselves in. Over time, as we become more familiar with the territory of the heart, we may begin to see the strength in compassion, gentleness, gratitude, generosity, and find it less threatening to let these qualities show. We can then experience the strength of being genuine firsthand, and gain confidence we can be authentic without being judged as weak.

190

Practicing Law to Serve Your Higher Goals

Strengthening our connection with the heart can also have implications for how we think about our professional lives generally, and how we view our relationship to the legal profession. Recognizing our hearts play a role in our professional lives, we can gain insight into what drew us to the legal profession in the first place and why many of us relate so strongly to our identity as lawyers. We can see more clearly the validity of our need to find meaning in the work we do, rather than simply buying into the all-too-common view of legal practice as nothing more than a way to make money or accrue external recognition.

Everyone loves to win, and of course we all need to pay our bills, but those aren't the real reasons most of us got into practicing law. Many, if not most of us, came to the legal profession because we wanted to serve a higher ideal. It may have been a particular issue like freedom of expression that drew you to legal practice. You may have wanted to represent a certain group of clients, like children, or people in financial distress. You may have wanted to serve justice by participating in the legal system in one way or another. Or you may simply have wanted to help people by solving the legal problems that are part of daily life or that come in the business world.

Over time, the pressures of legal practice and the unrelenting materialism of modern society may have taken you away from those original ideals, but they are still there—maybe not even so far from the surface. Strengthening your connection with the heart can reignite your connection with those ideals, and help you remember how you came to be in this profession. When you see yourself and your advocacy through the lens of heartfulness, you can see you are following a calling that has personal meaning.

Reading this, you may find yourself feeling very skeptical. In fact, you may wonder what meaning your work could possibly have for you after all these years, and all the daily frustrations, disappointments, and irritations you put up with just to get through your working day. To be clear, we're not saying your work as you currently experience it is a beautiful, profound, and meaningful exercise—but we do think it's very likely that the kernel of what drew you to the law is still there, and still resonant. To explore this idea, you can try this exercise: think of a project you've worked on recently that you liked. It doesn't need to be anything particularly amazing or extraordinary, but just something you liked working on. Ask yourself, what was great about that project? Write down the answer. Now, look at what you wrote down. Maybe it was the fact you were able to run the project on your own. Ask yourself, what's great about that? Was it the feeling of independence? Was it the realization you have the expertise to lead a project? Was it that you get along well with this particular client? Whatever it was, write it down. Now keep going—repeat this process five or six more times, each time asking yourself what was great about the last thing you identified. Now look at the last answer you've written down. Chances are you've identified a value that is deeply meaningful to you. And, it is connected to work you are doing now, however tangentially.

Reconnecting with the meaning in our work can let us see how much we actually value doing our work for its own sake—and this is a useful insight. If we aren't doing it solely for fame or fortune, then how we engage with our work on a day-to-day basis takes on profound importance. Seeing that our work itself has meaning for us, rather than only the external reward, can also help bring more sanity into our lives. In Week Three, we discussed the role of luck in our lives, and how meditation can help us come to a more realistic relationship with it. A corollary to that insight is if winning external recognition or financial success is what gives our work meaning, then we are powerless to bring meaning into our working lives, and entirely at the mercy of random, external forces. If we are offering our work in service to a higher goal or as an expression of our deeply held values, then we are in control and can access meaning in every minute of our working lives.

What if you look at your work through the new lens of valuing it for its own sake, and realize something is wrong? You've allowed yourself to stray too far from your original ideals, or maybe you've just changed. The mental clarity that comes from a regular meditation practice will also make you far less likely to adopt others' opinions unconsciously. With less of the bad advice of the world swirling around in your head, the more subtle voice of your heart has a chance to be heard and, with it, the insight into what is truly important for you. With the help of the heart, making necessary changes can be easier. Greater comfort with vulnerability may help you find the courage to try something new, where there are no guarantees. And lest you worry that following your heart will lead you to financial and professional disaster, remember that building a vision from a place of authenticity is absolutely essential for attaining the kind of achievements that are personally meaningful as well as impressive to others.

Processing Difficult Emotions

Strong and sometimes troubling emotions come up as part of legal practice and as part of life. We lawyers are routinely face to face with others' difficulty, and moving through the emotional fallout of this work can be challenging. We all also face our own emotional challenges as a result of our relationships, our life experience, and our personal history. It's important to get outside help for these challenges when that's what's needed. Connecting with the heart in a very elemental, physical way can help us process difficulty and find the strength to face situations directly when we would much rather flinch away from them.

We're including an exercise here that draws on the grounding quality of the heart to help process difficult emotions. Connecting with the strength and sweetness of the heart space can often allow us to stop fighting strong emotions, let them through us and also see what they have to tell us.

Mantra Repetition in the Heart Space to Help Process a Difficult Emotion

Settle yourself. Focus on the flow of your breathing for a few minutes.

Allow your breath to bring your attention into the heart center, the energetic center in the middle of your chest. Let your attention settle gently on this space.

Begin to repeat your mantra. Imagine the sound of the mantra is actually coming from your heart center. Allow that sound to pull your attention more fully into your heart center. Imagine the space is expanding each time you repeat the mantra. Allow yourself to imagine that with each breath, the heart is softening and widening.

Keeping the heart center in your awareness, very gently, allow yourself to connect with the distress you've been feeling. You may experience a flood of thoughts. Just watch them as phenomena, and, without trying to push them away, gently come back to the mantra. You may need to do this multiple times.

You may also notice your thoughts and your mantra present in your mind simultaneously. That's fine. You can allow your thoughts to be there, while letting the mantra be the main focus of your attention. Let go of any story lines that may come up.

Now, focus on the energy of the emotion you are feeling, the physical sensation of it in your body. Where is the feeling located? Is it in your head, your back, your heart? Is it located in your stomach or gut? What sensations are you experiencing? Does it feel prickly? Is there a buzzing or electric quality to it? Is there heat? Heaviness? Examine your emotion with a sense of tenderness and curiosity. Notice all of the different sensations you feel.

As you do this, allow yourself to remain aware of the mantra at the same time. If you can, let the mantra run in the background of your mind while you engage with your emotion. If that's too difficult, simply come back to the mantra periodically when you remember to do so. Let the sound of the mantra resonate in the space of the heart, grounding your attention there.

Now, hold the emotional feeling in your heart space. Let the mantra create a sweet, protected space for it, as if you were cradling it in your awareness. Sit with the emotion, feeling its energy while simultaneously keeping your focus opened out into the widening spaciousness of the heart.

Continue to sit until the energy of the emotion dissolves into your larger awareness.

———

One note on the word "strength," which we've used quite often in Week Seven to describe one of the key qualities of the heart: when we refer to the heart's strength, we are not talking about an aggressive or destructive quality. The strength of the heart is more subtle and far more powerful than aggression. If you continue to engage with your heart through your meditation practice and perhaps some of the exercises we've offered here, you may come to see the unique and disarmingly gentle capacity of heartfulness to support you in facing difficulty.

~

Heart-Centered Meditation
Using Mantra Repetition

I will meditate for _____ minutes, every day.

Mantra meditation instructions

Visit www.theanxiouslawyer.com for audio guided meditations.

1. Sit with a straight spine, in a comfortable position you can hold for the time you will be meditating. Commit to that posture.
2. Let yourself settle: Take a couple of deeper breaths, consciously releasing any tension you may be feeling with each exhale. Notice the sounds around you, the weight and feel of your body, any physical sensations you may be experiencing. Notice the state of your emotions and the quality of your thoughts. Enjoy the fact that you don't have to change any of this.
3. Bring your attention to the space of your heart. This is not the physical heart, but the energetic space at the center of your chest. Imagine your breath is moving in and out of that space. Let yourself feel the heart space expand with each inhale and soften with each exhale.
4. Now add a mantra to your breathing. Continue to use the mantra you selected in Week Six. Repeat the mantra silently, in coordination with the breath.
5. Meditate, allowing the sound of the mantra to resonate in the space of the heart. If the mantra falls away at some point, that's fine. Enjoy the silence and contentment of the heart space. If you notice you're distracted or are getting caught up in thoughts, return to the mantra.

~

Our Higher Goal

Offering our actions to a higher goal is a time-honored practice that is part of many spiritual traditions. The seemingly simple act of seeing our actions as service can have a surprisingly strong effect on how we experience our daily lives. By shifting the focus away from ourselves, we slip out of unconscious self-centeredness and may even find spaciousness that lets us act without being inappropriately worried over outcomes.

Identify a higher ideal or goal with meaning for you. It could be something as general as "peace in the world" or as specific as "a quick recovery for my friend who is ill." Spend a day consciously offering everything you do to this higher ideal or goal. Begin your day by consciously offering your thoughts, feelings, and actions to this goal. If you like, you can set an alarm with a soft bell to remind you to reconnect with your offering at a few different points during the day. Note how this practice affects your experience of your day in your meditation journal.

196

I will offer my actions to _____

_____

_____.

Meditation Log

Day	Time/Length	Notes: Sitting	Notes: Off the Cushion
Mon			
Tue			
Wed			
Thu			
Fri			
Sat			
Sun			

197

Gratitude

*True happiness is to enjoy the present, without anxious dependence
upon the future, not to amuse ourselves with either hopes or fears
but to rest satisfied with what we have, which is sufficient, for he
that is so wants nothing. The greatest blessings of mankind are
within us and within our reach.*

—Seneca

*If I had accepted what people told me I looked like as a negative yes,
then I would be dead. But I accepted it and I thought, well, aren't I
the lucky one.*

—Maya Angelou

THIS IS THE EIGHTH week of your program, the last week of formal meditation practice included in this book. Have the weeks flown by for you? Have you struggled to keep up? Either way, by working your way through the program outlined here, you've created a meditation practice for yourself.

This week you'll want to think about how to bring this program to a close in a way that's meaningful for you. You've purposely taken time out of your schedule for the past seven weeks to focus on meditation, and this last week is a chance to try something new, explore your edge or simply enjoy the practice you've built up to this point.

We'll complete our exploration of heart-centered practices this week by engaging an aspect of the heart that may have come to feel a little distant over years of legal practice: gratitude. We'll discuss some of the benefits of taking a posture of gratitude toward life, and consider how we can begin to reorient ourselves toward gratitude notwithstanding what we encounter in our professional lives. We'll also offer some off-the-cushion practices that can help you consciously re-engage with gratitude. These practices can be particularly useful if gratitude feels hard to connect with in the context of your current professional life.

Your Practice in This Last
Week of the Program

As you enter into the last week of the program outlined in this book, consider how you want to approach it. What do you want to add to your practice at this time? Take some time to think about what might be an appropriate way for you to bring these eight weeks to a close. We suggest you consider taking an approach to your practice that balances or contrasts with the way you've been engaging with the program up to this point:

- If you've been driving yourself to meditate, completing every single practice and exercise and digging into every question posed by the text, try taking it a little easier this week. What would happen if you took a gentler approach to your practice? And what would it mean for you to take a gentler approach? We're not suggesting you stop meditating, but you might be surprised to find that you can manage to meditate without taking a taskmaster's mentality toward your practice. Could you look forward to having nothing to do but sit still for a few minutes? Or allow insights to come to you instead of analyzing your experiences relentlessly? Try looking at this week as a chance to relax and enjoy the benefits of the practice you've built.

- If you've been holding back, meditating just a few minutes a day or skipping some days, see what would happen if you let yourself dive in completely. What if, for a week, you gave it your all? Consider taking a concrete step to support yourself to focus on your practice, like setting your alarm ten minutes earlier so you have some extra quiet time in the morning. You have deep reserves of will power if you've gotten yourself through law school. Try drawing on a little of that power to get yourself on the cushion every day this week.

- If you've been trying the program but keep getting sidetracked by other obligations, see if you can prioritize your meditation practice for a week. What if you skipped that networking breakfast so you could have an unhurried meditation time? Consider giving yourself the benefit of putting yourself and your practice first, just for these last few days. Also, you may want to look at any resistance to your meditation practice that may be playing a role here. Is there some hidden concern about what meditation will do? Are you concerned about what others will think? Take a look at what is stopping you from fully committing to this practice.

Besides changing your approach to your practice, also consider whether there's something in the program you haven't tried yet. If you haven't tried sitting for thirty-minute meditation periods yet, this week is a great week to give it a go. You may find it's easier than you think. Or if you haven't had a chance to engage deeply with the off-the-cushion practices, pick one out and make a point to spend at least ten minutes on it every day this week. You've had seven weeks of building your meditation practice, so anything you add now will benefit from the momentum you've created.

Finally, you may just want to savor the practice you've created. Maybe what you're doing is perfect right now, and changing things around would be superfluous. If that's your instinct, honor it and enjoy the continuity of your practice. Whatever you do, choose something that will make this last week special.

Challenges and Benefits of Gratitude

We've been focusing on the heart and its qualities for the past several weeks. The meditation practice we've been following, mantra repetition, has a natural tendency to bring focus to the heart, so in our time off the cushion we are consciously engaging with the heart's qualities, to strengthen and complement our sitting practice and help bring the benefits of that practice into our day-to-day lives.

Along with compassion, gratitude can be difficult for lawyers, who must use critical thinking much of the time. We pride ourselves on identifying problems and seeing pitfalls before others do and we may ask, how could gratitude help with that? Gratitude can seem like a naïve stance to take when you're operating in a world of sharp elbows. All day long, we deal with people who are out to further their own interests, often at the expense of our clients. Far from feeling grateful, we spend much of our time questioning others' motives and thinking through worst-case scenarios. Whatever our attitude toward life may have been when we started law school, only a few years of legal practice can be enough to fall out of the habit of feeling grateful.

It can also be challenging to feel grateful when our work puts us in contact with so much of what we may feel is ugly or disappointing. Lawyers literally paper over the world's messes, and we end up witnessing a lot of bad behavior and misfortune. How to be grateful for the disputes, crimes, deaths, betrayals, official misconduct, and financial reversals that make up the fabric of our days? But the challenges we may face in engaging with gratitude are precisely what make gratitude so very useful for lawyers. In fact, gratitude is such a powerful antidote for what ails so many lawyers, if you come away from this course having added only one new practice to your life, we suggest it be a strong and daily engagement with gratitude.

Gratitude Fix

Connecting in with gratitude can be the perfect antidote to a long and tiring day, or a good way to realign yourself after a stressful meeting. This short exercise can help you realign. You can spend about ten minutes on the following steps:

Settle yourself. Focus on the flow of your breath for a few minutes. Allow your eyes to close. Notice the sounds around you, first the louder and then the quieter sounds.

Once you feel settled, think of something or someone you're grateful for. It doesn't need to be anything big. It could even be something you think others would consider insignificant, like nail polish, the mute button on your phone, or the person at the airport information desk. As long as you genuinely appreciate it and are glad to have it in your life, it's fine.

Bring the person or thing you're grateful for into your mind's eye. Spend a few minutes just appreciating that person or thing. If you are thinking about a person, you could imagine yourself smiling at them and then their looking back at you and smiling. Enjoy the feeling of appreciation.

Now, think about what you did in order to bring that person or thing into your life. Even if all you did was allow yourself to be loved, or accepted your good luck, notice you did that. Appreciate yourself for what you did.

Spend a few moments enjoying the feeling of gratitude. If you like, you can imagine gratitude flowing out of you on your out-breath, and gratitude for yourself flowing into you on your in-breath.

Many of us are starved for gratitude, even though gratitude is a natural way to rejuvenate ourselves. In that sense, you can think of gratitude giving your mind and heart a spa day. Gratitude can help us reconnect with what is good and worthwhile all around us, perhaps even remind us about the very positive values that brought us to the practice of law in the first place. Taking time out consciously to feel grateful everyday can unharden some of the closed-off parts of yourself, and, contrary to what you might fear, will not reduce your critical edge. In fact, you may find giving yourself this freedom of thought allows you access to creativity and mental energy you'd locked down in an effort to be a tough and idealistic lawyer.

We've both seen the powerful effect gratitude has had on our own lives and those of other lawyers, and scientific research in this area validates this. A series of research studies conducted by scientists at the University of California, Davis showed that people who consciously engage with gratitude on a daily basis are more optimistic, happier, and have improved personal and professional relationships.[24] Perhaps, surprisingly, those research subjects were also physically healthier than their peers. Other studies that specifically focused on examining the physical benefits of gratitude have found people who practice gratitude sleep better, have healthier hearts, and stronger immune systems.[25]

Reorienting Our Minds with Gratitude

Practicing law hones our minds to focus on problems and dangers, to see the places where agreements are likely to fall apart or interests diverge. This starts in the first week of law school, where we are taught to "spot issues," and continues on throughout our professional life, where we grow accustomed to running through worst-case scenarios, questioning witnesses' veracity, and looking for mixed motives in those seeking to collaborate with our clients. While all of these exercises are necessary and often very valuable for our legal practice, over the years they can build negative habits of mind, which—if we don't take conscious steps to counteract them—can drain pleasure and meaning from our lives. A negative mindset can also make us less effective professionally, as it makes it hard to access our most creative thinking. We are, after all, most helpful to our clients when we go beyond pointing out potential dangers and pitfalls but can offer innovative solutions and wise advice.

Ideally, we'd like to engage our critical faculties when they're needed, and let them go when it's appropriate. While we need to be effective problem-spotters when that skill is called for, we also want to be able to fully engage in the expansiveness of creative thinking, fully enjoy our friendships, and connect with our sense of wonder when we have new experiences. To do this effectively, we may need to consciously disengage the reflexive, over-analytic, and negatively oriented mindset we've allowed to build up over years of legal practice.

This sounds simple, and yet most lawyers who've tried can attest to how very difficult it can be to combat the cynicism and negative thought patterns that build up over years of legal practice. Ironically, trying to take on negative thoughts directly can lead to reinforcing them. For example, if you notice yourself thinking your vacation is bound to be a disappointment, fighting that thought directly may simply kick-start your critical mind, which bombards you with a cascade of logical reasons and counterexamples designed to prove your vacation can't possibly meet your expectations. In part, this is a result of where you put your attention. Focusing your attention on "the disappointment of my vacation" gives that disappointment a more prominent place in your consciousness. It's also because the critical thinking skills we learn in law school dovetail with a tendency of the human mind to focus on the negative. We naturally tend to take for granted what we have and only pay attention to what we are unhappy with or those things that cause discomfort. This habit of focusing on the things that aren't right contributes to further irritation and unhappiness.

Karen's Experience:
Reconnecting with Gratitude

When my children were young I was working in the enforcement and litigation group of one of the banking regulators. My work was fascinating, and I felt I was doing good in the world by helping to reduce bad behavior in the financial sector, or at the very least, bringing that behavior out into the light. At the same time, I was frequently shocked and disheartened by what I saw. That may sound naïve, but this was years before the financial crisis brought corruption in the financial industry to the headlines, and I was genuinely surprised at the level of greed and the ethical lapses I came across in my work.

Almost all my cases brought me into contact with senior executives who were either dishonest themselves, or, more commonly, never bothered to understand the businesses they were supposedly responsible for. As long as profits kept coming in, bonuses were high, and no one asked how it all happened. I saw misrepresentation of risks to clients, misappropriation of funds meant for the government, public corruption, money laundering, executives who lied about the financial state of their banks, and plenty of instances of straightforward embezzlement. Over and over again, the people I interviewed for my cases—who came to my office dressed in beautiful suits and looking like upstanding citizens, with all the trappings of respectability—turned out to be lying or grossly distorting important facts I asked them about.

Over time, these experiences began leading to a deep-seated cynicism and negativity that began to infect my non-working life. I spent so much time wondering whether the people who came into my office were lying, I couldn't easily turn off that attitude when I walked out of work. I also saw so many bad events—business deals gone bad, personal betrayals, crises no one anticipated—that disaster began to seem routine, and that, in turn, colored my perceptions. Suspicion, mistrust, and worry were starting to feel like my default posture toward the world. During this time, when my kids would say, "Don't worry, Mom," I always answered, "Are you kidding? They pay me to worry. I worry for you for free." I was only half joking.

My meditation teacher at the time emphasized the importance of attending to the state of your mind: what you do with it and what you fill it with. In particular, she pointed to the need to consciously engage with gratitude, and to make gratitude a practice. She used an analogy that was meaningful for me: thinking of my mind as a room that I lived in. Did I want that room to be messy, disordered, and unattractive? Or did I want to bring some harmony and beauty into it? I began to think of my mind as the environment I was living in, and I tried to attend to it in the same way I kept my home and office in good order. That made sense to me—it's hard to be productive in a disordered office, or serve a nice dinner when your home is messy and ugly.

Following my teacher's advice, I tried to bring more harmony into my own mind by consciously feeling gratitude for what I had. I started with gratitude for my children, for my spouse; that was easy. Then I tried gratitude for my friends, for the colleagues I appreciated, for the apartment I was lucky to have. Still pretty easy. Then, gratitude for the city I lived in, which was so vibrant, and had so many corners of beauty. OK. How about the subway? Could I be grateful for that? Sure. It got me where I was going. Well, what about the stinky alcoholic at the end of the subway car, snoring and muttering to himself in his sleep? Hmm. That was a challenge. But there he was, a fellow human being.

I couldn't always find gratitude in my heart for every single thing I set out to appreciate. And I didn't consciously think of my gratitude practice as an antidote to a cynical worldview I wasn't entirely aware I'd taken on. But the experience of gratitude, and turning my attention toward gratitude on a regular basis, did have an interesting effect on my mental state: it lightened. I noticed I was taking a more balanced attitude toward the people and events in my life, both at the office and outside it, and, importantly, I began to notice that balance was realistic. My investigative work was exposing me to the worst behavior of people, not a representative sample of humanity. Life began to feel sweet again, and the best things in my life began to take a more prominent place in my attention than the worst.

206

This is where taking a stance of gratitude toward the world can be remarkably helpful. Reorienting your mind toward gratitude can help you loosen the pull of overanalysis without fighting it directly. You do this on the cushion through meditation practices like mantra repetition, which subtly emphasizes the heart and tends to strengthen your sense of connection with heart-centered qualities like gratitude. You do it off the cushion by consciously invoking gratitude throughout the day or through specific practices designed to help engage with gratitude, like the gratitude practices in this chapter. There are also additional resources on gratitude included in the Resources section of the book.

Engaging with Gratitude

Even for people who don't find themselves face to face with the conflicts and negativity that can come up in legal practice, taking a posture of gratitude toward life usually requires some effort, especially in the beginning. For those of us who practice law, it may take some time to even remember what gratitude feels like. Tuning in to the details of your day is a good way to begin.

Consider this: when you woke up this morning, what was the first thing that ran through your mind? What was your emotional and physical state? Did any of it even register? Chances are unless you woke up with some strong negative emotion or physical state (e.g., waking up and thinking about the hearing you lost yesterday), you probably have little recollection of your waking mind-state. However, when you take a step back, you can recognize the very act of waking up this morning is something to be grateful for—regardless of the hearing you lost yesterday, or even the frustrating set of interrogatories awaiting you at the office.

What if instead of waking up each morning with your mind racing off in 100 directions or immediately becoming absorbed in your long to-do list, you take a moment to bring a sense of gratitude for being given another day? After all, none of us know how many mornings we'll have left. One of the great surprises of gratitude is seeing how much there is to be grateful for. Once we turn the lens of appreciation on our daily lives, the many benefits we enjoy as a matter of course can feel almost overwhelming. Our sensory experiences, the beauty of nature and the ever-changing environment we live in come to us free of charge every day. We also enjoy the many benefits of modern society: clean running water, electricity, and the many technological advances that bring so much convenience into our lives.

We can be grateful for the people in our lives. Not just our loved ones, friends, and colleagues, but all the people we don't even know who make our day-to-day life possible, like the cashier at the check-out line at the local supermarket, or the thousands of people who have worked to make it possible for food to be in the supermarket: the farmers who grew the food and those who picked, packaged, and shipped it. We can even practice gratitude toward non-humans, such as pets, other animals, plants, and so forth. Or, taking this one step further, consider the amazing ecosystem that makes our existence possible.

We can bring gratitude to unpleasant events or situations as well. For example, if you have a pounding headache, you can give all of your attention to the pain or take a moment to be grateful for the rest of the body that's not hurting and is healthy. Or maybe your colleague has let you down in some way, perhaps by forgetting to update a document you need to meet a deadline. You can focus all of your attention on that person's shortcomings and how she has not lived up to your expectations; or you can use the moment to be grateful for having that colleague and consider the support you've gotten from her good work. Perhaps her insights, so different from yours, have allowed you to make successful arguments you never would have seen if you'd been working on your own. A simple shift in focus like this can often be enough to wash away a feeling that you are struggling on your own and replace it with the sense that you are on a team—a much more enjoyable, and realistic, view of your situation.

Gratitude can even be brought to bear in very painful situations. When a tragic event strikes, for example, death of someone who is close to you, you may understandably view everything about that event through the lens of grief and pain. Even a devastating event, however, will bring something to be grateful for, and focusing on that can be enormously helpful. You may be grateful for the outpouring of sympathy and support you receive from friends and family. Perhaps you can be grateful for your ability to feel so deeply. Being grateful doesn't mean you're happy about the situation, or you don't feel the pain it brought about. Quite the contrary. What we are suggesting is that in every situation, there is always something to be grateful for, and seeing that may help in finding a means to cope or relieve the intensity of our pain.

Connecting the Dots

In the lines below, write down tragic or traumatic events in your life. Then write down the highlights or the best moments of your life. Consider moments where you experience deep joy or bliss. Once done, consider if there are any links between the negative event and positive event. You may notice that if the negative event did not occur, the positive event may not have happened either.

Negative, tragic, or traumatic in your life:

1. _____

_____

2. _____

_____

3. _____

_____

Positive, joyful, or happiness in your life:

1. _____

_____

2. _____

_____

3. _____

_____

Connecting the dots: Is there a thread or a way in which the negative and positive events are connected? If so, jot down the connection. It's entirely possible that there are many steps in between the negative and positive event—not just one link.

_____

_____

_____

_____

_____

After you get into the habit of gratitude, you can try connecting with it in situations that normally send you down the rabbit hole of irritation and worry. When you notice your mind obsessively thinking about your opposing counsel and what he did (or failed to do), you can catch yourself and shift your mind by asking yourself: Despite what is happening now, what am I grateful for? Ironically, these seemingly small shifts can be the ones that have the biggest effect on your life. As you become more skillful at engaging gratitude, you may notice you take the bumps in the road of life less seriously.

Gratitude, Ease, and Enjoyment

Besides making the challenges of life easier to bear, experiencing gratitude on a regular basis contains a deeper lesson, one that points us to an important truth. A wonderful aspect of gratitude is that it doesn't require anything—no equipment, no achievement, and no changes need to be made in order for gratitude to be possible. The practice of gratitude is simply cultivating appreciation for what you have right now.

The simplicity and ease of gratitude are tonics that counter a message many of us have received our entire lives: that we must strive to accomplish anything worthwhile. By the time we find ourselves practicing law, this message has become a drumbeat running constantly in the background of our lives. It may be so deeply ingrained in us we don't even realize how fully we've internalized it. We may find we instinctively don't value anything that comes easily, no matter what its intrinsic worth may be. This attitude can corrode our lives, causing us to neglect friendships and loving relationships and demean the value of time spent relaxing, daydreaming, or not pursuing a particular goal, even though these moments are the very ones in which we most often encounter our greatest creativity and insight.

Making a Daily Connection with Gratitude

Connecting with gratitude on a daily basis can have a powerful effect on your lived experience. One of the best things about practicing gratitude is that, by definition, you don't have to do anything special or add anything to your life in order to do it. The whole point of a gratitude practice is simply noticing what you already have that you appreciate.

What follows is a simple gratitude practice you can do with a journal.

- Settle yourself. Just for the next few minutes, let go of what you have to do or take care of. Take a couple of deeper breaths, noticing the movement of the breath in and out of your body. Let yourself become aware of the moment you're in right now.
- Consider what is already good about your life as it is. Let yourself notice what you appreciate now, or what opportunities are available to you. These things don't need to be grand. Some of the most meaningful things to think about are those things you might take for granted: running water, the ability to go for a walk, a pet, a friend, your memories, a favorite tree.
- Choose one thing you're grateful for. See if you can think of it as a gift instead of something that just sits in the background of your life. Consciously acknowledge it by saying, "I am grateful for the gift of [that thing/person/place]." Repeat this process at least two more times.
- Record what you are grateful for to help you anchor your thoughts. You can, if you want, include entries on gratitude in your meditation journal.

211

When we practice gratitude, we're cultivating joyfulness. Often, we only allow ourselves to experience joy when we attain certain accomplishments or achievements. But the joyfulness we experience from just being grateful isn't contingent on a win or success, and the truth is we don't have to do or achieve anything in order to experience joy. It's available to us at any time. It can be nothing more complicated than the act of savoring the morning cup of coffee, appreciating the sunshine, and enjoying the time we have to relax before the day kicks in. It can be gratitude for our car and having the means to be able to afford it. It can be having a body and mind capable of driving. This isn't to say that accomplishments or achievements shouldn't be valued—they certainly should be. All we're suggesting is that in our gratitude practice we can experience some much-needed ease by accessing the pleasures of the ordinary, but often important, details of our lives.

Expressing Gratitude for Yourself and Your Meditation Practice

Similar to the compassion practice where we directed compassion externally and then practiced compassion for ourselves, we can practice gratitude for ourselves. Your life, your health, your mind, all of your abilities, as well as your unique personal traits and abilities all offer many opportunities to experience gratitude. We can begin to explore this practice now, by using your meditation practice as a focal point.

You've put quite a bit of time and effort into meditation. Now, as you come to the last week of this program, take some time to consider the benefits you've received from your meditation practice, and extend appreciation to yourself for bringing those benefits into your life. Here are some questions you may want to think over:

- What have you come to enjoy most about your meditation time? The quiet? The time away from goals and deadlines? The chance to do something for yourself?
- Is there a meditation practice you particularly enjoy? What is it about that practice that speaks to you?
- Has your meditation practice supported you in dealing with a specific challenge? Has an insight from your practice been helpful at a particular moment?
- Is there something you've been able to change that's eluded you in the past? Are you more able to connect with ease than you have in the past?

Obviously, there's no right answer to any of these questions. They're just pointers for considering what you appreciate about the practice you've created for yourself. Whatever it is, take some time to allow yourself to be grateful for your meditation practice and what it's brought into your life.

You can also take some time to appreciate your mind. Over the past seven weeks, you've spent some dedicated time with your mind. It may have resisted and baffled you, but it's also made itself more apparent to you. Hopefully after sitting with your own mind on a regular basis during this program, you can better appreciate that it isn't just an invisible automaton, executing your orders in the background of your life. Take some time to appreciate your mind and all it's done for you. It's a powerful tool that's taken you through your education and professional training. It's enabled you to work at a profession that has meaning for you and has helped pay your bills. And now, after watching it more closely, you're likely better able to see some more of its complexity, fluidity, and individuality. Take a minute to appreciate the depth and mystery of your mind.

Finally, we invite you to take a moment to appreciate yourself for taking on this program. We can imagine that there have been times when it hasn't been easy! The practice of meditation takes courage, especially if like many lawyers you've spent your entire career suppressing or denying your inner world. Appreciate yourself for taking the plunge and giving meditation a serious try. The benefits of meditation you are happy to have received came into your life because you were willing to begin this practice and keep at it for as long as you have.

As we wrap up Week Eight of our practice, remember, this is only the beginning of what will hopefully become a lifelong practice. As one of our meditation teachers was fond of saying, the last class is the longest because it's the first day to a lifelong journey. May your practice continue to serve you.

Seated Meditation Using Mantra Repetition

I will meditate for _____ minutes, every day.

This week, continue to practice mantra repetition, using either the meditation instructions from Week Six or Week Seven.

Visit www.theanxiouslawyer.com for audio guided meditations.

~

Gratitude Journal and/or Jar

Journaling or writing down what you are grateful for is a wonderful way to cultivate and strengthen your gratitude practice. Each day this week, write down one thing you are grateful for. Alternatively, you can start a gratitude jar, jotting down what you are grateful for on a small piece of paper and placing it in the jar. The gratitude jar is a lovely practice because it can serve as a visual reminder of how much you have to be grateful for and you can also randomly pull out a slip of paper from the jar during difficult times.

Meditation Log

Day	Time/Length	Notes: Sitting	Notes: Off the Cushion
Mon			
Tue			
Wed			
Thu			
Fri			
Sat			
Sun			

Taking Your
Practice Forward

That last thing is what you can't get, Carlo. Nobody can get to that last thing. We keep on living in hopes of catching it once and for all.

—Jack Kerouac

YOU'VE NOW COMPLETED OUR eight-week meditation program. Congratulations! We hope the program outlined in this book has been helpful in beginning a meditation practice that will go on for years. This week, we'll consider how things may have changed for you over the past eight weeks. We'll also share some things you can expect from your meditation practice as you continue forward, and ideas about how to continue to pursue and deepen your practice.

How Has Your Perspective Changed?

Whether or not you're fully aware of it, you're in a very different place than you were eight weeks ago. You've spent eight weeks meeting yourself and your mind in the unique environment created by the practice of meditation, and eight weeks working to bring the insights gained in the meditative state to your daily life through off-the-cushion practices. This is long enough to have received some real benefits from meditation, and those benefits are lasting. Recent studies have shown that measurable changes can be seen in the brains of people who complete an eight-week meditation course—so, in some small way, you are quite literally a different person at the end of a course like this one.[26] And not only are you physically different, you are likely experiencing the world differently. For many people a meditation class may be the first time they have regularly set aside time to do nothing "productive," be with themselves, or to have a regular period of silence, and the effects of taking that time can be surprising and far-reaching.

If you never meditated before beginning the program, now you have a sustained experience of what a meditation practice is like. It may not have been anything like you thought it would be: maybe it was easier and better than you were expecting; maybe you struggled far more than you imagined you would. But importantly, whatever your experience of meditation practice has been, it's now real, and that makes it more valuable than any idealized notion you might have had about what it would be like to start meditating.

If you used this program to get back into meditation or rejuvenate an established practice, you've spent eight weeks following a fairly structured meditation program and had a chance to engage with a number of different meditation methods, some of which may have been new for you. You've also had a chance to hear our perspective on meditation practices you may have been engaging with for some time, and perhaps that gave you new views on something you already know well. You've also been consciously connecting your meditation practice with your daily life through the off-the-cushion practices and other exercises in the book, which may or may not be something you've done in the past.

However you came to this program, it's worth taking some time at this natural moment of transition to consider what's changed for you. You may have been so immersed in the task of getting yourself to the cushion you haven't had a chance to notice in what ways your perspective and day-to-day experience of life has evolved as a result of what you've been doing. Try taking a few minutes right now to think over the past eight weeks of meditation and how it may have affected your outlook, habits, and interactions even in this relatively short time. Here are some questions you may want to consider:

- Reconnect with your intention from Week One. Do you have more clarity or insight about your intention?
- Thinking back to before you began the meditation program, have you noticed any changes in your daily experience?
- What is the biggest change you've noticed since beginning to meditate?
- Consider your day-to-day work life. Has anything changed since you began meditating?
- Have you made changes to any personal habits over the past eight weeks? If so, did you make any of those changes intentionally to help with your meditation practice (e.g., going to bed earlier so you could get up to meditate)? How do you feel about those changes—would you continue them? Did any other changes come about as a result of meditating?
- How are you interacting with those you are closest to? Do you see any difference since starting to meditate?
- What was the most surprising thing about meditation?

We suggest you record these reflections in your meditation journal, so you can come back to them in the future.

Stages of the Meditation Path

What should you expect as you keep going with your practice? We've alluded to the fact that the meditation process has an internal logic that evolves over time, and that's something most people who continue to meditate consistently will experience.

There have been attempts to map out how the insights of meditation unfold, from Christian traditions that teach that the dark night of the soul is followed by deeper wisdom, to Buddhist traditions that map elaborate levels of insight to be attained by the practitioner. None of these maps has ever gained general currency, most likely because the meditation process is individual for everyone. No one else's description of how a meditation practice evolves will be perfectly accurate for you; you're the only one who can map your experience. That said, there are some relatively predictable stages many people go through in the course of their meditation practice. Many people experience something like the following sequence:

- First, we experience a sense of longing. This may take the form of feeling restless, that something is just not right, or maybe a sense of dissatisfaction with what used to make us very happy. We start looking to make a change of some kind.
- Eventually, we start a sitting practice.
- After we've been sitting for a while, we have a big opening. We gain insight into ourselves, our lives, our relations with others, or perhaps all three.
- Again, after some time, we experience difficulty in our meditation practice. This may feel quite similar to the restlessness that led us to sit in the first place.
- We may feel frustrated, or we may make changes to our practice.
- If we keep going with our practice, we eventually reach another moment of insight. We see more deeply into the questions that brought us to meditate in the first place.

220

This process tends to repeat itself over and over again: (1) feeling good, practice easy; (2) feeling bad, practice difficult or frustrating; and (3) feeling neutral, followed by new insight. Every time we go through this cycle, we deepen our understanding.

Over time, the deepening insights of meditation can bring freedom from the sense of alienation most modern people take as a given. We begin to see much of the fear, anger, and cynicism we've accepted as part of the human condition are more optional than we knew. As that knowledge becomes more and more real for us, we can live with a greater and greater sense of freedom, while also experiencing a deep connection with the world and with others. For us, this deepening understanding has been the most genuine source of satisfaction in our lives—far beyond any kind of professional recognition or material gain.

Stick with It!

Thinking about stages of the practice may feel abstract to you right now, and that's fine. Our main purpose in mentioning them is to encourage you to keep at your practice, even if you hit some bumps. This is an important message to internalize now and you can return to it when you're experiencing difficulties in your practice.

Many people finish an eight-week introductory course on meditation like the one outlined here feeling absolutely great. They've mastered the basic techniques of meditation and they've been sitting every day for almost two months in a row. The first taste of the clarity, contentment, and ease this practice brings can be intoxicating. New meditators often report being astonished at what their practice has done for them in such a short time. They can hardly believe the sweetness of the silence they find inside themselves. They're amazed by the flashes of contentment and even joy they feel during meditation or afterwards. Bad habits may fall away easily or they may be able to see through misconceptions they'd been walking around with for years. They may find themselves noticing beauty in their daily environment that had never been apparent before: the smile of a store clerk, the nondescript brown bird hopping around by the bus stop, the sliver of sunlight breaking through a dull cloud cover might all suddenly look breathtaking.

This is a very special time. While there will be wonderful times in your practice, deep insights into yourself and profound understanding, the initial joy of discovery and enthusiasm that often comes with a new meditation practice comes only once, and doesn't last forever. So if you fall head-over-heels in love with your practice early on, savor it. And if that early feeling of intoxication never particularly comes up for you, don't worry. It's not required nor is it a sign of a successful meditation practice. In fact, the greatest satisfactions of a sustained meditation practice don't even kick in until well beyond the honeymoon phase.

Just as the early, love-struck phase of a romantic relationship gives way to more complexity and depth, so too one's experience of meditation can evolve into a more balanced but deeper commitment to practice. If you keep going with your practice—and we hope you will—inevitably, at some point, you'll encounter difficulty of one kind or another. Meditation may start to feel dry or boring, or maybe one of the meditation side effects we discussed in Week Three surprises you or makes you feel uncomfortable.

221

Sadly, many people stop meditating when they encounter these sorts of challenges in their meditation practice, because they think the difficulty they're experiencing must be a sign they can't meditate. We can tell you for certain, from our own personal experiences, this isn't so! Tempting as it is to judge your meditation practice by how good it feels, this would be a mistake. If you think about any worthwhile endeavor you've taken on, whether it's learning a sport or understanding an arcane area of law, there are always times of challenge, and meditation is no different. The difficulties people experience in a meditation practice are usually transitory, and if you keep going with your practice you'll likely come to a new phase of ease and deepening insight in not too long.

In summary, if there is a single piece of advice we could give you about meditating, it would be this: keep doing it.

Unfolding Insights and Evolving Goals

222

In addition to the classic insights of meditation, many people also experience profoundly personal transformative moments at various points in their practice. While the specifics of those transformations can't be predicted—after all, they reflect the personality and values of the person involved—what can be said is that most people who meditate for long periods of time go through changes they see as benefits of their practice, and that they didn't anticipate. The transformative experiences you have may also affect the way you view your practice, shifting the goal posts you initially set for yourself. What follows are some examples of the kinds of changes we've seen in ourselves and our peers as a result of our respective practices.

Reducing Our Reactivity

Part of the self-knowledge that comes with a meditation practice is familiarity with our own triggers. Meditation practice helps us interact more skillfully with these triggers and have fewer knee-jerk reactions, by improving our awareness of the moment of choice. We connect with the moment of choice over and over again in meditation, in part so we can notice that brief space between our automatic reaction to something and a considered response. Often, we reflexively feel we need to do *something* to try to *fix* a situation when, in fact, we only do more harm by saying or doing something in that moment. Again, this need to do something may just be a habitual reaction. Instead of jumping into *doing* mode, we can observe what is going on in our mind with a bit of distance and see our initial reaction for what it is—simply thoughts, which we can choose to act on or not.

For example, you may have a particular opposing counsel you have great difficulty working with. Like every lawyer, you probably have at least one attorney who comes to mind immediately when you think about difficult working relationships. When you think about this opposing counsel, does your heart beat just a little faster? Can you feel any sensations such as heat rising to your face, your stomach tensing, or any other physiological response? What is the thought process that goes through your mind when you think about this person? What is the narrative?

Chances are if your opposing counsel is setting you off regularly, it's because he's triggering some kind of automatic reaction on your part. As you uncover these triggers, the hidden landmines of your mind, you can set your intention to protect or free your mind from these irritations. With some practice, you can begin to see that your story about your opposing counsel is something you've created and have a choice about believing. Perhaps instead of immediately connecting with that story, you can view his actions not as a personal assault against you or your client but rather a reaction to your behavior, reaction to his client, or some other reason unknown to you. You may be able to bring a sense of detachment and compassion knowing his anger isn't directed at you. The ability to gain distance from your thoughts and looking at your experience with a wider lens helps allow you to view the situation from different perspectives. As you practice doing this, you'll better be able to tap into your creativity and consider different ways of resolving the issue or working with this difficult opposing counsel.

Most importantly, you can begin to take ownership of your own reaction—the thoughts, the narrative, the feelings, and emotions you have about this situation or opposing counsel—and recognize you have the ability to choose your response. Often, the wisest course of action is to practice being with your own reaction until clarity emerges.

223

~

The Mindful Lawyer

There is no single formula for bringing mindfulness into your legal practice. Fair to say, it's a constant effort. Here are some suggestions for thinking about the intersection of mindfulness and the law.

- Understanding we have a finite amount of energy, and therefore respecting our own energy. In this way, we can be mindful of our own boundaries.
- Mindfulness as a place to retreat. When we feel as though the ground beneath us is about to give and we're spiraling out of control, mindfulness can serve as our anchor.
- Using mindfulness as corrective measure. When we're feeling out of balance from working too much, not taking the necessary time to care for ourselves, or not spending enough time out of the office, being mindful can help correct the imbalance.
- Combating vicarious trauma or compassion fatigue. We can get lost in other people's problems or pain and lose sight of self-care. Use mindfulness to notice when we're giving too much of ourselves and bring it back into balance.
- Letting go of unproductive, unhelpful thoughts. Our mind is constantly producing thoughts. Mindfulness allows us to discern productive and helpful thoughts from the unproductive, unhelpful thoughts.

~

More Intentionality

Meditation builds habits that allow us to slow down our minds and not live in a constant state of high alert. From this perspective, our meditation practice can help us to prioritize and give our attention to what we value in life. For example, many people begin their meditation practice to become more efficient at work. For lawyers, who usually bill in 0.1-hour increments, becoming more focused, efficient, and concentrated at work is an understandable reason for starting a meditation practice. Meditation helps settle the mind; so instead of feeling as though your mind is constantly in the middle of a tornado, you can find a sense of peace. You'll soon notice that being able to calm the mind and gain clarity can help you get better at just about everything. It not only helps you be better at work but will probably help you get better at golf, too, if that's what you want to do.

In addition to increasing your ability to direct your mind to your task, you may also notice you become more intentional about how you spend your time. As lawyers, we have a tendency to rush from one activity to another without giving much consideration to whether what we're rushing toward is truly important in that moment. We're so driven by forward movement and busy with the act of *doing*, we rarely pause and ask the question, "Is what I'm doing aligned with my values?" We continue to do more, simply for the sake of doing more instead of asking ourselves about the *why* behind our actions.

If you had to list ten things you value the most in your life, those things that are truly important to you, what would be on that list? Now, look back to the past ten days and ask yourself, "How much time did I spend doing things that are aligned with my values—those things I consider the most important?"

As you build the habit of pausing and turning your attention inward, you may naturally begin to question how you spend your day and prioritize your time. It's possible things you believed were important lose that feeling of importance or you begin to evaluate the tasks that fill your day by a different yardstick. For example, instead of being concerned about how other people will view you and making choices designed to gain external validation or approval, you may begin to attend to your own inner source of wisdom.

As your practice deepens, you'll begin to see you have control over cultivating and creating a positive mental state. You'll also begin to cherish and care for your mind so you're less subject to external influences and more aware of what's truly best for you. Living in accordance with what's important to you and what you truly value helps you feel more grounded and happier.

225

Opening to Bigger Questions

In meditation practice, we create a safe space for larger life questions such as:

- What is this life all about?
- Why am I here?
- What is the purpose of my life?

- What is my mission?
- What is the impact or difference I want to make?
- How can I cultivate a deep sense of joy and happiness in my life?

As your journey into meditation unfolds, you may connect or reconnect with your personal values, or your personal sense of ethics. This may initially feel uncomfortable because we lawyers are so focused on precedents and legal knowledge that we rarely consider our own personal ethical guidelines. If you notice this shift in perspective, we encourage you to allow yourself to make room for this exploration. The practice of law, with all of its ethical and moral challenges, makes for a wonderful space to engage with the insights of meditation. It's precisely the difficult challenges that make the practice of law so interesting.

Stepping Outside of Story Lines

In this book we've focused on how we can engage with meditation as lawyers. It can be quite valuable to consider how our role as lawyers affects our relationship with meditation. Ultimately, though, we want our meditation practice to help us grow as human beings, outside of any particular role we may play, however compelling that role may be. It can also be particularly useful for lawyers to remember they do have an existence separate from their role—we are a group that tends to identify very strongly with our profession.

This short exercise is a chance to consciously step away from the story lines that often come to define us, and simply enjoy the experience of being oneself, outside of any role or story. To do the exercise, you'll need paper and something to write with. Ideally, you should sit in a pleasant place while you're doing the exercise, but you can do it anywhere.

- Without taking too much time to think, write down the world's story about you. How does the world see you? Write out all the good and all the bad. Don't censor yourself, be falsely modest, or try to make yourself better than the world actually sees you. You won't have to show what you're writing to anyone, so there's no need to hold back.

- After you finish, take a moment to read over what you've written. Now, tear up the world's story about you. Tear the paper you've written on into tiny shreds. You can also burn the paper if you are in a place where you can do so safely. Throw the remains of the story away.

- Sit quietly for a few minutes. Allow your eyes to close, and take some slower, deeper breaths. Once you feel settled, allow yourself to feel the feeling of being yourself, without anybody's story defining you. Let go of all story lines and any expectations. Feel what it feels like to be you. This is not what your clients, colleagues, spouse, family, or friends think about you. It's not who you wish you were, who you want to become, or any of your achievements, failures, or plans, but the simple feeling of being you, in this moment.

- Connect with the very basic and natural sense of being yourself. You may not have done this since you were a child, so remembering something very simple from your childhood may help you engage with this feeling. You might remember what it was like to wake up in the morning, or walking to school. (Don't focus on a memory that is too interesting or that you have strong feelings about, because it will distract you from the exercise.) If you're experiencing any particular sensation, like feeling the warmth of sunlight or the support of a chair or sofa, that may also help ground you in the feeling of being yourself in this moment. Enjoy the simplicity of existing without any story line.

- After a few minutes, reflect on this experience. What possibilities could emerge without your current stories about yourself? How did it feel to tear up the stories that have built up around you? To step outside of all those roles and story lines? Who would you be if you lived without any story?

227

The questions that come up for you may also deepen over time. It's not unusual to consider questions around death and dying, including your own mortality, when you begin to explore life's purpose or meaning. This is also common as you begin to accept the impermanence of life, which inevitably means recognizing the natural cycle of life—from birth until death. The topic of death and dying is one that makes most people uncomfortable. Despite knowing cognitively that all of us are going to die, this is a topic we deny or fight thinking about. We encourage you to *be with* these questions if they come up for you. At the same time, there's no need to rush or force the process. Always be gentle and kind with yourself. Engaging with life's deeper questions can be challenging but it also can bring a great sense of satisfaction.

Jeena's Story: Finding a Purpose-Driven Life

As your mindfulness practice unfolds and you have an opportunity to listen to your inner voice, you may start to have questions about your higher purpose. By sitting quietly everyday, you make space to ask yourself questions such as "What is the positive impact I'd like to make in the world?" If you notice this in your meditation practice, know that it's perfectly natural. It may feel alarming to allow these questions to surface because lawyers are trained to seek answers. However, when it comes to answering these bigger questions about life, it's not about finding an answer or even answers but rather holding the question. In other words, it's about the journey—not the destination.

Why Are You Here?

Albert Einstein said, "Insanity is doing the same thing over and over again and expecting different results."

When I look back at my life, I recognize I was doing precisely what Einstein said. I kept working, striving harder, doing more, trying to accomplish more, and trying to check more items off of the accomplishment list. However, I was *doing* more, just for the sake of *doing*. I didn't have a purpose.

I worked incredibly hard at the law firm jobs I've had, even harder at the State Attorney's office, and hardest of all—at my own firm. I thought making partner, climbing the ranks, and having more clients would make me feel fulfilled, but, of course, it didn't. It's like winning a pie-eating contest where the prize is more pie. You better make sure you really like pies before entering the contest. I don't like pies and, predictably, I became increasingly despondent.

I wasn't exactly unhappy. I just felt lost. I felt overworked, and constantly exhausted. Then I returned to a practice I had abandoned since law school: *meditation*. Through meditation, I was able to calm my mind, which was constantly operating in overdrive. Once I found stillness, I had the space to examine my life.

"Why are you here? What makes you feel alive? What would truly make you happy? What is the unique gift of yourself that you are bringing to all of us?"

When my friend Kit Newman asked me these questions, I cried. I cried because *no one had ever asked me those questions*. More importantly, I cried because *I had never asked myself those questions*.

These questions unlocked something inside of me—that part of myself which had been hidden, suppressed, and neglected all of my life.

This was three years ago, which is to say, this finding your purpose business—it's a process. Initially, I had some vague idea of wanting to teach mindfulness and meditation to lawyers. That idea blossomed over time and now I have more clarity on my life's mission.

229

~

The unexamined life is not worth living for a human being.

—Socrates

~

It's so easy to go through life without ever pausing to critically examine it, to ask the tough questions about your life's meaning, purpose, mission, and goals. It requires that we unplug from the constant noise, to stop, and to reflect. I've found this is really hard for lawyers because *we identify so much of who we are with what we do*. If you let go of your identity as a lawyer, who are you?

Not About Happiness, But About Purpose

Let me pause here to address an important distinction. When I talk about finding your life's purpose, I'm not talking about constantly chasing after fleeting moments of happiness. What I'm talking about is intentionally thinking about and exploring your greater purpose for being alive.

At the end of your life, as you reflect on your journey, what do you want to say you've accomplished? What is the difference or impact you want to make?

Role of Resiliency and Courage

Making room, pursuing, and exploring your life's purpose isn't an obvious thing to do for most lawyers. It certainly wasn't for me. I was the follow-the-rules and stick-to-the-script lawyer. There was a certain protocol, certain pattern, certain roadmap I was *supposed* to follow.

When I decided to break the mold and define for myself what success looked like, to step into my life's mission and purpose, I met a lot of resistance. There was a lot of "What the hell is she talking about," and admittedly a lot of "I have no idea what I'm doing," as well as self-doubt.

Figuring out your purpose isn't obvious. It's not a singular destination. It's a lifelong journey and exploration. Sometimes, you have to try something on to see if it fits—to see if it feels right. You're not a failure if you try something on and decide it doesn't fit. You're not a bad person for wanting to do your life's work.

Here are two things I've learned from committing to live a purpose-driven life:

1. Living your purpose means you have to exercise your resiliency muscle because you're going to be breaking rules and social constructs. You'll be met with obstacles and naysayers. You have to be resilient. You have to be able to bounce back from adversities.
2. You must be courageous. It takes guts to say that the thing you've worked so hard to achieve, the thing you've been striving for, the dream you've been living wasn't meant for you. It takes courage to stand up to those who say you can't do this or you're crazy.

It's easy to be a bystander offering running commentaries on your actions. As far as responding to these naysayers, I'll quote my favorite author, Brené Brown:

"If you are not in the arena also getting your butt kicked, I'm not interested in your feedback."

Life Transitions

Study hard, go to a good school, find clerkship, find the ideal job, get married, have children. These are some of the many things that have likely been on your life's checklist. As we grow older and check items off the list, we may arrive at a deeper questioning of what we are meant to accomplish. You may find one day you've finished checking all the boxes and wonder, now what? This time that many people go through is popularly considered a midlife crisis.

Whether we're experiencing a midlife crisis, a quarter-life crisis, or just considering making a change, meditation can be very helpful in navigating the difficult choices we find ourselves facing. Just as with life's bigger questions, meditation practice can create a space where we feel more comfortable reexamining our life choices. This reexamination process can be very challenging for lawyers, as we've generally spent most of our lives pursuing outward success and giving short shrift to the kind of introspection that is useful at these times.

Meditation practice can help us develop a healthier attitude toward change, which many professionals tend to find quite uncomfortable. As you become more skilled in observing your mind, you'll notice your mental state changes—constantly. You begin to understand on a deeper level that everything changes, including your body, thoughts, feelings, and your mind. At different times and in different company, you may notice your thoughts and actions change. Over time, your desires and opinions also change.

Instead of resisting the flow of life and its inevitable constant, which is change, you begin to accept what is—without struggling against it. This isn't to suggest you become a passive victim of your life; accepting what is actually has the opposite result, which is by accepting what you cannot change, you become more skillful at stepping into the arenas where you can exercise agency. You can also begin to let go of judgment you may have about wanting to make changes in your life. For example, you may be able to see you're actually done with a particular job even though it was completely right for you years ago when you started at it, and understand there's no need to judge yourself for that. You can see change as a natural part of life and spend less time dwelling on what is lost in the change and appreciate where you are and what you have—right now. In this way, meditation can ease life's natural transitions.

Next Steps

Now that you're done going through the program in this book, you may be wondering what's next on a practical level. We told you to stick with it, but what exactly does that mean? Basically, all you have to do is keep going! You've got the basics down, so you can have confidence you know all you need to have a long and rewarding meditation practice. Here are just a few practical points that may be helpful in keeping your practice going.

Revisiting Your Intention

If you set an intention for yourself at the outset of this program, now is a great time to return to it. Do you see that intention playing out in your practice thus far? Consider how this initial intention looks to you now in light of your practice over the past two months. Do you want to deepen your commitment to this intention? Revise it? Or maybe you want to begin this new phase of your practice with a new intention. Anything you decide to do regarding your intention is good. Again, remember writing down any new intention or revision to your original intention will force you to clarify it and help you connect with it by creating a concrete anchor with it in your mind.

Settling on a Meditation Style

Which meditation practice will you use? Now that you've had a chance to sample a number of different meditation practices, we suggest you pick the one you feel the most connected with and stick with it for a sustained amount of time. Spend at least six months on that practice; that's the minimum you'll need to get deep enough to really get to know it and internalize its qualities. Even if you decide to change methods later, spending a sustained amount of time on any practice will let you start to see your own mind better, and that will leave you with lasting benefits. Changing meditation practices too frequently, especially in the beginning, means you'll be very caught up in mastering new techniques rather than getting deep enough to gain genuine insight.

Some Alternative Styles and Methods of Meditation

There are many other styles of meditation in addition to the ones covered in this book. Each has its own unique qualities, so once you feel your meditation practice is up and running, you may want to investigate to see if another method or tradition is best for you. What follows is a non-exhaustive list of some of the more popular styles of meditation:

Centering prayer—Historically, many people in the West connected with meditative practice through contemplative forms of prayer, and this form of prayer is currently enjoying a renaissance. Contemplative prayer practice differs from vocal or active prayer in that the mind is quieted during the prayer period. Thomas Keating, a Trappist monk, developed the method of centering prayer, a form of contemplative prayer intended to be accessible for many.

Centering prayer has become extremely popular across many religious traditions, and there are now quite a number of interfaith and ecumenical centering prayer groups as well as many based in Christian traditions. A good introduction to centering prayer can be found in Father Keating's book, *Open Mind, Open Heart.*

233

Zen—Much of what we encounter as mindfulness practice in the West has its roots in Zen Buddhism. The Zen tradition has been particularly adaptable to a secular Western context, because of its emphasis on the meditator's direct experience. Zen focuses on practice rather than study of Buddhist doctrine, making it relatively accessible to those who are unfamiliar with Buddhist teachings.

As practiced in America today, Zen has almost as many different styles as there are teachers. Nonetheless, it is fair to say American Zen continues to retain the flavor of its Japanese roots, which tends to bring simplicity, austerity, and discipline to the way it is practiced. The focus of most Zen practice communities is on *zazen*, a type of seated meditation. Zazen may or may not include reflection on a series of *koans*, seemingly paradoxical questions or statements designed to circumvent the intellect (e.g., what is the sound of one hand clapping?) and enable the practitioner to see reality more directly, without the barrier of mental concepts. A fundamental aspect of Zen practice also includes interaction with an accomplished teacher, or Zen master.

While there are many excellent introductory books on Zen, the best way to get a taste of Zen practice is to try it. There are Zen centers and meditation groups in many U.S. cities and towns, so if you are curious about Zen, consider attending an introductory session or regular sitting program.

Dzogchen, Mahamudra—These "practiceless practices" from the Tibetan Buddhist tradition were traditionally considered advanced, esoteric techniques that could only be taught after years of preparation. Under the current Dalai Lama's influence, they have been made more available to students of all levels. Now there are even retreats specially geared to teaching Mahamudra practice to beginning meditation students.

While Mahamudra and Dzogchen both employ various techniques to help settle the mind, the core of both practices is to drop all techniques and focus on the nature of awareness itself. Many people believe this very plain, stripped down form of meditation goes back to the time of the Buddha. Because of its simplicity, this practice is more accessible for Western students than other Tibetan practices that may require complex visualizations or rituals.

Anam Thubten is a teacher of Mahamudra who is particularly accessible for Western students. There are introductory talks and guided meditations available online on his website. (See Resources section.)

Tonglen—Tonglen is a Tibetan practice in which the meditator imagines taking away the pain of others by breathing in pain, then breathing out happiness and well-being and sending it out to those who need it. It differs from the Metta practice we covered in this book, in that Metta is exclusively focused on sending good wishes, whereas in tonglen, the practitioner consciously imagines taking on the suffering of others with the intention to transform it. Tonglen is intended to open the heart, overcome the fear of suffering, and connect with our natural compassion for ourselves and those around us. Tonglen can be challenging and may initially seem counterintuitive, but it is a powerful practice that can be transformative. If you are interested in exploring Tonglen practice, Pema Chodron is a meditation teacher in the Tibetan tradition who has written extensively on Tonglen practice. She has also made many resources on Tonglen available online.

If after trying one practice for some time you decide you'd like to explore something different, there are many great meditation traditions to choose from. The break out section above describes some of the larger meditation traditions besides the ones covered in this book. We've also included books and other resources from various meditation traditions at the end of the book.

Books, Retreats, and Finding a Teacher

Many people are very satisfied working exclusively from meditation books for years. If you continue on with your practice, there will likely come a time when you decide you want to find a meditation teacher, but you can allow this to happen organically. As long as you're happy with your practice, you can use the advice you get from meditation books like this one and the many excellent books written by others. We've listed some of them in the Resources section at the end of this book.

Usually people decide they want to find a meditation teacher because something in their practice has changed. You may decide to seek out a teacher when your practice feels like it's become significantly deeper, or if you have experiences you don't entirely understand. Or you may find deeper questions are coming up for you and want the benefit of someone with greater experience to talk them over with.

If and when you do decide to find a meditation teacher, the most important criterion to use is your own judgment. Your meditation teacher should be someone you personally respect and are comfortable with. Work with someone who you believe, to the best of your ability, to have had direct experience of some of the deeper insights of meditation. A good meditation teacher should be able to speak about the trajectory of the meditation path from experience rather than theory.

In choosing a teacher, do take a few obvious precautions: a teacher should be clear about your relationship: there should be no question that he or she in some way controls your progress. Avoid anyone who asks you to take his or her expertise on faith, or who asks you to make exorbitant payments or donations. Use your common sense, maintain responsibility for yourself and your experience, and you'll be fine.

In addition to finding a teacher, many people enjoy finding a regular meditation group to attend. People often find meditating with others can help them settle more quickly and arrive at a deeper state of meditation

235

than when they sit on their own. There can also be great benefit in having a community of support. Even though it is gaining in popularity, meditation remains outside our cultural mainstream with its materialist focus. Having a community of like-minded people to sit with can provide you with moral support and help maintain your practice. Many cities and even smaller towns have a number of groups that meet regularly to meditate. Some are tied to a specific tradition; others are entirely ecumenical. A quick Internet search will likely turn up a few in your area.

Another way of deepening your engagement with meditation can be to go on a meditation retreat. Retreats can vary greatly in terms of time, style, and, of course, format. Many meditation centers will host half- to full-day non-residential retreats, while retreat centers will host longer retreats from a weekend to several months. While going on retreat can be a wonderful experience, as we said earlier, retreats are entirely optional. If it's not realistic for you to take time away from work and family for an extended time, you needn't worry your practice will suffer. Meditation retreats run the gamut from very strict and structured to relatively open; accommodations can be very austere or quite comfortable. Some meditation retreats are held in silence; others actively encourage participants to reflect on and share their experiences. Going on a retreat with a specific teacher can be a great way of getting to know that person's teaching style and expertise, so you may want to choose a retreat on that basis. Being clear in your own mind what you're looking for, and what you want to get out of a retreat, before signing up will help you have the best experience possible.

Go Deep and Have Fun!

We hope you've enjoyed your initial foray into meditation—and that this book has been a useful support. For us, it's been very meaningful to create a meditation book especially geared for lawyers. Our larger hope in doing so is that through meditation and related practices, we can cultivate a healthier relationship to our work: that we can create space to explore our minds fearlessly and with a sense of adventure; that we begin to value the role of our feelings and emotions in our personal and professional lives as well as that of our reason; that we can begin to acknowledge the importance of our own vulnerability; and that we come to understand the benefit of creating a quiet space in our daily life to turn our attention inward and reflect—getting to know our inner world.

As you continue to meditate, our wish for you is that your practice will bring you ease, delight, and more and more access to your own wisdom. Enjoy the journey you've started. You are now the scientist of your own mind—this is your investigation to conduct. No one can say how your meditation practice will unfold—and that's the fun of it. Fundamentally, this practice is a journey of self-discovery. Thankfully, the process of getting to know oneself better is a lifetime project. There are always new depths to uncover.

Resources

Introduction to Meditation

Swami Anantananda, *What's On My Mind?* (1996)

Pema Chodron, *When Things Fall Apart: Heart Advice for Difficult Times* (2000)

Jack Kornfield, *A Path with Heart: A Guide Through the Perils and Promises of Spiritual Life* (1993)

Jon Kabat-Zinn, *Wherever You Go, There You Are* (2005)

General Meditation

Sally Kempton, *Meditation for the Love of It: Enjoying Your Own Deepest Experience* (2010)

Dalai Lama, *The Art of Happiness* (2009)

Chogyam Trungpa, *Cutting Through Spiritual Materialism* (new ed. 2002)

Shunryu Suzuki, *Zen Mind, Beginners Mind* (1993)

The Science of Meditation

Sharon Begley, *Train Your Mind, Change Your Brain: How a New Science Reveals Our Extraordinary Potential to Transform Ourselves* (2007)

Richard J. Davidson, *The Emotional Life of Your Brain* (2013)

Rick Hanson, *Hardwiring Happiness: The New Brain Science of Contentment, Calm, and Confidence* (2013)

The Mind and Life Institute is a non-profit organization founded with the encouragement of the Dalai Lama and focused on exploring the intersection between the scientific investigation of the mind and Buddhist meditation practice. The organization sponsors research and organizes events around topics related to the scientific study of meditative practice. Their website includes resources such as books, videos, and a calendar of events. https://www.mindandlife.org

Compassion

Paul Gilbert, *The Compassionate Mind: A New Approach to Life's Challenges* (2010)

Kristin Neff, *Self-Compassion: Stop Beating Yourself Up and Leave Insecurity Behind* (2011)

Gratitude

240

The Greater Good Science Center, based at the University of California at Berkeley, has a focus that includes the practice of gratitude. Their website includes instruction, studies, and courses on the gratitude practice. http://greatergood.berkeley.edu

Brother David Steindl-Rast, a Benedictine monk, has founded a global organization, A Network for Grateful Living, focusing on gratefulness as an engaged mindfulness practice. http://www.gratefulness.org

Meditation in the Workplace

Stephen Cope, *The Great Work of Your Life: A Guide for the Journey to Your True Calling* (2012)

David Gelles, *Mindful Work: How Meditation is Changing Business From the Inside Out* (2015)

Steven Keeva, *Transforming Practices: Finding Joy and Satisfaction in the Legal Life* (2009)

Joel and Michelle Levy's Wisdom at Work website contains resources, links, and various programs designed to harness the insights of meditation in the workplace. http://www.wisdomatwork.com

Janice Marturano, *Finding the Space to Lead: A Practical Guide to Mindful Leadership* (2014)

Tim Ryan, *A Mindful Nation: How a Simple Practice Can Help Us Reduce Stress, Improve Performance, and Recapture the American Spirit* (2013)

Sharon Salzberg, *Real Happiness at Work: Meditations for Accomplishment, Achievement and Peace* (2013)

Other Meditation Practices Not Covered in This Book

Centering Prayer:

Thomas Keating, *Open Mind, Open Heart* (2006)
More resources on centering prayer can be found at: http://www.contemplativeoutreach.org

Mahamudra:

The Dharmata Foundation supports the work of Anam Thubten, a teacher of Mahamudra style meditation practice. The foundation's website includes talks, books, retreat schedules, and Anam Thubten's teaching schedule. https://www.dharmata.org

Tonglen:

Pema Chodron, *Tonglen, the Path of Transformation* (2001)
More information about tonglen practice can be found in other books by Pema Chodron, and on the Pema Chodron Foundation website: http://pemachodronfoundation.org

Personal Inquiry

Brene Brown, *Daring Greatly: How the Courage to Be Vulnerable Transforms the Way We Live, Love, Parent and Lead* (2015)

Viktor E. Frankl, *Man's Search for Meaning* (1997)

Arianna Huffington, *Thrive: The Third Metric to Redefining Success and Creating a Life of Well-Being, Wisdom and Wonder* (2015)

Author's Note

Note on Suicide from Jeena

As I travel across the United States to talk to lawyers about mental wellness, self-care, and mindfulness, the topic of suicide often comes up. I'll sometimes ask the audience to raise their hand if he or she has been touched by suicide. It's not unusual for more than three-fourths of the audience to raise their hand.

One person shared with me that once you know someone who has committed suicide, it makes you realize that it's a possibility—for anyone. This has been true for me. I'll sometimes find myself wondering how painful life would have to become before I decide to take my own life. While I certainly know I can endure and survive through a lot, the idea of suicide is no longer an impossibility. I share this because I think it's important to talk about our life experience—both the joyous and the painful.

However, knowing someone who has committed suicide also forces you to recognize how interconnected we truly are. The shock, the horror, the pain, the disbelief, the grief of knowing someone who has committed suicide makes me wonder if the person *truly* knew the far-reaching ripple effect of his or her action, if he or she would've taken his or her life anyway.

I recall a conversation I had with Rachael Barrett, Executive Director of Dave Nee Foundation, a nonprofit that was started after Dave Nee, a law student committed suicide. She shared that often, she'll meet attorneys who make callous statements such as "well, maybe Dave shouldn't have gone to law school if he couldn't handle the pressure."

We as a profession can do better and *should* do better to support one another—our fellow sisters and brothers. Being a member of the Bar is a wonderful privilege and an opportunity to make the world a better place, even if slowly, one client at a time. It's also a wonderful opportunity to deepen our relationship with one another, to not see each other as competitors or enemies but part of a deeply interconnected community.

If you know of an attorney who is struggling, please encourage him or her to get help. Almost all states have some form of Lawyer Assistance Program (LAP). If you are the one that's struggling, please reach out to someone you can trust. This can be a family member, friend, a colleague, a therapist, or LAP.

It's only when every single attorney makes a commitment to himself or herself to care for his or her own mental health that we can begin to make systemic changes within our profession. While not everyone will suffer from a mental illness, we all have a mental health that requires tending to.

It is my greatest wish that you be happy, you be free from suffering, that all beings be happy and free from suffering.

Acknowledgments

Jeena's Acknowledgments

I am grateful for the many teachers in my life who have played a role in deepening my meditation and mindfulness practice. My first meditation teacher and therapist was Rolf Sovik at the Himalayan Institute who planted the seed of meditation, which sprouted at the precise moment when I needed it the most. Thank you Rolf for modeling what it means to be a compassionate human being. Doctor Mark Abramson has the incredible gift of teaching mindfulness with so much grace and beauty. Thank you Mark for teaching me to be kind to myself. Robert Cusick created a safe space for me to explore the intersection of law practice and compassion. Robert, thank you for allowing me to struggle with the question of how I can be compassionate toward my opposing counsel and other difficult people. Thanks to Karen Zelin for the Mindfulness Based Stress Reduction teacher training class. Karen, you radiate with so much warmth, kindness, authenticity, and genuineness. I am grateful to you for teaching me how to struggle with taking the teacher seat, to do it with grace and courage and, at the same time, know how to be with the inevitable stumbling and difficulties.

To my husband who has been my number one supporter, who has tirelessly and joyfully read and edited almost every word I've ever published. Thank you for loving me. I could not have produced this work without your love and support. I cherish every morning I get to wake up next to you.

To my mom, dad, sister, and brother for their love and role in shaping me to be who I am today. I'm so grateful to you.

To Karen Gifford for co-creating this book with me. I'm constantly surprised by your insights and wisdom. I'm grateful we met so randomly at the Happiness Retreat.

To our editor, Jon Malysiak for his patience and encouragement.

Finally, I am grateful to all the lawyers who have supported and encouraged this work. For being brave enough to embark on this journey into meditation and mindfulness. May this effort spread and benefit all.

Warmly,
Jeena

Karen's Acknowledgment

This book simply would not have happened without the vision, enthusiasm, and tenacity of my co-author Jeena Cho. When Jeena approached me to work with her, her idea for a book that would present meditation to lawyers straightforwardly and on their own terms was immediately and immensely appealing. We didn't know each other well at that point, and the friendship that developed through our work together has been one of the great rewards of a project that has deep personal meaning for both of us. No one could ask for a more thoughtful, supportive, and insightful co-author.

Immense appreciation for my meditation teachers, formal and informal. I will never be able to fully express my gratitude to Gurumayi Chidvilasananda for all she has meant in my life, including introducing me to a meditation tradition and philosophy of profound depth and value. Alan Chapman has helped me to better integrate what I learned in the yoga tradition into the Western and humanist context that is my heritage.

Special appreciation for my husband, my dearest meditation buddy, who urged and then nagged and cajoled me to begin a meditation practice at a time when I was a pretty anxious lawyer.

Jon Malysiak, our editor at Ankerwyke, has read through successive versions of this book and given us wise advice and insights at each stage. Laura Duggan's editorial insights were invaluable.

246

Notes

1. Chiesa and Serretti, "A systematic review of neurobiological and clinical features of mindfulness meditations," *Psychological Medicine*, August 2010, http://journals.cambridge.org/action/displayAbstract?fromPage=on line&aid=7826360&fileId=S0033291709991747

   Garrison et al., "Effortless awareness: using real time neurofeedback to investigate correlates of posterior cingulate cortex activity in meditators' self-report," *Frontiers in Human Neuroscience*, August 2013, http://journal.frontiersin.org/article/10.3389/fnhum.2013.00440/abstract

2. Goyal et al., "Meditation programs for psychological stress and well-being: a systematic review and meta-analysis," *Journal of the American Medical Association internal medicine*, March 2014, http://www.ncbi.nlm.nih.gov/pubmed/24395196

3. Carlson and Garland, "Impact of mindfulness-based stress reduction (MBSR) on sleep, mood, stress and fatigue symptoms in cancer outpatients," *International Journal of Behavioral Medicine*, December 2005, http://link.springer.com/article/10.1207/s15327558ijbm1204_9

   Kim et al., "Effects of meditation on anxiety, depression, fatigue, and quality of life of women undergoing radiation therapy for breast cancer," *Complementary therapies in medicine*, August 2013, http://www.ncbi.nlm.nih.gov/pubmed/23876569

   Creswell et al., "Mindfulness meditation training effects on CD4+ T lymphocytes in HIV-1 infected adults: a small randomized controlled trial," *Brain, Behavior, and Immunity,* February 2009, http://www.sciencedirect.com/science/article/pii/S0889159108003085

   Astin, "Stress reduction through mindfulness meditation effects on psychological symptomatology, sense of control, and spiritual experiences," *Psychotherapy and Psychosomatics,* 1997, http://www.karger.com/Article/Abstract/289116

4. Mitchell, "Dr. Herbert Benson's relaxation response," *Psychology Today,* March 29, 2013, https://www.psychologytoday.com/blog/heart-and-soul-healing/201303/dr-herbert-benson-s-relaxation-response
    Redwood, "Interview with Herbert Benson, MD," *Health Insights Today,* Fall 2008, http://www.healthinsightstoday.com/articles/v1i3/benson_all.html

5. Szalavitz, "Q&A: Jon Kabat-Zinn talks about bringing mindfulness meditation to medicine," *Time,* January 11, 2012, http://healthland.time.com/2012/01/11/mind-reading-jon-kabat-zinn-talks-about-bringing-mindfulness-meditation-to-medicine/

6. "Meditation's positive residual effects," *Harvard Gazette,* November 13, 2012, http://news.harvard.edu/gazette/story/2012/11/meditations-positive-residual-effects/

7. Kahn and Polich, 'Meditation states and traits: EEG, ERP, and neuroimaging studies," American Psychological Association, *Psychological Bulletin,* March 2006, http://psycnet.apa.org/?&fa=main.doiLanding&doi=10.1037/0033-2909.132.2.180

8. Matthew A. Killingsworth* and Daniel T. Gilbert, "A wandering mind is an unhappy mind," *Science,* November 12, 2010

9. Healy, "Brain's default mode network may hold key to better psychiatric diagnoses," Los Angeles *Times,* August 30, 2010, http://articles.latimes.com/2010/aug/30/health/la-he-brain-side-20100830

10. Healy, "This is your mind on meditation: less wandering, more doing," Los Angeles *Times,* November 22, 2011, http://www.latimes.com/health/la-heb-meditation-mind-wandering-20111122-story.html
    Brewer et al., "Meditation experience is associated with differences in default mode network activity and connectivity," *Proceedings of the National Academy of Sciences,* October 4, 2011, www.pnas.org/cgi/doi/10.1073/pnas.1112029108

Brewer et al., "What about the 'self' is processed in the posterior cingulate cortex?" *Frontiers in Human Neuroscience,* October 2, 2103, http://journal.frontiersin.org/article/10.3389/fnhum.2013.00647/abstract

11. Condon et al., "Meditation increases compassionate responses to suffering," *Psychological Science*, 2013, https://pccondon.files.wordpress.com/2014/10/condon-et-al-2013-meditation-increases-compassion.pdf

12. Begley, *Train Your Mind, Change Your Brain: How a New Science Reveals Our Extraordinary Potential to Transform Ourselves*, Ballantine Books, 2007, ISBN 978-1-4000-6390-1
Davidson,*The Emotional Life of Your Brain*, Penguin, 2013, ISBN 978-0-452-29888-0
Goleman, "Finding happiness: cajole your brain to lean to the left," New York *Times,* February 4, 2003, http://www.nytimes.com/2003/02/04/health/behavior-finding-happiness-cajole-your-brain-to-lean-to-the-left.html

13. Andersen, Liu, and Kryscio, "Blood pressure response to transcendental meditation: a meta-analysis," *American Journal of Hypertension*, March 2008, http://www.ncbi.nlm.nih.gov/pubmed/18311126

14. American Heart Association, "Beyond medications and diet: alternative approaches to lowering blood pressure: a scientific statement from the american heart association," *Hypertension*, April 22, 2013, http://hyper.ahajournals.org/content/suppl/2013/04/22/HYP.0b013e318293645f.DC2.html

15. Rabin, "Can meditation curb heart attacks?" New York *Times*, November 20, 2009, http://well.blogs.nytimes.com/2009/11/20/can-meditation-curb-heart-attacks/?_r=0

16. Schneider et al., "Stress reduction in the secondary prevention of cardiovascular disease randomized, controlled trial of transcendental meditation and health education in blacks," *Circulation,* November 2012, http://circoutcomes.ahajournals.org/content/early/2012/11/13/CIRCOUTCOMES.112.967406

17. Ong and Sholtes, "A mindfulness-based approach to the treatment of insomnia," *Journal of Clinical Psychology*, November 2010, http://www. ncbi.nlm.nih.gov/pmc/articles/PMC3060715/

18. Vedanthan et al., "Clinical study of yoga techniques in university students with asthma: a controlled study," *Allergy and asthma proceedings*, Jan-Feb 1998, http://www.ncbi.nlm.nih.gov/pubmed/9532318

19. Alexander et al., "Transcendental Meditation, mindfulness, and longevity: an experimental study with the elderly," *Journal of Personality and Social Psychology*, December 1989, http://psycnet.apa.org/journals/psp /57/6/950/

20. Davidson et al., "Alterations in brain and immune function produced by mindfulness meditation," *Journal of Psychosomatic Medicine*, July-August 2003, http://www.ncbi.nlm.nih.gov/pubmed/12883106/
    Barrett et al., "Meditation or exercise for preventing acute respiratory infection: a randomized controlled trial," *Annals of Family Medicine*, July-August 2012, http://www.annfammed.org/content/10/4/337.full

21. Hanh, *Healing is Possible Through Resting*, July 1997, http://acharia. org/downloads/Healing_is_Possible_Through_Resting.pdf

22. Sakai, "Study reveals gene expression changes with meditation," University of Wisconsin *News*, December 4, 2013, http://news.wisc.edu/ study-reveals-gene-expression-changes-with-meditation/

23. Brown, "The Power of Vulnerability," June 2010, http://www.ted .com/talks/brene_brown_on_vulnerability

24. Eammons et al., "Counting blessings versus burdens: an experimental investigation of gratitude and subjective well-being in daily life," *Journal of Personality and Social Psychology*, February 2003, http://greatergood .berkeley.edu/pdfs/GratitudePDFs/6Emmons-BlessingsBurdens.pdf

25. "In praise of gratitude," Harvard *Mental Health Letter*, November 2001, http://www.health.harvard.edu/newsletter_article/in-praise-of-gratitude
    Digdon and Koble, "Effects of constructive worry, imagery distraction, and gratitude interventions on sleep quality: a pilot trial" *Applied*

Psychology: Health and Well-Being, July 2011, http://onlinelibrary.wiley
.com/doi/10.1111/j.1758-0854.2011.01049.x/abstract

McCratey et al., "The effects of emotions on short-term power spectrum analysis of heart rate variability," *American Journal of Cardiology*, February 1996, http://www.ncbi.nlm.nih.gov/pubmed/7484873

26. "Meditation's positive residual effects," *Harvard Gazette*, November 13, 2012, http://news.harvard.edu/gazette/story/2012/11/meditations
-positive-residual-effects/